MENTAL HEALTH AND STUDENT CONDUCT ISSUES ON THE COLLEGE CAMPUS:

A Reading

By Gerald Amada, Ph.D

The Higher Education Administration Series
Edited by Donald D. Gehring and D. Parker Young

COLLEGE ADMINISTRATION PUBLICATIONS, INC.

College Administration Publications, Inc.,
830 Fairview Road, Suite D, Asheville, N. C.
28803-1081

Library of Congress Cataloging-in-Publication Data

Amada, Gerald.
  Mental health and student conduct issues on the college campus : a reading /
by Gerald Amada.
      p. cm. — (The higher education administration series)
  A collection of articles that were originally published between 1972 and 2001.
  Includes bibliographical references.
  ISBN 0-912557-25-7
    1. College students—Mental health services—United States. 2. Counseling in
higher education—United States. 3. College discipline—United States.   I. Title.
II. Series.

RC451.4.S7 A46 2001
378.1'9713—dc21

                                                            2001047357

The views expressed in this book are those of the individual authors and are not
necessarily those of College Administration Publications, Inc.

This publication is designed to provide accurate and authoritative information
in regard to the subject matter covered. It is sold with the understanding that the
publisher and author are not engaged in rendering legal, accounting or other professional service. If legal advice or other expert assistance is required, the services
of a competent professional person should be sought.

—*from a Declaration of Principles jointly adopted by a committee of the American Bar Association
and a committee of publishers.*

This book is dedicated with love to
Rena and Leonard Amada
and
Frema and (in memoriam) Herbert Amada

Table of Contents

Preface

This book is an omnibus of articles that have been published in professional journals and books over a period of approximately thirty years, spanning the entire time I was a director of the City College of San Francisco Mental Health Program. As will become apparent to the reader, these articles deal with clinical, administrative, philosophical, and ethical issues that, in my view, college counselors and clinicians must courageously face on a regular basis. The articles are arbitrarily presented in chronological order, which will perhaps give the reader a fair sense of both the evolution of the clinical program in which I worked as well as the progression of my clinical interests and concerns over the course of my college career.

I wish to express my apologies to the reader with respect to the occasional overlapping and redundant material that appears in several of these articles. This flaw is found especially in the introductory portion of these articles where it had, in each case, been necessary to provide background information about the City College of San Francisco Mental Health Program before launching into the central topic of the article. Readers who find the rereading of such material overly soporific are urged, for the sake of their own mental alacrity, to move hurriedly on to the meatier portions of these articles.

As, over the years, these articles began to accumulate in number, I was frequently asked by friends and colleagues where I found the inspiration, the emotional seedbed so to speak, to generate publishable writings. Whenever I was asked such a question, my thoughts harked back to a concert I had attended many years ago. Malvina Reynolds, the prolific and acerbic folk singer and songwriter was asked by a member of her audience where she found the inspiration to write so many wonderful songs. Without hesitation she replied, "I tend to write a song whenever I am angry about something important, which means that I write a song about once every day." Although I am not nearly as prolific or gifted as the enchanting Malvina Reynolds, I find that the main emotional wellspring for my writings is indeed my anger, my deep dissatisfaction with social and institutional conditions that undermine and incapacitate the delivery of social and psychological services to those who most need them, that is, the victims of injustice, poverty, neglect, and misusage. Having confessed my anger, I must also express my heartfelt wish that readers regard these articles not so much as war cries but rather as awakening tocsins that ring out for radical changes in the way colleges deal with the behavioral and emotional needs of their students.

The first article, *Social Work in a College Mental Health Program,* was written in deference to the contributions social workers and social work as a discipline made to the organization and development of the City College of San Francisco Mental Health Program. The discipline and profession of social work study and attend concertedly to the nature and workings of organizations and institutions; for this reason the insights and energies of social workers in our program were indispensable to its success and deserve great credit and gratitude. This article is a tribute to them.

The article entitled *The Paucity of Mental Health Services and Programs in Community Colleges* was inadvertently instigated by a board member of my college. During a board meeting in which I was clamoring for the augmentation and permanency of our program, this board member challenged me by stating that I had no data that substantiated a need among community college students for on-campus psychological services. That same week I undertook the research that resulted in this article and later used the data derived from this research to restate and fortify the argument for a permanent mental health program on our campus. It, along with many other factors, had a positive influence upon the eventual outcome: program permanency.

The article entitled *Crisis-Oriented Psychotherapy: Some Theoretical and Practical Considerations* was written around the time I realized that our clinic could no longer afford the luxury of providing open-ended therapy to students. Within just a few years there were simply too many students for too few staff. As our staff shifted gears toward limiting the quota of sessions to students, I felt impelled to develop a theoretical and practical model that would maximize the value of these number-limited sessions to students without, hopefully, seriously shortchanging them. At least for myself, this model provided a useful guidepost in dealing with the exigencies of time-limited therapy.

Mental Health Consultation on the College Campus was written after I had spent a considerable amount of time assisting the administrative, instructional, and classified staff of the college with a variety of issues and concerns. After learning that many college mental health programs did not devote substantial time to such extramural activities, I thought it apt to publicize this important dimension to our program with this article.

I wrote *The Interlude Between Short- and Long-Term Psychotherapy* soon after a conference with one of my supervisees. During this meeting I had spent some time explaining to him why I thought many clients decamped—sometimes unwisely—from psychotherapy soon after overcoming the crisis that originally prompted them to enter treatment. The supervisee was obviously fascinated by my remarks and pressed me for elaboration. Inspired by our discussion, I afterward searched for published information on this subject and, not having found any, decided to write this article.

Organizing a Community College Mental Health Program was written as an introductory chapter to a book I had edited on college mental health services. My hope in writing this chapter was that it would provide inspiration and vital information to those who were contemplating and planning the institutionalization of psychological services on their own campuses.

The article entitled *Overcoming the Problem of Face-saving: Outreach Services to Chinese Students* was written by clinical social worker Art Hom and myself. I am grateful to Art not only for the many wonderful cultural insights he provided for this article but also for providing me with a rich cultural education throughout the process of our collaboration on this article.

Why People Distrust Psychotherapists was written soon after I had read a book by a renowned psychoanalytic author who stated, unequivocally and quite convincingly, that most patients enter psychotherapy with a profound, albeit hidden, conviction that the entire psychotherapeutic enterprise is destined to fail. I had often intuited such lurking fears from my new patients, but, for whatever reason, had never understood or articulated them with the bold clarity of this author. After much thought, I accepted his clinical perspective as something close to a truism and then, not satisfied with the finality of such a state of affairs, I decided to investigate the reasons for the nihilism of entering patients. This article is the product of my investigations.

Altogether there are five articles in this book on the subject of dealing with the disruptive college student—*Dealing with the Disruptive College Student: Some Theoretical and Practical Considerations; Coping with the Disruptive Student: A Practical Model; The Role of the Mental Health Consultant in Dealing with Disruptive Students; The Disruptive Student: Some Thoughts and Considerations; The Disruptive College Student: Recent Trends and Practical Advice.* The breadth and multiplicity of the articles on the disruptive student in this book reflect my intense interest in and commitment to resolving this widespread institutional problem. Although it was never in my job description (or my wildest pipe dreams) to investigate or consult on this subject with anyone, I was for many years called upon by my colleagues at City College of San Francisco to assist them in dealing with disruptive crises. As I learned more about the systemic sources of this problem I wrote two books and several articles on the subject that have been widely regarded as highly remedial and pathbreaking. Based upon my discoveries and recommendations I have been invited to speak at over seventy colleges and universities, which provided me with rich and inimitable opportunities to learn about the diverse ways these institutions struggle to maintain reasonable civility on their respective campuses.

Anxiety was written with and at the behest of Dr. Paul Grayson, who co-edited the book in which it appeared. I am grateful to Paul for his generous collaboration throughout the process of publishing this article.

I wrote *Date Rape on the College Campus: The College Psychotherapist as Activist* soon after I had dealt with a harrowing case of date rape that involved two women students on my campus. Based upon this experience I concluded that cases of rape, due to their inherently harrowing nature for the victims, may require college psychotherapists to serve as advocates for their patients; with the police, the college administration, the victims' families, and, if appropriate, with the state legislature (to help enact protective legislation for potential victims).

The Role of Humor in a College Mental Health Program was solicited by Dr. William Fry, who, at the time, was co-editing a book on humor in therapy. Dr. Fry had read in the *San Francisco Chronicle* an excerpt from my book, *A Guide to Psychotherapy*, which explained and illustrated the role of levity and humor in therapy. He evidently liked this material and requested that I write a chapter on the role of humor in a college mental health program for his forthcoming book. I must admit that I derived more pleasure and sheer fun from writing this article than any other I have ever written.

You Can't Please All of the People All of the Time: Normative Institutional Resistances to College Psychological Services is based upon research undertaken when I had been working on my Ph.D. dissertation. My dissertation was a retrospective study of the historical development of the City College of San Francisco Mental Health Program. The institutionalization of this program was aggressively and sometimes brutally resisted by the then college administration and I set out, in my dissertation, to make theoretical sense of this opposition. I learned from this study much about institutional authoritarianism and mischief and, by depersonalizing my professional experiences in this manner, I found

I could gain a useful and salutary emotional distance from and perspective on what I had gruelingly experienced.

The Formulation of a Therapeutic Paradigm: A Professional Odyssey was written at the behest of Dr. Leighton Whitaker, Editor of the *Journal of College Student Psychotherapy*. I was deeply flattered that Lee selected me for the honorific opportunity of explicating and publicizing my therapeutic paradigm but I must confess that no article before or since has caused me such a degree of anxiety and self-consciousness as this one. The frightful personal self-exposure required by this article served as a heavy counterweight to my narcissistic wishes to rave about my self-revered paradigm and nearly caused me to decline this unique assignment.

I wrote *Disqualifying Specified Students from the Campus Psychological Services: Some Considerations and Guidelines* soon after one of my colleagues in the Mental Health Program argued in favor of continuing to offer services to a student who had: (a) sabotaged the staff's every effort to help her (by regularly missing appointments and flouting all therapeutic recommendations); and (b) conducted herself in a highly unacceptable manner while in the waiting room of the clinic. In my opinion, there had been too many cases, over the years, of students whose outrageous behavior in counseling sessions and in outer offices of the clinic had been masochistically tolerated by staff and I wanted to do something about it, once and for all. Thus, this article was written to provide college psychotherapists and counselors with reasonable and legally sound criteria for disqualifying specified students from the counseling center.

Liberal Censorship on Campus: A New Form of McCarthyism? was written soon after my return from a university at which I spoke on the disruptive student. A professor in the audience raised a question regarding the abridgement of speech. I pointed out that speech in classrooms may be legally abridged if the abridgement is related to the time, place, or manner of the speech. However, I cautioned the questioner, ordinarily speech should not be abridged based upon its content. The questioner rejoined by saying he would deal with bigoted speech by telling the bigot to simply "shut up." I chose, in the interest of time, not to debate or prolong this discussion. When I returned home, however, I found myself to be quite angry over what I now refer to as the "New McCarthyism." I recalled from my previous campus lectures that there were many professors who, in order to apotheosize their political correctness were willing to vitiate the constitutional rights of students. It is my hope that this article will serve in some small way to restore sanity and constitutional regard wherever college administrators and instructors appraise the social and political viewpoints of their students.

In summary, I wish to point out that it is a privilege to share this publication with my colleagues. I hope you will enjoy the articles and benefit from the concepts and perspectives in this book and will feel free to contact me in order to share your thoughts and responses to what you will read in the following pages.

Gerald Amada

Acknowledgments

This book is a collection of works, previously published, for which the original publishers have generously given their permission.

Social Work in a College Mental Health Program.

Reprinted with permission of University Press of America from *Social Casework.* November, 1972. © 1972 by Family Service Association of America.

The Paucity of Mental Health Services and Programs in Community Colleges.

Reprinted with permission of University Press of America from *Journal of the American College Health Association.* June, 1975. © 1975 by Heldref Publications.

Crisis-oriented Psychotherapy: Some Theoretical and Practical Considerations.

Reprinted with permission of University Press of America from *Journal of Contempory Psychotherapy.* Spring-Summer, 1977. © 1977 by Journal of Contemporary Psychotherapy.

Mental Health Consultation on the College Campus.

Reprinted with permission of University Press of America from *Journal of American College Health Association.* April, 1983. © 1983 by Heldref Publications.

The Interlude Between Short- and Long-term Psychotherapy.

Reprinted with permission of University Press of America from *American Journal of Psychotherapy.* July, 1983. © 1983 by American Journal of Psychotherapy.

Organizing a Community College Mental Health Program.

Overcoming the Problem of Face-saving:
Outreach Services to Chinese Students.

Why People Distrust Psychotherapists.

Dealing with the Disruptive College Student:
Some Theoretical and Practical Considerations.

Anxiety.

Date Rape on the College Campus:
The College Psychotherapist as Activist.

Coping with the Disruptive College Student:
A Practical Model.

The Role of Humor in a College Mental Health Program.

The Role of the Mental Health Consultant in
Dealing with Disruptive Students.

The Disruptive College Student: Some Thoughts and Considerations.

**You Can't Please All of the People All of the Time:
Normative Institutional Resistances to
College Psychological Services.**

Reprinted with permission of *Journal of College Student Psychotherapy*.
1995. © 1995 by The Haworth Press, Inc.

The Disruptive College Student: Recent Trends and Practical Advice.

Reprinted with permission of *Journal of College Student Psychotherapy*.
1997. © 1997 by The Haworth Press, Inc.

The Formulation of a Therapeutic Paradigm: A Professional Odyssey.

Reprinted with permission of *Journal of College Student Psychotherapy*.
1998. © 1998 by The Haworth Press, Inc.

**Disqualifying Specified Students from the
Campus Psychological Service:
Some Considerations and Guidelines.**

Reprinted with permission of *Journal of College Student Psychotherapy*.
1999. © 1999 by the Haworth Press, Inc.

Liberal Censorship on Campus: A New Form of McCarthyism?

Reprinted with permission of *Journal of College Student Psychotherapy*.
2001. C 2001 by the Haworth Press, Inc.

About the Author

Dr. Gerald Amada was one of the founders and a director of the Mental Health Program, City College of San Francisco and is now retired after a thirty-year career at that college. He also has a private psychotherapy practice in Mill Valley, California. He received the M.S.W. degree at Rutgers University and Ph.D. in social and clinical psychology at the Wright Institute, Berkeley, California. He has published eight books and over fifty articles and book reviews on the subjects of mental health, psychotherapy, and disruptive student issues.

His latest books are: *A Guide to Psychotherapy* (Ballantine Books/Random House); *The Mystified Fortune-Teller and Other Tales From Psychotherapy, The Power of Negative Thinking* (Madison Books); and *Coping with Misconduct in the College Classroom: A Practical Model* (College Administration Publications). In 1994, Dr. Amada published *Coping with the Disruptive College Student: A Practical Model.* He has been lecturing on college campuses throughout the United States and Canada on the subject of the disruptive college student for over 20 years.

Dr. Amada has been a book reviewer for the *American Journal of Psychotherapy,* University Press of America, the San Francisco *Chronicle,* and the *Journal of College Student Psychotherapy.* He is a member of the editorial board and is book review editor of the last-mentioned journal. He is the recipient of the 1984 Award of Excellence in the category of administrator, Post Secondary Education, conferred by the National Education Special Needs Personnel, Region 5, which comprises 18 states.

Dr. Amada enjoys and feels challenged by the opportunity to share strategies and principles for fostering civility on the college campus.

Anyone interested in contacting Dr. Amada regarding the subjects discussed in this book or about the possibility of conducting a campus workshop on disruptive student issues may reach him at phone number 415-479-8889, or e-mail to *mgamada@earthlink.net*

by Gerald Amada and Jacqueline Swartz

Social Work in a College Mental Health Program

*Casework services aid students who grew up
in racial ghettos and poverty areas, handicapped
by different linguistic and cultural backgrounds*

Social workers are rarely found in a college setting, even though the diversity of their training and knowledge of community resources would seem to make them singularly appropriate as helping professionals for college students. At City College of San Francisco, social workers worked productively in a variety of ways within the context of the Mental Health Program, a pilot program designed to offer psychological services to the students. It is sponsored jointly by the California Medical Clinic for Psychotherapy and the Westside Mental Health Services of San Francisco. This article describes the ways in which social workers were utilized in the Mental Health Program. It is hoped that such utilization, although unique at this time, will serve as an encouraging model for use in the future.

SETTING

The Mental Health Program functioned in and was shaped by the particular context of the college in which it operated. City College of San Francisco is a two-year school with an open admissions policy. It offers two basic programs: (1) an academic curriculum designed to enable students to transfer to a four-year college or university, and (2) vocational and paraprofessional training programs in a variety of areas, including police science, dental assistance, and hotel and restaurant management. The only academic requirement traditionally has been a high school diploma, but the school's policy has changed in recent years to include the recruitment and tutoring of disadvantaged people who would otherwise not attend college.

City College, like other urban community colleges, has a student population which reflects the diversity of the city itself; 1970 statistics indicate that more than one-half of the students are from racial minorities. Twenty-six percent are Oriental, 14 percent black, 7 percent

1

Latin American, and 5 percent are American Indian, Filipino, Samoan, Korean, or other than Caucasian. Over 24 percent of all City College students are supported by public assistance. Among those who do not receive this aid, 17 percent have family incomes of under $300 per month; another 15 percent have total family incomes ranging from $301 to $500 per month.

Ninety percent of the students are between the ages of seventeen and twenty-nine, an age group particularly susceptible to a variety of medical and social problems including venereal disease, drug and alcohol abuse, and unwanted pregnancy. Moreover, many City College students have grown up in racial ghettos or poverty areas, and large numbers are handicapped by linguistic and cultural backgrounds that are sharply different from the white middle-class world they are entering, usually for the first time, as college students. These differences are often compounded by financial and personal problems, poor housing, criminal records, heavy drug use, an impulsive live-for-the-moment orientation developed in reaction to the largely ungratifying world in which they have always lived, and many years of experiencing schools as hostile and frustrating places.

Although special educational services including financial stipends and vocational counseling have been available to selected students for several years, prior to 1970 health services at City College consisted of one public health nurse. As a result of her efforts and those of social workers from a local clinic for psychotherapy, grants were received to pay salaries of staff members recruited to establish an innovative mental health program for students at City College.

PROGRAM

The Mental Health Program was established with the following guidelines. Psychological services would be offered with the goal of promoting growth and development by giving students the opportunity to explore problems that interfered with school, work, and relationships with family and friends. The racial composition of the staff would approximate that of the student body. Appointments would be available to any student without delay and at no charge, and consultation would be available to faculty and staff. Emphasis would be placed on providing short-term crisis services in order to insure the availability of appointments. Mental health records would be kept separate from all other student records, and the highest degree of confidentiality would be maintained.

DIRECT SERVICES

The need for effective brief psychotherapy has been widely surveyed, and research indicates that current treatment methods cannot possibly fill the ever-increasing demand for psychiatric care.[1] At City

College of San Francisco, exploration of student utilization of community resources revealed that facilities off campus have proved insufficient to meet the often urgent needs of students at the time service is requested. In addition, the most seriously disturbed students, and particularly those who need help on an emergency basis, cannot cope with the eligibility requirements, bureaucratic complications, and long waits for service which are often necessary to obtain low-cost services off campus.[2]

Short-term Individual Therapy

The Mental Health Program is geared toward providing short-term crisis therapy mainly on an individual basis. Because the majority of students are in their late teens or early twenties, there were certain problems or themes which emerged with marked regularity. Critical career choices, difficult relations with parents, complex marital choices and decisions, economic pressures, academic stresses, conflicts in relation to drugs and sex, and identity crises were found to constitute problems common to this age group. After a small number of sessions —usually two to five—students very often reached a satisfactory resolution or mitigation of their crises and required no further treatment. Students whose problems did require long-term therapy were referred to agencies in the San Francisco area.

From January 1970 through June 1971, two thousand individual treatment hours were provided to a total of six hundred students by four psychiatric social workers, three psychiatrists, and eight trainees from several disciplines. There were a significant number of students who presented emotional disturbances of a severe nature. In some instances it was necessary to see these students two or more times a week in order to provide sufficiently intensive treatment. Many of the students who came for treatment revealed overwhelming reality problems, such as lack of money for food, the necessity to work long hours in addition to studying and attending classes, and living conditions so crowded that studying was impossible. Attention was given to social and economic factors or agents of disturbance, and, accordingly, intrapsychic disorders were placed in perspective. Thus the clinical work was done in the context of social problems.

For example, Glenn is a twenty-five-year-old, married, second-year student who was referred to the Student Health Services by the Dean of Students. For about one year he had been seriously abusing himself with amphetamines which resulted in physical enervation, a marked deterioration in his academic performance, and a tenuous marital situation. Glenn had already been admitted to a state university for his junior year, contingent upon successful completion of his current courses. However, due to extreme fear and confusion, Glenn disenrolled from several of his courses prematurely and thereby jeopardized his chances to attend the university. It was only several days later that he recognized the gravity of his action.

Since there were only two months remaining in the semester, the therapist immediately offered regular and frequent sessions to Glenn. Initially, Glenn was advised about the various ways in which he could gain reenrollment in his courses. He approached the appropriate college administrators, who granted his request to reenroll. Throughout the first several sessions, therapy was directed toward supporting Glenn's efforts to reduce his drug intake. Although he could not sustain total drug abstinence, he was able to gradually reduce drug usage to a more tolerable level, enabling him to cope more competently with his course work.

After several sessions, emphasis was placed upon his marital relationship. In the last stages of this brief therapy, Glenn was encouraged to attend more actively to the early origins of his psychological problems. This investigation revealed important repetitive patterns of self-destructive behavior, many of which were clearly derived from early conflicts within the family matrix.

Another important context for therapy was the campus setting which varied according to where the crisis occurred. Therapists found themselves called to classrooms, offices, campus grounds, the cafeteria, and the library. In addition to seeing students in these various locations, it was often necessary to respond with the instructor or administrator present. An additional feature of the college setting involved extramural contact with students in therapy. Staff had to be prepared for accidental contact and could not rely on maintaining the anonymity possible in a clinic. For example, it was likely that a therapist might meet in the library a student who had discussed problems he would not want to reveal outside the privacy of the office. Sensitive issues arose that had to be dealt with in an extramural contact in which it was important to maintain confidentiality as well as the continuity of the relationship. Therapists learned to take cues about whether or not students wanted to be acknowledged outside the office.

Still another factor related to the college setting concerned dress. Staff found that although appearance issues could be explored in long-term therapy, it was easy to alienate students by clothes which caused the therapist to be dismissed as an authoritarian establishment figure. This experience, repeated often enough, motivated staff to alter their dress in closer accordance with campus norms. Although the therapists did not attempt to dress like college students, they wore clothes that were casual and comfortable to them; as a result, they were better able to relate to the students they saw. This method of handling the problem of appearance suggests alternatives to the rigid conformity often required for social workers. Particularly when dealing with the disadvantaged in their own setting, formal business attire can create avoidable barriers between the client and the social worker.

Group Psychotherapy

In addition to individual therapy, group psychotherapy was conducted by two psychiatric social workers on campus. These groups were developed to assist students whose problems were largely in the area of interpersonal relations. Group members were encouraged to express feelings, share insights, and test perceptions with their college peers. Because of their particular social conflicts, a significant number of students derived far more benefit from the group psychotherapy experience than they could possibly have gained from a more socially limited one-to-one relationship with a therapist. Millard Ryker states:

> For a peer-oriented student in the throes of a situational crisis, where better to find the support so necessary to resolve it successfully than in a warm, concerned group of peers . . . Peers, with whom most college students are primarily concerned, are present so he may test his interactional skills and shape his identity. Authority figures, in the persons of the therapists, are also present to lend sanction to these activities and to provide a testing ground for relations with authority figures in the student's true environment, such as parents or college professors and deans. In summary, then, a group could provide support for the members as they meet the various inevitable crises of college life and also provide an atmosphere in which they may shape and test their emerging identities.[3]

Careful screening of applicants played a large part in the success of the groups. This processing resulted in the exclusion of students who either lacked adequate motivation or were potentially disruptive.

INDIRECT SERVICES

Social workers were extensively involved in a wide variety of training and consultation assignments. From September 1970 to June 1971, they supervised two graduate students in social work, two graduate students in vocational rehabilitation, and one psychologist with a master's degree, all of whom received training in psychotherapy. Time spent in supervising this group of trainees had the desired results of quantitative and qualitative improvement in mental health services to City College students.

In addition to traditional training in crisis therapy, conferences dealt with such issues as how best to relate to minority students in their own milieu. Minority social workers in particular were active in reaching various ethnic groups on campus, and trainees were encouraged to explore outreach possibilities. Many of these students were discouraged from seeking therapy because of the office setting and procedures, even though they involved no waiting list or eligibility requirements. Often these contacts were effective stepping stones to more formal and intensive office contact between the minority social workers and students.

The general visibility of the social workers was a necessary key to encouraging minority students to utilize the mental health service. It was found that "informality and professionalism can be extremely compatible, and indeed more penetrating than the usual formally structured therapist-client interaction."[4] This approach, involving contact with students in their own milieu, generated an increase in black student intake from 9 percent of the total intake in the period from January to March 1970 to 23 percent during the period from May to June 1970.

Social workers proved adept at relating to the college as a whole. They offered consultation to faculty and administrators who requested information or advice about dealing with student mental health needs. Faculty members were able to utilize information and suggestions on how to modify teaching techniques, for example. In some instances when instructors were at a loss to know how to deal with an overt crisis in the classroom, through consultation they were able to see the situation more clearly and approach the student with more awareness. In this way it was sometimes possible to avert formal treatment.

This goal was consistent with the indirect method of helping as many students as possible while minimizing the number of patients. In those instances when instructors were involved with students whose problems were too serious for the faculty member to handle, they were often relieved to be able to refer students to competent professionals, thereby avoiding problems that interfered with their academic responsibilities.

In their outreach to faculty and administrators, social workers found that education was important in removing the stigma often attached to therapy and in making psychological services a creditable part of the Student Health Services. In talking to counselors it was emphasized that students in therapy should not be treated differently from other counselees and should be given no special dispensation or privilege. In response to faculty and student interest in the Mental Health Program, social workers gave classroom guest talks which were valuable in introducing the service in its most palatable form. These talks, focusing on what constitutes mental health, often resulted in students' relating the information to their personal lives and consequently making appointments to see the lecturer. In addition, social workers offered their services as advisors to student groups, and this outreach service was most helpful to minority organizations.

ADMINISTRATION OF THE PROGRAM

All major administrative duties were carried out by a social worker whose job it was to coordinate the Mental Health Program, assign trainees to supervisors, and make liaisons with the faculty, administration, and students. That the social worker-administrator was effective in coordinating a multidisciplinary team is perhaps reflective of a wide social perspective which can be seen as the result of a training orientation that includes components from various disciplines. Such an orientation may well be the most eclectic in the mental health field. The administrator was able to be responsive to the flexible and innovative design of the program, which exacted its own type of leadership.

For instance, since the Student Health Services have no eligibility requirements, the response of staff must be tailored to student needs rather than to agency philosophy. Constant evaluation of the effectiveness of the program is necessary, especially to enable students to see a therapist as quickly and as smoothly as possible. As Shirley Cooper states, "The waiting period between a patient's application move and his therapy is, in most instances, an artifact to good therapy."[5]

Another reason for the necessity of remaining flexible is the endless variety of clients. Although therapists in the program see only students, the City College population includes a diversity of students in terms of age, background, and sophistication about therapy. Unlike the situation at most clinics, diagnostic categories are left wide open at the Student Health Services.

An additional consideration involves hiring. Because of the nature of the setting and population, it is crucial to select staff who are appropriate and who feel comfortable at City College, a milieu that is strikingly different from the isolated environment of most four-year colleges and universities. Staff, it was found, should be sympathetic to the problems of youth, especially within the context of poverty, and should be aware of the constant and rapid changes occurring in contemporary American society. It is also important that staff be responsive to the cultural and ethnic differences of City College students. This emphasis on responsiveness might mandate certain techniques, for example, the open-door policy used successfully by minority social workers.

REFERRALS

Because of the limitations on space and staff time, referrals were necessary if long-term therapy was indicated or if other services such as public assistance seemed appropriate. City College, like other community colleges, offers either limited services, referrals, or no services whatsoever. Social workers were particularly valuable because of their expertise in making referrals and their awareness of social service agencies, family service agencies, psychiatric clinics, public welfare agencies, and private practitioners. They were often instrumental in informing students of benefits they were not aware of, in addition to oiling the machinery of eligibility and entrance procedures. Thus, if the social worker saw that a student would eventually benefit from long-term therapy, he or she would begin contacting clinics while the student was still in short-term treatment. By the time the immediate therapy ended, the student could be seen at a clinic without an interim waiting period. Such a lapse is often harmful and sometimes causes students to end treatment after only a few sessions.

Therapists felt that the referral procedure sometimes included implications of rejection for the student, especially if a therapist-student relationship had developed. Attempts were made to convey to the student the fact that the relationship could not continue for practical reasons and that the student could better meet his or her needs elsewhere. It was made clear that referrals were made for objective reasons and were related to the needs of the other students and not because the student's problems were unwelcome or because he or she had done anything to offend the therapist. The impact of referrals was minimized by having the names of people in agencies available to the student. Also, it was helpful for the therapist to inform the student of the limitations on services at the beginning of treatment.

A significant number of students came to the Mental Health Program to learn about the vocational opportunities and training requirements in the field of social work. The social worker role in the college context was seen as desirable and represented a good advertisement for the social work profession.

Endnotes

1. Karl K. Lewin, *Brief Encounters* (St. Louis: Warren H. Green, Inc., 1970).

2. Alan Leavitt, Judith Carey, and Jacqueline Swartz, Developing a Mental Health Program at an Urban Community College, *Journal of the American College Health Association,* 19:200 (June 1971).

3. Millard Ryker, Group Work with Students in a University Mental Health Service, *Journal of American College Health Association,* 18:296 (April 1970).

4. Ken Davis and Jacqueline Swartz, Increasing Black Students' Utilization of Mental Health Services, *American Journal of Orthopsychiatry,* 42:771-76 (October 1972).

5. Shirley Cooper, Emergencies in a Psychiatric Clinic, *Social Casework,* 41:134 (March 1960).

The Paucity of Mental Health Services & Programs in Community Colleges: Implications of a Survey

The City College of San Francisco Mental Health Program began as a pilot project designed to offer psychological services to students. Since its inception in January, 1970, 3,000 different students have been provided about 8,000 hours of individual and group psychotherapy. In addition, staff psychotherapists have been extensively involved in a wide variety of training and consultation assignments.

Consultation services are also readily offered to student organizations, faculty and administrators who request information and advice about dealing with student mental health needs. Each year graduate schools of social work and rehabilitation counseling place students in the Mental Health Program for training in psychotherapy. Psychiatric residents from local training facilities also serve in the program and are available to prescribe and dispense psychiatric medications.[1]

Experience has demonstrated that there are several critically important reasons for an on-campus mental health service. First, staff working on campus are immediately available to cope with emergency situations and can develop special knowledge of students, faculty and the college environment. Mental health facilities off-campus have frequently proven insufficient in meeting the students' often urgent needs at the time service is requested.

Furthermore, the most seriously disturbed students, particularly those who need help on an emergency basis, cannot cope with the eligibility requirements, bureaucratic complications and long waits for service which are often necessary to obtain low-cost services off-campus. Also, at City College of San Francisco, the sizable (20,000 day and evening students) and heterogeneous make-up of the student body results in its having become a community itself, and one requiring its own mental health services.

9

A further impediment to the utilization of off-campus health services is the understandable reluctance of some students to identify themselves as patients. These students might, however, be ready to seek help from persons who are closely identified with the college. Other complications often arise in connection with families which are unfamiliar with and often opposed to psychological services outside the college itself; low income and foreign families often tend to view the need for psychological services as threatening or shameful.

The City College of San Francisco Mental Health Program was originally subsidized by federal and private foundation grants. Two and one-half years after the inception of the program, a grant from the college district provided additional funding. Since the fall of 1974, the Mental Health Program has received funding exclusively from the San Francisco College District.

The experience of organizing and implementing a community college psychological service stimulated interest in gaining an overview of the extent and nature of mental health services throughout the entire community college system in California, with obvious implications on a national scale.

METHOD

A survey was devised to evaluate current mental health programs on California's junior college campuses. The survey was initially conducted by mailing questionnaires to all public and private junior colleges listed in the California Junior College Association Directory; a total of exactly one hundred schools. Fifty-one of these schools responded to the written questionnaire. By undertaking telephonic contacts with the remaining schools a one hundred percent response to the questionnaire was achieved.

Although the mailings were addressed to the college dean of students, responses were provided by a wide variety of knowledgeable and authoritative college representatives, including deans, nurses, counselors, health officers and psychotherapists. Respondents were asked the following questions:

1. Are mental health or psychological services offered on your campus?

2. If such services are offered, could you describe the extent of these services?

3. If mental health services are not offered, do you think there is an appreciable need for such services on your campus?

4. Are psychologically-oriented services provided by the academic counseling department on your campus?

5. If psychologically-oriented services are offered on your campus, roughly what percentage of counseling service time is devoted to intensive psychological intervention or psychotherapy?

6. Is there an official policy in relation to having the counseling or any other department provide psychotherapy to students?

7. Please indicate the level of enrollment, including day and evening students.

8. In what manner and by what departmental service are psychiatric emergencies (i.e., uncontrollable or severe drug and psychotic reactions) coped with?

9. Is there a campus service which provides psychiatric medications?

10. If there is no campus service which provides psychiatric medications, do you think that there is an appreciable need for establishing such a service?

11. If mental health services are provided on your campus, what is their source of funding?

12. Is consultation, with respect to the psychological needs of students, provided to the college faculty and administrative personnel?

13. If such consultation is not available, do you think there is an appreciable need for such a service on your campus?

RESULTS

1. *Are Services Offered.* In response to this question, 62% of the junior colleges indicated that they did not offer mental health or psychological services on campus.

2. *Extent of Services.* Thirty-eight junior colleges provide mental health services, ranging from two to ninety hours per week. The average number of hours of psychological services provided by these programs was twenty-seven per week. The total number of service hours for all one hundred colleges was 1,010 per week.

3. *Need for Services.* Of the sixty-two junior colleges which do not provide mental health services, fifty-three or 85%, responded "Yes" to this question.

4. *Psychologically-oriented Services.* In response to this question 52% of the schools responded "Yes."

5. *Percentage of Counseling Time.* Representatives at six of the fifty-two schools in which counselors devote some percentage of their time to psychologically-oriented service refused to estimate the percentage of time counselors devote to this activity, other than to indicate that such assistance to students was "minimal." At the forty-six other schools the estimated range of time devoted to this type of service was from 1% to 50%; the average for all forty-six schools was 23%.

6. *Official Policies.* In response to this question, 90% of the schools replied "No." Of the ten schools which replied "Yes," eight stated that there was a policy which prohibited counselors from providing

psychotherapy. Two schools indicated there was an official policy in favor of an on-campus psychotherapeutic service.

7. *Enrollment Figures.* The enrollment figures ranged from a low of 250 to a high of 31,461 day and evening students per college. Total enrollment for all California junior colleges, excluding City College of San Francisco, is approximately 780,000 students.

8. *Psychiatric Emergencies.* In response to this question, all one hundred colleges responded similarly. Psychiatric emergencies were generally referred to the person on campus who was regarded to be officially responsible for, or most knowledgeable in handling such matters. If the emergency required service off-campus, the college then arranged for transportation to a community psychiatric facility. In most such instances attempts were made to enlist the assistance of potentially helpful persons, such as family members, police and ambulance service personnel. No junior college reported maintaining a campus facility which provided round-the-clock physically secure care for students who required this kind of service.

9. *Medications.* In response to this question, 91% of the schools indicated that there was no campus service which provided psychiatric medications.

10. *Need for Psychiatric Medications.* Of the ninety-one schools which did not provide psychiatric medications, one indicated uncertainty as to need, thirty-six indicated no appreciable need and fifty-four or 59% indicated an appreciable need for this modality of service.

11. The following is a breakdown of funding sources for the thirty-eight schools which did provide on-campus mental health services.

Table I

Source of Funding	Number of Schools
District Funding	18
Student Health Fee	11
County Funding	3
State Funding	2
Privately Donated Services	1
Joint District & County Funding	1
Joint District Funding & Privately Donated Services	1
Joint District Funding & Student Health Fee	1
	N = 38

12. *Consultation.* In response to this question, 54% of the junior colleges indicated that they did not provide consultation to the faculty and administration, with respect to the psychological needs of students.

13. *Need for Consultation.* Of the fifty-four schools which did not provide consultation, forty-eight or 89% indicated that an appreciable need existed for such a college service.

DISCUSSION

The fact that *almost two-thirds* of California's junior colleges do not provide on-campus mental health services in itself invites further study. This figure, coupled with the findings that 85% of those schools which lack these services also indicate an appreciable need for on-campus mental health services, further dramatizes a glaring gap in the educational system. Another way of viewing this issue is to consider full-time mental health positions in terms of forty hours a week of service and convert into full-time positions the total number of mental health service hours per week provided collectively by all of the state's junior colleges (1,010 hours). By doing this we discover that there are only twenty-five "full-time" mental health positions on all of California's junior college campuses. The ratio of campus psychotherapists to the 780,000 junior college students throughout the state is approximately one psychotherapist for every 31,200 students!

Two factors are often adduced in an attempt to minimize the significance of junior college mental health services. Firstly, it has been argued, college counselors capably meet the psychological needs of students. That this is not the case has no bearing on the qualifications or competency of college counselors. In fact, most seem to provide highly effective counseling services.

Nevertheless, academic counseling is not psychotherapy. Psychotherapy requires a different (not better) set and range of professional skills and techniques. This has been implicitly recognized in the California educational codes which state that "counseling services shall assist each student in the college in the following ways: (a) to determine his educational goals and (b) to make a self-appraisal toward his goals."[2] Although psychotherapeutic services often incorporate these educational objectives, the goals of psychotherapy are frequently broader or depart, to some extent, from immediate educational considerations. In any case, although psychologically-oriented work is undertaken by counselors at 52% of the junior colleges in this study, the average percentage of time devoted to such intervention is only 23%. Furthermore, most of the fifty-two schools which provide psychologically-oriented counseling services readily acknowledge that although these services are often intensive, they should not be deemed psychotherapy.

Other objections sometimes raised against on-campus mental health services relate to low student enrollment and the availability of community psychiatric facilities. In some instances small student populations appear not to warrant on-campus psychological services. In other instances, the ready availability and physical propinquity of community psychiatric services would appear to render an on-campus mental health program ineffectual and a duplication of community services. Despite these possible objections to on-campus psychological services, it is clearly significant that of the sixty-two schools without these programs, fifty-three or 85% reported the need for them.

The results presented in Table II indicate, as expected, that those schools with larger student populations (over 10,000 students) tend

Table II
Schools Offering Mental Health Services

Size of Enrollment	Yes	No
0 - 4,999	6	23
5,000 - 9,999	8	20
10,000 - 14,999	9	0
15,000 - 19,999	12	9
20,000 - 24,999	2	1
25,000 - 29,999	0	2
30,000 - 34,999	1	1
	N = 38	N = 62

to provide on-campus mental health services more often than those schools with smaller student populations (under 10,000 students).

The data presented in Table III suggest that an appreciable need for an on-campus mental health service does not necessarily reflect a large student population. Although the largest number of colleges which indicated no appreciable need for mental health services had

Table III
Schools Expressing Appreciable Need for Mental Health Services

Size of Enrollment	Yes	No
0 - 4,999	16	7
5,000 - 9,999	20	0
10,000 - 14,999	5	1
15,000 - 19,999	8	1
20,000 - 24,999	1	0
25,000 - 29,999	2	0
30,000 - 34,999	1	0
	N = 53	N = 9

enrollments under 5,000 students, sixteen, or about 70% of those schools with enrollments below 5,000 students, indicated an appreciable need for these programs. The fact that size of enrollment does have some bearing on the need for psychological services is demonstrated, however, by the finding that 37, or about 95% of the thirty-nine schools which lack on-campus psychological services and have enrollments over 5,000 students, indicated the need for these services.

The finding that 90% of the junior colleges lacked an official policy with respect to the delivery of on-campus mental health services suggests that such services could be relatively easily instituted and implemented on those campuses which lacked them, providing that adequate funds and physical facilities were made available.

Although all the junior colleges had an established procedure for coping with psychiatric emergencies, the absence of round-the-clock, physically secure and carefully supervised facilities for students in crisis raises important questions. How much less stigmatizing would protective care in a campus facility be than in a community psychiatric hospital? What are the potentially harmful effects which result from the delays, public exposure and clamor which ordinarily accompany psychiatric hospitalization in the community? Many universities have developed 24-hour infirmary facilities in response to just such considerations. It may be necessary for the junior colleges to follow suit.

It is significant that fifty-four or 59% of the ninety-one schools which do not maintain programs which provide psychiatric medications, indicated an appreciable need for this modality of service. This figure demonstrates the need amongst these schools to investigate opportunities for funding, medical supervision and licensure and developing physical facilities for the safe impoundment of psychiatric medications. If these conditions can be met, it is apparent that psychiatric drugs can be a timely and helpful treatment modality, particularly when used in conjunction with ongoing psychotherapy.

The figures in *Table I* indicate that eighteen or 47% and eleven or 29% of the thirty-eight schools with mental health services received funding for these programs from the college district and student health fees respectively. The lack of uniformity in the funding sources of junior college mental health programs reflects the necessity of each college to generate its own funds in order to subsidize these services. Faced with this dilemma, the colleges have either failed to establish the programs at all or have generated funds according to the particular financial resources and limitations of the college. Viewed from a state-wide perspective this form of individualism has resulted in a patently inequitable, chaotic and inefficacious system of funding junior college mental health programs. Figures in *Table I* additionally indicate that 74% of California's junior college mental health programs are subsidized exclusively by college district funds.

The data provided in *Table IV* indicate that programs financed by college districts tend to provide more hours of psychological service than programs subsidized by other sources. The fact that such a widespread precedent for this use of district funding already exists, suggests that the likelihood that those fifty-three junior colleges which indicate an appreciable need for on-campus mental health services would readily institute psychological services if adequate funds for these programs became available to the various school districts.

Table IV
Weekly Hours of Psychological Service

Source of Funding	0 - 19	20 - 39	40 - 59	60 - 79	80 - 99
District Funds	4	4	8		2
Health Fee	6	3	2		
County Funds	2		1		
State Funds	2				
Joint District Funding and Health Fees				1	
Joint District Funding and Privately Donated Service		1			
Joint District and County Funds	1				
Privately Donated Services	1				
	16	8	11	1	2

N = 38

The finding that 89% of the junior colleges which lacked psychological consultation indicated an appreciable need for such a resource is noteworthy. The potential value of psychological consultation was highlighted by many college officials who reported faculty and administrators frequently felt alarmed or confused over how to cope with emotionally disturbed students.

The findings of this survey have implications which reach far beyond the borders of California. If we can justifiably assume that the colleges included in this survey are relatively representative of other junior colleges in the nation, there then seems cause for carefully evaluating the status of mental health services on all junior college campuses throughout the country. The urgency for such studies must be recognized because "while most categories of colleges and universities are growing in number, by far the greatest increase is in public junior colleges. During the 1960s such schools increased in number from 330 to 650 (97%)."[3]

The incidence of mental health problems on the nation's college campuses is tragically high and widely acknowledged by those attempting to assist students psychologically. Farnsworth, for example, estimated that for every 10,000 students:

1,000 will have emotional conflicts of sufficient severity to warrant professional help.

300 to 400 will have feelings of depression severe enough to impair their efficiency.

100 to 200 will be apathetic and unable to organize their efforts—"I can't make myself want to work."

20 to 50 will be so adversely affected by past family experiences that they will be unable to control impulses.

15 to 25 will become ill enough to require treatment in a mental hospital.

5 to 20 will attempt suicide, of whom one or more will succeed.[4]

Staff psychotherapists at City College of San Francisco regard these figures as an underestimation of the extent of emotional difficulties with which students must contend.

SUMMARY

This survey and most epidemiological studies of college students demonstrate a profound need for on-campus mental health services which can offer psychological assistance immediately, confidentially and intensively. The implications of the survey are national in scope. Such programs demonstrably depend upon the expenditure of considerable funds. Whether mental health services are offered under the campus aegis of the counseling department or student health service probably should be determined by the particular administrative priorities, orientation, resources and limitations of those respective departments. What undoubtedly is required is state and federal legislation which will allocate to junior college districts funds for organizing the mental health programs for which they are expressing an appreciable need. Only by this means can the psychological needs of community college students receive the recognition and respect to which they are entitled.

A note of thanks to Mr. Peter Brett for help in collating and editing this material and to Ms Susan Bain for organizing and typing the final copy.

Endnotes

1. Amada G, and Swartz J: Social Work in a College Mental Health Program. *Journal of Social Casework*, 53:528533, 1972.

2. *California Community Colleges, State of California*, Title 5, Part VI Register 70, No 16, (4/18/70), 618.

3. Glasscote R, et al, Mental Health on the Campus, *Joint Information Service of the American Psychiatric Association and the National Association for Mental Health,* 1973.

4. Farnsworth D: *Psychiatry, Education, and the Young Adult.* Charles C. Thomas, Illinois, 1966. 349.

Crisis-oriented Psychotherapy: Some Theoretical and Practical Considerations

Since its inception in January, 1970, over 3,000 different students have been provided about 8,000 hours of individual and group psychotherapy at the City College of San Francisco Mental Health Program. Although no arbitrary quota was placed on the number of therapeutic sessions to which students were entitled, each semester the average number of contacts per student was below three. City College students, particularly those in their late teens and early twenties, evidenced overriding concerns with respect to their emotional independence-dependence. Such concerns often resulted in a tendency to utilize therapeutic services on a relatively tentative and brief basis. The experience of organizing and implementing a community college psychological service which primarily offers short-term psychotherapy stimulated theoretical interest in identifying those characteristics which distinguish crisis-oriented psychotherapy from other modalities of treatment.

A frequent question put to staff members of the Mental Health Program is, "Do you provide psychotherapy services or must students who require long-term assistance go elsewhere?" The presumptuous phrasing of the question, by implication, imputes to short-term psychotherapy a lesser status and importance than to long-range modalities of psychological intervention. Such a denigrating perspective actually does a serious disservice to the process, patient and psychotherapist involved in crisis-oriented therapeutic encounters.

WHAT IS A CRISIS?
It is an emotionally significant event or radical change of status in a person's life which is disruptive of his usual mode of adaptation. Time-limited or crisis-oriented (fewer than nine sessions) psychotherapy is generally justified on two bases. First, funding and personnel

shortages in many community psychiatric agencies require a form of psychotherapy designed to reach maximum populations. Thus, by structuring services toward the short-term resolution of psychological crises it is possible to effect adequate caseload turnover. By avoiding inordinately long treatment waiting periods an agency enhances its prospects for therapeutic success.

As indicated by Lewin, "the long wait for treatment insures that only the most regressed and dependent people remain, since those with any ego strengths have made arrangements for therapy elsewhere, a process of case selection which almost guarantees therapeutic failure" (Lewin, 1970).

A second valid basis for providing short-term psychotherapeutic services is the indisputable fact that the foremost concern of the vast majority of prospective psychiatric patients is immediate psychological relief and not basic personality transformation. It is manifestly illogical and self-defeating to gear a therapeutic philosophy and set of clinical techniques primarily to the luxuries of long-term contact when the preponderance of psychiatric patients are more amenable to short-term modalities. The fact that short-term psychotherapy is ubiquitously the mainstay of public and private psychiatric services makes it imperative to examine and delineate those clinical characteristics which are peculiar to short-term intervention.

It is ordinarily sensible and therapeutic to regard any cause or reason a psychiatric patient employs for seeking psychotherapy as a legitimate expression of a personal crisis which requires prompt psychotherapeutic help. There are exceptional instances when psychotherapy is unwarranted and contraindicated due to external coercive demands upon the patient; however, such circumstances are relatively rare and a subject for another discussion. Although the verbalized emotional concerns of the patient who enters psychotherapy may not constitute the "actual" crisis, there are few therapeutic pitfalls to genuinely regarding the patient as someone who is indeed in a state of crisis. A psychotherapist who, regardless of theoretical orientation, approaches all new patients as persons in crisis will be in a position of readiness to help overcome the patient's and his own tendency to emotionally trivialize important but sometimes subtle psychodynamic factors.

To regard all initial contacts as crisis-engendered does not in the least imply an alarmist or pessimistic viewpoint. On the contrary, such a perspective implies a hopeful conviction that a genuine resolution of the precipitating crisis will restore even the most seriously disturbed patient to a level of psychological functioning which the latter regards as adaptive and viable. Therefore, to aspire with the patient toward crisis-resolution is frequently in total accordance with both the ostensible and unexpressed wishes of the patient.

A common criticism of crisis-oriented psychotherapy is that it tends to neglect or minimize the importance of long-standing, basic personality conflicts. This is untrue both on practical and theoretical grounds. The short-term psychotherapist carefully evaluates and incorporates characterologic factors in formulating a diagnosis and in implementing the treatment plan. He may detect repetitive patterns and themes which stem from early childhood that require explication and dynamic interpretation.

Although time limitations may preclude the emergence and fruitful interpretation of many deep-seated and steadfastly resisted emotional conflicts, basic personality factors are not left untouched in brief clinical encounters. As a matter of fact, effective crisis-intervention will not only reduce psychological pain but will frequently produce important insights into the personality which enable the patient to forcefully discover how and why he falls prone to crises. Such discoveries can have the highly salutary effect of fortifying the patient against future psychological mishaps and, thus, serve as inestimable sources of self-esteem which enhance the potentialities of personality. The following case exemplifies this point.

A female student, age 21, in an initial session described feelings of depression which, although long-standing, became particularly acute during the time of a family reunion from which she voluntarily excluded herself. Her reason for estranging herself from her family was to avoid contact with her father whom she had not seen in over seven years. During this session the patient revealed that at age 14 her father had expressed a desire to have regular sexual relations with her, for which she would be financially remunerated. Shocked, dismayed and humiliated, she immediately decamped, vowing never to see him again; a pledge she faithfully kept. However, the patient grew more depressed each subsequent year and found herself increasingly desirous of a reconciliation.

In discussing her current feelings toward her father, the patient admitted both rage and an attitude of forgiveness. She revealed that her primary apprehension in seeing her father again was that he would again "proposition" her. In response to concerns raised by the patient, the therapist set out to assist her with four interconnected questions: (1) What was the status of her father's mental condition when she was 14?; (2) Would she benefit psychologically from a substantive reconciliation with him?; (3) How should she respond in the event that he were to attempt a sexual overture?; and (4) Should she remind her father of the incident which originally estranged them in order to mend old wounds?

Brief exploration revealed that the patient's father underwent multiple psychiatric hospitalizations during her adolescence. In discussing the nature of those hospitalizations it became clear that his behavior seven years before was a psychotic manifestation. Gradually she began to view him in a more objective and less condemnatory light. From this recognition flowed the determination to see her father again. She independently resolved that all sexual overtures would be dealt with firmly and emphatically. Because she herself could not decide whether to remind her father of the earlier debacle, she was encouraged by the therapist to totally avoid mention of the incident if possible. The patient then scheduled a second session for a week hence.

The patient reported the following week that she had enjoyed a remarkably unproblematic visit with her father. He was kind and considerate, albeit occasionally disoriented. In parting, they planned to see each other often. The patient expressed the exhilarated feeling that a mountain had been lifted from her shoulders and that her staggering depression had vanished. No future therapeutic contacts were scheduled and none eventuated. A year later the therapist and student met accidentally on campus, affording the former the opportunity to learn that she and her father had further solidified their relationship and that she continued to be free of debilitating depressions. School performance, social relationships and vocational effectiveness were also mentioned as areas in which marked improvement took place. She made unsolicited reference to the transformative value of the psychotherapy.

The following discussion deals with the therapeutic philosophy and techniques which are inherent in brief psychotherapy. The considerations referred to here are not exhaustive and are not exclusively applicable to short-term treatment. The intent here is merely to adumbrate the distinguishing features and thrusts of short-term psychotherapy and not to place unnecessary restraints upon the options available in long-term work.

ATTENTION TO TIME-LIMITATIONS

Particularly in psychiatric agencies which give statistical evidence of a preponderance of short-term cases, the psychotherapist is well disposed to regard the initial interview as potentially his last session with the patient. Such a therapeutic stance should not be cause for impotent anxiety, premature interventions or professional pessimism. Rather, it is a realistic recognition of the fact that the psychotherapist must actively mobilize his clinical skills in a manner commensurate with the unique potentials and demands of a markedly time-limited contact. A psychotherapist who is sensitively attuned and responsive to the possibility of early termination will enhance his chances for therapeutic success. Furthermore, his heightened attention to time (perhaps in the form of highly pointed questioning, lively and supportive interpretative responses and a willing opinionatedness) not only will promote therapeutic impact but will also improve the prospects that the patient will return for additional services if warranted. Ironically, many patients fail to return for much needed subsequent psychotherapeutic sessions *precisely because* the psychotherapist casually and mistakenly assumed he would have ample future contact with the patient.

ESTABLISHING A CHRONOLOGY

One of the first tasks of crisis-intervention is to establish a chronology or sequence of important psychological events. The psychotherapist presumes that a significant interpersonal or intrapsychic event has "broken the camel's back" in precipitating the crisis. Although he should not be overly stringent in delimiting the patient's discussion of overall concerns, he must determinedly strive to gain a coherent, sequential picture of the precipitants of the crisis. By thoughtfully tracing the events which have undermined the patient's emotional life the patient gains a functional awareness of what psychological and pragmatic steps are necessary in order to reverse the destructive process and restore his equilibrium.

UTILIZATION OF ANCILLARY SERVICES

A patient in acute psychological crisis often has a variety of needs which can be met only through the provision of a variety of ancillary services. Examples of such services are the legal, welfare, medical, dental, vocational and educational resources of the community. Commonly, in long-term psychotherapy there are contraindications to directly assisting the patient in gaining access to community agencies. Such intervention can unduly contaminate the long-term therapeutic relationship or foster an inordinate dependency upon the therapist which is inimical to the patient's growth.

In short-term therapy, however, certain types of crises may not be amenable to an approach which is exclusively psychological, in the narrow sense of the term. For example, a patient who is about to be evicted from his apartment may suffer acute separation anxieties which require psychological intervention. It may serve his interest to also receive timely legal, housing and economic assistance. The crisis interventionist who is conversant with those agencies of the community which provide such services is in an advantageous position to help the patient with a referral, particularly if the latter lacks the knowledge or sophistication to initiate the enlistment of community agencies himself. The minimal risk of relationship contamination and the fostering of excessive dependency in short-term psychotherapy is taken in order to reap the more immediate benefit of crisis-resolution.

HEIGHTENED THERAPEUTIC ACTIVITY

Determined structuring of a crisis-oriented interview is based upon the willingness and ability of the psychotherapist to be relatively active. An active psychotherapist is not necessarily disputatious, rude, or inhibitory. On the contrary, persons in crisis tend to justifiably regard the psychotherapist's non-intrusively active manner as an indication of interest, involvement and encouragement. It has been observed that certain passive forms of therapeutic intervention, such as protracted listening and wooden neutrality, give rise to a patient's expectations that he can and should delay resolution of his crisis, sometimes resulting in unduly lengthy and frustrating therapeutic work. Conversely, an active psychotherapist in a time-limited clinical situation will convey implicitly and explicitly a realistic expectation that an early resolution of the presenting crisis is achievable. *Often it is exactly that expectation which serves as the primary therapeutic agent.*

MAINTENANCE OF A POSITIVE RELATIONSHIP

A time-limited therapeutic encounter requires that the therapist seek to maintain a positive relationship with the patient. Such a posture does not preclude exploration of aggressive, hostile attitudes which are necessarily engendered by the therapeutic milieu. However, by permissively allowing or fostering intense and prolonged negative feelings toward the therapist in abbreviated therapeutic work, the psychotherapist defeats his own credibility as a source of psychological benefit. In crisis-oriented work it is incumbent upon the psychotherapist to quickly gain the patient's trust and confidence in his competence. The patient's relatively positive feelings for the psychotherapist's personality and clinical skills will be, in large part, the principal springboard to restoring homeostasis.

USE OF THE CONTEMPORARY CONTEXT

In long-term psychotherapy it is often appropriate and desirable to encourage temporary regression through the patient's recollections of childhood experiences. The psychotherapist, by relevantly comparing and applying contemporaneous events to the patient's recent and distant past, helps him regress to an irrational thought process which permits the formulation of a new conception or an especially clear delineation of a problem.

Even a single therapeutic session can generate extensive historical material and intense irrational thought processes. As suggested above, such regression can serve to enhance the self-awareness and growth of the ego. However, in brief psychotherapy, time-limitations may leave the patient highly vulnerable to the ambiguity of his regressive thought processes. Rather than utilizing the regression toward realistic ends, he may become victimized, for lack of therapeutic time, by an inability to adequately return to rational thinking. Therefore, in brief psychotherapy, it is necessary to make a conscientious effort to place historical data and irrational associations in a proper contemporary context. This is not to suggest that brief therapy discourages or ignores regressive activity, but only that the patient's regressive thoughts be readily applied to his current dilemma in order that he can begin effectively broaching the immediate task of crisis-resolution.

THE ROLE OF APPAREL, VERNACULAR
AND OFFICE FURNISHINGS

The appearance, speech and office furnishings of the psychotherapist are frequent catalysts of significant, symbolic responses in the patient. Long-term psychotherapy tends to afford abundant opportunity to address and explore those responses. However, when in short-term psychotherapy the office appearance, speech and apparel of the psychotherapist inadvertently alienate the patient, there may be too little time to profitably elicit and resolve the latter's antagonism.

The author is not recommending that the short-term psychotherapist dress, speak and furnish his office in total conformity with the norms of his patients, whatever they might be. However, in dealing with patients primarily on a short-term basis, it is particularly important to be unflaggingly cognizant of the role of these factors and to consider possible alternatives of personal apparel, speech, and office appearance which do not offend or alienate.

RELINQUISHMENT OF ANONYMITY

In brief psychotherapeutic encounters which have an arbitrarily appointed termination date, the psychotherapist should be prepared to relinquish a degree of his professional opaqueness and anonymity. Obviously, there are definite therapeutic risks in sharing personal information with the patient. Nevertheless, the psychotherapist who provides brief services may be more therapeutically effective if he can discreetly and selectively shed some of his persona. Often therapeutic failure results from an unnecessarily uncharitable coyness and retentiveness on the part of the short-term psychotherapist. Given the fact that certain personal information about the psychotherapist cannot prudently be imparted and that all such personal data is potentially contaminating and subject to misusage, a too rigid adherence to total anonymity may severely alienate the patient, subvert the patient-therapist alliance and thereby neutralize all therapeutic advancements.

FLEXIBLE SCHEDULING

Brief psychotherapy in particular requires a responsive flexibility of scheduling. Unlike the predictable regularity of scheduled sessions which is common to conventional long-term psychotherapy, crisis-oriented services must be geared to a wide variety of scheduling options. The expected range may reasonably be from multiple sessions within the same day to an arrangement by which the psychotherapist is placed on an availability basis in order to trouble-shoot crises whenever and however they arise. In addition, the length of sessions may vary in accordance with the patient's emotional needs and tolerance. A psychotherapist who "stands on ceremony" by insisting that all patients utilize his services only at regular, convenient intervals will inevitably and necessarily exclude large numbers of treatable patients from his practice.

TELEPHONE ACCESSIBILITY

Brief psychotherapeutic intervention in particular frequently requires a special willingness on the part of the psychotherapist to be reached by telephone. As indicated by Mackinnon and Michels (1971), the telephone plays an important role in contemporary psychiatric practice. Although patients in crisis may not actually avail themselves of telephone access to the psychotherapist, the fact that they are encouraged to contact him in the event of an emergency, often allays anxiety and works toward resolving the crisis. Dealing with psychological crises in a time-limited modality especially requires an explicitly reassuring, protective and nurturing professional attitude. Offering himself generously for emergency telephone contacts effectively betokens and conveys such a therapeutic attitude to the patient. The therapeutic impact of this attitude has been particularly evident to this author when he himself has taken the initiative to contact his crisis-ridden patients by telephone.

THE PROVISION OF INTELLECTUAL "HANDLES"

The provision of intellectual "anchors" or "handles" is an especially useful therapeutic tool in brief psychotherapy. Many confusional states make it impossible for the patient to define or clarify his feelings. At times words will be misapplied to feelings such as a reference to "annoyance" when the patient actually feels rage. Commonly the misdesignation of words to feelings will further exacerbate disruptive emotions. The patient feels a nebulous, indefinable, unnameable fear for which he cannot account. He then finds it impossible to master or manage feelings which he cannot rationally circumscribe.

The following example is relevant: a student patient at the College Health Center returned for a second session in a much improved psychological condition. When asked by the psychotherapist what he thought were the reasons for his gains, he remarked glowingly that he discovered why he was upset. He stated, "It's because I'm anxious." Puzzled, the psychotherapist probed for deeper, more complicated explanations, tending to debunk the student's contribution to the matter. After considerable fruitless investigation, it became clear that the student was basically correct. He had constructively applied to himself a term (anxiety) used by the psychotherapist in the first session. The word was pregnant with important meaning to the student and helped to demystify his fears and inhibitions. The crisis interventionist must recognize the overwhelmingly destructive effect of bewilderment upon the patient and conscientiously seek to supply him with the ballast of a definitive working vocabulary with which he can explain and govern his own feelings.

THE PROVISION OF ADVICE

The role of advice-giving as a psychotherapeutic technique is controversial. This author recognizes a high degree of validity to Oscar Wilde's witty aphorism that: "To give advice is foolish. To give *good* advice is fatal." Nevertheless, there are certain junctures in crisis-oriented psychotherapy when advice-giving is essential. For example, a patient who possesses a weapon with which he plans mayhem may require directives to relinquish the weapon and submit to hospitalization. A patient with a too severe superego who is unwittingly suffering through repeated academic misfortunes may benefit from advice to disenroll. A patient who has prematurely and unwisely terminated psychotherapy elsewhere may need overt encouragement to return to his former therapist.

Traditional psychotherapists have been rather allergic to supplying advice to their patients on the grounds that it is inefficacious and fosters unhealthy dependence. In short-term psychotherapy the hazard of fostering undesirable dependency is recognized and carefully weighed against the potential benefits of crisis-resolution through corrective decision-making. Especially in crisis-intervention work it is important to appreciate the fact that certain psychiatric patients cannot disencumber themselves of severely impoverishing entanglements without being authoritatively advised to do so. Although time-limitations will probably not allow for the development of intense dependency conflicts such as frequently evolve in long-term treatment, *it is usually best that advice be accorded sparingly, gingerly, and optionally in order that the patient feel free to go his own way.*

A SPECIAL REPERTOIRE

Finally, short-term psychotherapy requires a special repertoire of clinical styles and interventions which are professionally and personally exacting. It may necessitate unorthodox therapeutic interventions such as allowing friends, instructors and other significant persons to directly participate in the therapeutic process. It may require that the psychotherapist meet with the patient in an extramural setting such as a classroom, school. cafeteria or the patient's own home (Amada and Swartz, 1972).

In certain crisis-serving psychiatric facilities the practitioner must expect to encounter patients with whom he will have to intervene physically in order to prevent personal harm to the patient or himself. In certain instances he might gain considerable therapeutic mileage by offering patients cigarettes or refreshments.

This is not to imply that the author advocates that the psychotherapist become a dilettante or prestidigitator who deftly plies a therapeutic bag of tricks to charm and placate his crisis-ridden patients. Although special clinical circumstances sometimes warrant unorthodox interventions, the clinician must exercise particular discretion and care when he departs from conventional therapeutic procedures.

Although the goals of long-term and crisis-oriented psychotherapy may, in some therapeutic situations, coincide or overlap, the two modalities mandate disparate therapeutic approaches . In sum, the standard of clinical adeptness and sophistication requisite for undertaking effective short-term psychotherapy is unique, and perhaps even more difficult to achieve than that which inheres in long-term psychotherapy.

References

Amada, Gerald and Swartz, J. Social Work in a College Mental Health Program. *Journal of Social Casework*, Vol. 53 (1972), 528-533.

Lewin, Karl K. *Brief Encounters*. St. Louis: Warren H. Green, Inc., 1970.

Mackinnon, Roger A., and Michels, Robert. *Psychiatric Interview in Clinical Practice*. Philadelphia: W. B. Saunders, 1971. 63.

Mental Health Consultation on the College Campus

The City College of San Francisco Mental Health Program (MHP) began as a pilot project designed to offer short-term, crisis-oriented psychological services to students. Since its inception in January 1970, over 6,000 different students have been provided with approximately 15,000 hours of individual and group psychotherapy. In addition, staff psychotherapists have been extensively involved in a wide variety of training and consultation services.[1]

The primary and most obvious purpose of an on-campus mental health program is to provide direct psychological services to students. A second and broader purpose of such a program is to effect attitudinal and institutional changes within the college that will be conducive to the psychological well-being of students. This article will describe specific activities of the MHP which have been undertaken principally for the purpose of effecting psychologically beneficial changes in the educational environment.

Each semester a staff member of the MHP meets with classes of police science students who are responsible for on-campus law enforcement. This consultation provides these students with dynamic insights into the behavior of the emotionally disturbed student and familiarizes them with a range of practical strategies for dealing humanely with disruptive behavior.

Recently the services of the MHP were utilized by the Radiologic Technology Department in order to evaluate that department's procedures for interviewing students who applied for enrollment. Following a period of observation and evaluation of current procedures, a staff therapist recommended methods for refining and standardizing criteria for admission. The faculty were also assisted in restructuring their interviews in order to gain a more objective assessment of student candidates.

Each semester a staff therapist lectures to classes in the engineering department. Since most of these students would soon be entering the corporate sector of the economy, these lectures were conducted to acquaint them with the psychology of corporate organizations.

A bilingual Chinese-American therapist attended classes made up predominantly of recent Chinese immigrants. Through the medium of the Chinese language he was able to help some of these students overcome their traditional resistance to utilizing formal psychological services.[2]

The MHP has for over a decade conducted lectures in the English and Health Education Department. These presentations frequently entail a description of the services of the MHP. Other, more topical, lectures entail a review, from a psychodynamic perspective, of literature assigned in the course.

For a period of two years a staff therapist served on the Student Review Board, a committee officially designated to review and evaluate students' petitions for a change of grade. The adversary nature of the student-instructor relationship during these proceedings frequently caused each to feel apprehensive about the prospect of receiving fair treatment from the committee. The therapist's role was at times of considerable importance in assisting other committee members and the "adversaries" themselves in resolving their disagreements.

Consultation services of the MHP were also provided to the on-campus child care facility. Workshops were organized for the parents, with particular emphasis placed upon teaching and encouraging empathic responses in their child-rearing practices.

Frequently, the MHP is called upon to provide consultation in unusual situations which require immediate intervention. For example, a student who suffered from Gilles de la Tourette's disease was repeatedly distracting his instructor and classmates by involuntarily emitting a barking sound. The instructor requested suggestions for coping with this student, and on the basis of this consultation, was able to arrive at a non-punitive resolution of the problem.

In many human organizations a segment of the labor force which is commonly overlooked is the classified staff; e.g., clerical and janitorial personnel. To acknowledge and correct this oversight, a MHP therapist organized and developed a workshop for this classified staff. The workshop focused upon methods for dealing effectively with the stresses of work in the college setting.

A MHP therapist has conducted regional conferences for counselors and administrators of other California community colleges. The conferences were devoted to teaching the principles and techniques of crisis intervention.

A staff therapist has served on the California Community Colleges Chancellor's Task Force on the Emotionally Disturbed Student and was editor of its position paper. The position paper provided guidelines and abstract recommendations for understanding and coping with the emotionally disturbed community college student.

The work of two MHP therapists on an earlier chancellor's task force led directly to the first incorporation into California's educational codes of references to crisis-intervention services as an essential component of community college student health services.

In summation, mental health consultations on the college campus constitutes vital services to the entire academic community. They, obviously, neither prevent mental illness, nor eliminate the need of many students, even those who are quite functional, for formal psychological treatment. These services do, however, have far-reaching impact in fostering an educational environment which will promote the emotional well-being of students.

References

1. Amada G. The paucity of mental health services and programs in community colleges: Implications of a survey. *J Amer Coll Health* 1975 June; 23(5): 345-349

2. Amada G, Hom A. Overcoming the problem of face saving: Outreach services to Chinese students, In *Mental Health on the Community College Campus*, Amada G. (ed). Washington, D.C., University Press of America, 1978

The Interlude Between Short- and Long-term Psychotherapy

The interlude between short- and long-term psychotherapy is ordinarily characterized by the following developments: (1) an increasing vagueness with respect to formerly circumscribed psychological goals; (2) the assumption on the part of the therapist of a less·active role in the treatment process; and (3) the emerging centrality of the transference relationship to the therapeutic process.

The resolution of crisis in the early phases of psychotherapeutic treatment may give rise to certain new and sometimes unwieldy dilemmas that require the vigilant attention and understanding of the clinician. As the regressive impact of the crisis diminishes and the patient develops better ego functioning, he may spontaneously experience a significant loss of his former intense commitment to the therapeutic process and to the therapist himself.

TERMINATION OR PROLONGATION

As the patient improves, the therapist must determine the following: (1) The extent to which the patient has substantively overcome, and perhaps even psychologically matured from, his personal crisis. For example, is the patient seemingly manifesting self-control, lightheartedness, and adequacy as a defense against conflicted feelings towards the therapist (i.e., "flight into health," or "transference cure")?[1] Or, conversely, has the patient undergone a genuine and salutary resolution of his crisis, thus requiring no further psychotherapeutic intervention? (2) Does the psychotherapist recommend or at least support the discontinuance of psychotherapy or should he favor its extension for the purpose of further exploring pathological and/or problematic personality issues?

Whether the therapist recommends termination or prolongation of therapy will likely depend upon his assessment of the degree to which the patient has genuinely resolved his crisis. If, in the therapist's opinion, the patient has achieved reasonable resolution of his crisis and, furthermore, the patient evidences minimal interest in undertaking ongoing psychotherapy, the therapist's options are narrower and more obvious. In this event, in all likelihood, the decision to discontinue treatment will be reached as a mutual and incontestably satisfactory course of action. According to MacLean et al., a patient's explicit knowledge of the planned discontinuance of time-limited therapy may even serve as a possible spur to his psychological improvement.[2]

However, when the therapist and the patient jointly recognize the necessity or potential benefits of prolonging their relationship, there are certain theoretical and practical considerations which, quite naturally, assume clinical importance. This paper will attempt to present those considerations that the author regards as particularly relevant in dealing with the transitional phase between short- and long-term psychotherapy.

THE INCREASED AMBIGUITY OF
THERAPEUTIC PURPOSES AND GOALS

The patient who initially enters psychotherapy ordinarily harbors rather explicit and circumscribed psychological objectives to which he aspires, albeit, often with great difficulty. These objectives may, for example, include relief from depression and anxiety, freedom from a problematic personal relationship, or the improved self-control of intense, eruptive emotions.

Although the patient may manifest a degree of concern with the inner workings of his own personality (workings that perhaps played a significant role in precipitating the crisis in the first place), these concerns often assume secondary importance to the patient seeking immediate resolution of psychological stress.[3] Therefore, unless basic personality issues are introduced into the psychotherapeutic process prior to or at the point of the patient's resolution of crisis, the resolution itself may leave the patient with a dread that a dangerous void awaits him in the therapy. At this therapeutic juncture the patient might validly inquire of the therapist, "Well, now that I've gotten over that tough hurdle, where do we go from here?"

How the psychotherapist responds to this query will depend upon several factors: (1) The extent to which the therapist has already piqued and enlisted the patient's interest in his own personality in the earlier phases of the therapy; (2) the level of motivation, sophistication, and insight that the patient manifests regarding his own personality; and (3) the patient's amenability to the furtherance of psychotherapeutic work.

The therapist who is queried with, "What do we cover now?" should not automatically assume that all such probings are manifestations of an infantile wish to be gratified or controlled. Nor should he too perfunctorily interpret such a question to be the characteristic feigned ignorance of the passive-aggressive personality. Naturally, the psychotherapist must carefully consider such possibilities before responding to his patients. In the event that he perceives the patient's probings for clarification as an unrealistic quest for reassurance, it may indeed be wise to call attention to and analyze the unconscious motives and defenses that underlie the patient's behavior.

Other, perhaps more salient considerations may arise at this juncture in the therapeutic process. The therapist, especially during the transitional phase of therapy, might validly consider the following question: To what extent can a patient who is relatively uninitiated to therapy realistically understand and foresee such an extraordinarily complex experience, an experience that the therapist himself has grasped and mastered only after many years of disciplined training? Logic and common sense require that the therapist take into account the fact that the patient who has never undergone long-term treatment will find many aspects of continuing therapy to be unintelligible and bewildering.

As Reik has suggested, a considerable degree of the challenge and psychological benefit to be derived from psychotherapy is provided by the unexpected vicissitudes and surprises that invariably emerge during the course of treatment.[4] Furthermore, many psychotherapists who have extensive experience in providing long-term treatment will readily admit that a good number of the turns, setbacks, advances, and outcomes that take place during therapy are entirely unpredictable and sometimes quite uncanny.

Is the psychotherapist, for these reasons, to remain totally noncommittal in his posture towards the patient seeking clarification regarding the future workings and results of long-term treatment? I think not. The following are some of the therapeutic interventions that I have found particularly useful and beneficial to patients who are considering long-term treatment after a course of brief psychotherapy.

REALISTIC OPTIMISM

One of the foremost and obvious concerns of the patient is whether he will "get better." Such a wish may encompass hopes for symptomatic relief, improved insight and understanding, greater sociality, enhancement of creative expression, etc. Whether the patient's hopes for "getting better" are realistic or magical, he is entitled, especially during the transitional phase of therapy, to receive some indication from his therapist regarding the latter's capacity and desire to help him.

Naturally the therapist should neither convey categorical promises, predictions, and guarantees to the patient, since such an approach is inherently fraught with painful disappointment and disillusionment, nor express, implicitly or explicitly, a woodenly neutral or pessimistic outlook to the patient lest he, thereby, erect a formidable barrier to therapeutic success. The therapist's poor morale and indifferent outlook will unavoidably instill in his patient similar attitudes and, consequently, will be deterrents to the treatment. In such a circumstance the therapist would probably do well to refer the patient to another clinician. If, *and only* if, the therapist genuinely and realistically believes that he can help his patient, then there are few hazards, particularly during the transitional phase of therapy, attached to his imparting such a conviction to the patient. This vital conviction should be transmitted without reference to rigid timetables for psychological change.

The mere fact that the therapist truly believes and is willing to impart that he can help the patient "become better" will very possibly establish itself as the most fundamental underpinning of the therapeutic process itself. Naturally, the incredulous patient will attempt to rebut and perhaps even subvert the therapist's optimistic convictions. If so, the therapist will need to deal with these suspicious and negativistic reactions by helping the patient explore their diverse origins, and thereby, consider the possibility of developing an alliance with the therapist.[5] Again, the hope and optimism of the therapist, when genuine and convincing, is essential to assisting the patient who is passing, with deep feelings of doubt and futility, through the transitional phase of therapy.

EXPLANATIONS REGARDING THE SHIFT FROM RELATIVE ACTIVITY TO RELATIVE INACTIVITY

The psychotherapist engaged in crisis-oriented psychotherapeutic work ordinarily tends to be relatively active in his stance towards the patient. As the patient resolves and overcomes his initial crisis he commonly will require less zestful activity on the part of the therapist. He will perhaps begin to realize that largely through expressing and exploring his concerns in therapy he can acquire greater self-esteem and interpersonal satisfaction. Consequently, the therapist may concomitantly and deliberately prepare himself for gradually assuming a more retiring and unstructured role. It is at this watershed period in the treatment that a particular clinical intervention may be warranted.

Is the therapist to assume that the patient possesses sufficient understanding of the therapeutic process to realize the rationales and bases for the therapist's growing withdrawal from him? Hardly. It is conceivable that the psychologically sophisticated patient will correctly interpret the therapist's reasons for his planned withdrawal. It is equally likely that the patient confronted with the therapist's unexplained withdrawal will come to his own, perhaps quite unfounded, conclusions regarding the basis for this shift in their relationship.

For example, he may erroneously conclude that the therapist has been developing a dislike for him or that he has offended and disturbed the therapist with his emotional problems. He may, therefore, perceive the therapist's altering role as retaliatory and punitive; as harsh punishment for some vague impropriety or personality trait that the therapist cannot brook. If he possesses an adequate degree of confidence, the patient may query the therapist about the unexpected shift between them and thus demystify the phenomenon. If he does not possess such confidence, he may frantically and prematurely terminate his treatment.

What is required of the therapist when he discerns that the patient is dealing with this crossroads in the treatment with undue trepidation and suspicion? As in the case of the patient's aforementioned doubts regarding his capacity to "get better," the therapist might explore and interpret the various origins and transference significance of the patient's distorted imaginings about their perceptibly altered relationship.

However, the patient who reaches such an impasse in the therapy may require a rather clear explanation from the therapist relative to the rationales, goals, and implications of the therapist's increasingly passive interactive posture. An explanation of the goals and purposes of the therapist's modified stance may serve to enhance the patient's awareness of the therapeutic process itself, further promote the growth of a positive transference and ultimately enlist the patient's ego in effectively resolving his concerns. In any case, it is probably a mistake to automatically assume that the patient clearly discerns the therapist's actual reasons for reducing his activity level. Although the therapist should be alive to the patient's imaginings and suspicions regarding his modified stance, acute anxiety reactions may often be precluded by simple statements regarding the rationales for the change.

EXPLANATIONS REGARDING THE GROWING CENTRALITY OF TRANSFERENCE-RELATED ISSUES

As the patient and therapist continue to regularly interact, over a period of time their relationship spontaneously intensifies and eventually assumes a quite central position, both within and without the therapy itself, in the emotional life of the patient.[6] As the therapeutic relationship heightens in emotional importance, the patient quite naturally develops more highly charged attitudes and feelings towards the therapist, only some of which may be conscious and self-explanatory. Because these attitudes increasingly occupy central importance in the patient's emotional life, they come to possess the potential for either undermining or furthering therapeutic objectives.

As the patient's feelings and attitudes towards the therapist intensify, the therapist must commensurately assume the onus for eliciting and interpreting them. To avoid this task will often invite one of two results: (1) The patient will soon become overwhelmed by inexplicable and, therefore, unmanageable emotions and rather than broach this matter with the therapist, will bolt, i.e., will prematurely terminate his treatment: or (2) the patient will deal with his mysterious and uncontrollable feelings towards the therapist by withholding them from the therapist and acting them out in other "safer" relationships. This tendency can result in quite compulsive and self-defeating behavior and, as a result, serves to "prove" to the patient that therapy only tends to aggravate his problems. In this manner, premature termination may be decided upon by the patient as his only logical and viable course of action.

During the interlude between short- and long-term treatment the therapist must exercise particular discretion in how he elicits and interprets the patient's attitudes towards him. A therapist who too matter-of-factly and unexpectedly attempts to plumb such feelings may not sufficiently appreciate the degree of dread that many patients harbor over expressing these emotions. Many patients have never spoken openly and directly of their "true" feelings towards others. Consequently, even the gentlest invitation by a therapist for a patient to reflect upon and verbalize feelings towards him may arouse exaggerated suspicions, concerns, and apprehensions. For example, the patient may misperceive the therapist's probings as indications of the therapist's displeasure or impatience with him, i.e., that the therapist is personally upset with the manner in which the patient is treating him. Or, an unduly insecure and suspicious patient may be inclined to regard the therapist's interest in his emotional reactions to their relationship as an artifice, used to gain the patient's trust or affection as leverage for later retaliation.

How, then, does the therapist deal with the dilemma of igniting interest in and discussion, of the therapeutic relationship and, at the same time, responding to the patient's inner turmoil over expressing his thoughts on such a highly charged issue?

CASE EXAMPLE

A forty-five-year-old woman entered therapy for the first time while suffering from severe depression. In her marriage she was harried and denigrated by her husband. When she objected to this mistreatment, he ridiculed her objections and called her "crazy." This sometimes caused her to doubt her sanity. Eventually she ceased objecting and suppressed her rage. In discussing her childhood, the patient described her father as tyrannical and terrifying. He would repeatedly ridicule the patient, drive her to despair and tears and then accuse her of being a self-pitying sourpuss.

After several sessions the patient evidenced an increase in anxiety and wariness towards the therapist. Her speech became studied and she tended to prevent the therapist from completing his comments. Since this tendency persisted and intensified, the therapist called attention to it by asking whether something troubled the patient about their sessions. The patient immediately became more anxious and leery, demanding to know why the therapist was bringing up the matter.

The therapist shared his observation that the patient seemed increasingly anxious during their sessions and wondered whether she might have concerns about him that were associated with the inhumane treatment she had received from her husband and her father. The patient hurriedly acknowledged that the very same thought had occurred to her, but quite suddenly fell into a state of panic and with great vehemence demanded to know why the therapist was calling attention to how she felt about him. (It seemed that the patient's troubled relationships with her husband and her father caused her to view the therapist's inquiry as a harsh criticism calculated to demean and humiliate her.)

The therapist realized that further interpretations of the patient's suspicions about his intentions would only aggravate rather than neutralize them. It was clear that the patient's fears could be defused only by an explanation of the therapist's behavior.

At this point the therapist told the patient that he had several reasons for inquiring into her feelings about him. First, if these feelings were troublesome to her, they would tend to inhibit her freedom of expression during the sessions and, consequently, would reduce the benefit to be derived from therapy. Second, by more fully understanding the nature of her relationship to the therapist, the patient would very likely gain insights into the other important emotional relationships in her life.

Finally, by resolving many of the fears and inhibitions she felt towards the therapist, the patient would probably experience less insecurity and dread generally. In short, the therapist's comments were formulated with the following purpose in mind: (1) To provide the patient with an understanding of the therapeutic relationship as a microcosm of her earlier, significant emotional relationships and (2) to assist the patient to realize that the therapeutic relationship, if adequately understood, could be a valuable springboard for psychological growth.

The patient considered the therapist's remarks for several minutes and then conceded that, although she did not fully understand "how all this works," it seemed to make sense. Her fears greatly subsided. Although there were many times throughout the remaining course of therapy when the patient became highly suspicious and enraged by the therapist's references to the therapeutic relationship, she often found the therapist's above-mentioned explanation to be a reliable basis for reexploring her feelings about him.

The intervention described in the case example had several weighty advantages. It appealed to the patient's "observing ego" and, therefore, served to neutralize her most adverse reactions.[7] It also reflected the therapist's willingness to share with the patient some of the underlying dynamics of the methods he intended to use to help her, thus, providing some impetus to the patient for sharing the inner dynamics of her own thoughts and concerns. Perhaps most importantly, such an intervention may be legitimately perceived by the patient as an earnest gesture or "gift," offered by the therapist to promote and cement what is basically a genuine human relationship. For this reason, such an intervention, when used properly, can have considerable value in fostering the therapeutic alliance. That alliance will undoubtedly become a central element in enabling patient and therapist to surmount and resolve the special dilemmas which they will face during the interlude phase of therapy.

SUMMARY

The interlude between short- and long-term psychotherapy is a critical period, fraught with possible pitfalls as well as therapeutic opportunities. During this transitional phase certain discernible shifts may take place in the therapeutic process. Among these changes are: (1) an increasing vagueness with respect to formerly circumscribed goals and outcomes; (2) the assumption on the part of the therapist of a less active role in the treatment process; and (3) the growing centrality and significance of the transference relationship to the therapeutic process.

Each of these shifts will very likely evoke strong and sometimes frightening reactions in the patient. These reactions can often be effectively broached and resolved through discussion and interpretation of their earlier origins. An effective auxiliary approach, however, is the willingness of the therapist to impart to the confused or frightened patient his rationales for being less definitive regarding therapeutic goals, less active in pursuing those goals, and more explicitly interested in the patient's attitudes towards him.

References

1. Firestein, Stephen K. *Termination in Psychoanalysis.* International Universities Press, New York, 1978.

2. MacLean, G., MacIntosh, B.-A., Taylor, A., and Gerber, M. A Clinical Approach to Brief Dynamic Psychotherapies in Child Psychiatry. *Can. J. Psychiatry,* 27:113, 1982.

3. Amada, Gerald. Crisis-Oriented Psychotherapy: Some Theoretical and Practical Considerations. *J. Contemp. Psychother.,* 9:104, 1977.

4. Reik, Theodore. *Surprise and the Psychoanalyst.* Paul, French, Trubner, London, 1936.

5. Greenson, Ralph. *The Technique and Practice of Psychoanalysis.* International Universities Press, New York, 1967.

6. Amada, G. *A Guide to Psychotherapy.* University Press of America, Washington, D.C., 1983.

7. Wallerstein, Robert S. *Psychotherapy and Psychoanalysis.* International Universities Press, New York, 1975.

Organizing a Community College Mental Health Program

This chapter will attempt to describe and explain the complex process of establishing and maintaining a mental health program on an urban community college campus—City College of San Francisco. The unique background of this program was profoundly affected by the particular college and city in which it is located.

CITY COLLEGE OF SAN FRANCISCO

City College of San Francisco is a two-year community college of approximately 14,000 day students and 9,000 evening students. It has an open admissions policy. It offers two basic programs: (1) an academic curriculum designed to enable students to transfer to a four-year college or university, and (2) vocational or semiprofessional training programs, including police science, dental assistance, and hotel/restaurant management. Particular emphasis in recent years has been placed upon the recruitment and tutoring for disadvantaged people who would otherwise not attend college.

City College, like other urban colleges, has a student population which reflects the diversity of the city itself. Statistics for the Spring 1985 semester indicate that more than one-half of the students were from ethnic minorities. 31% were White, 40% Asian, 11% Black, 9% Latin American, 7% Filipino and 2% other origins. In 1970 (the year of the inception of the Mental Health Program) 17 per cent of all students had family incomes under $300 per month; another 15 per cent had total family incomes ranging from $301 to $500 per month.

In the Spring 1985 semester the median ages of all students, day and evening, was 27 years. As Carey and Rogers point out (1973), this youthful, urban student population is a group which is particularly susceptible to a variety of medical and social problems, including ven-

41

ereal disease, drug and alcohol abuse, and unwanted pregnancy. Many City College students have grown up handicapped by linguistic and cultural backgrounds that are sharply different from the White, middle-class world they are entering, perhaps for the first time, as college students. These differences are compounded by financial and personal problems, poor housing, criminal records, heavy drug use, an impulsive live-for-the-moment orientation developed in reaction to the largely ungratifying world in which they have always lived. For many students, schools are hostile and frustrating places.

For the younger student, City College represents a transition from high school to the assumption of an adult role in the community. In addition to mounting responsibilities, the student will have to cope with the complexities of sexual liberation and the prevalent use of drugs —issues around which he must develop a personal philosophy and courage. The older student may face a different set of dilemmas: academic skills may be rusty, although a wealth of personal experiences can be a great asset. Yet all students will face a formidable world, often with much uncertainty and fear.

THE CITY OF SAN FRANCISCO

City College is strongly shaped and influenced by the city in which it resides. San Francisco, like so many other large American cities, is constantly undergoing many processes of social change. The city's 1975 population of 776,000 was crowded into 45.4 square miles: the highest population density in the state and one of the highest in the nation (14,707 per square mile).

San Francisco is unique in its multi-racial and ethnic mix, with more "other nonwhite" than Black population. Ethnic group estimates for 1975 follow the trends experienced during the decade 1960 to 1970, with a decrease, 61,186 or 12.0% in the White population and an increase of 13,212 or 6.5% in the nonwhite groups in 1975 over 1970. Blacks gained nearly one and one-half per cent, while the Chinese showed a numerical increase of 4,504, Filipinos 4,406 and other nonwhite groups, 1985.

Although San Francisco has a declining population (47,974 or 6.7% from 1970 to 1975), it suffers from chronic housing and job shortages. The housing problems are compounded by property costs which have risen rapidly in the last decade. It is estimated that nearly 16 per cent of San Francisco households pay between 25 and 34 per cent of their income for rent and about 30 per cent pay more than 35 per cent of their income for rent.

In addition to changes in the ethnic composition of the city, there have been other changes in the city's population structure. San Francisco's residents are becoming, synchronously, younger and older.

San Francisco consistently has a higher death rate than California and surrounding counties chiefly because of the age structure of its population. In 1975, almost 15% of its population was at least 65 years of age.

Also reflecting the age and ethnic composition of the city are the leading causes of death for its residents. While the four leading causes of death (diseases of the heart, malignant neoplasms, cerebrovascular disease and accidents) are the same as those statewide and nationally, it is significant that the fifth leading cause of death in the city is cirrhosis of the liver. This compares with a seventh rank nationally and a sixth rank in California for this disease. Suicide is the seventh leading cause of death in San Francisco as compared to its tenth rank nationally.

In 1975, San Francisco had one of the highest case rates of tuberculosis in the country. Statistics of the Department of Public Health reveal an overall case rate of 51.7 per 100,000 (345 cases), with the Filipino (226.8 per 100,000) and Chinese (101.3 per 100,000) ethnic groups showing the highest rates of this disease.

In the late 1960s, San Francisco was a leading center of counterculture activity. Thousands of young people descended upon the city in hopes of a better life than was offered in the suburbs of America. Unfortunately, many personal tragedies resulted from the huge influx of teenage youth. Harassment from the law enforcement agencies left many with criminal records. Others suffered from severe drug abuse and the terror instilled by the oppressively open sexual mores which prevailed in the groups with which they associated. Many are still struggling to re-enter the mainstream of the economic and social systems. Some of that once rebellious group became students of City College.

RATIONALES FOR COLLEGE MENTAL HEALTH SERVICES

Farnsworth (1966), using a variety of data at Harvard University (a relatively low-risk student population), estimated that for every 10,000 students:

1,000 will have emotional conflicts of sufficient severity to warrant professional help.

300 to 400 will have feelings of depression severe enough to impair their efficiency.

100 to 200 will be apathetic and unable to organize their efforts—"I can't make myself want to work."

20 to 50 will be so adversely affected by past family experiences that they will be unable to control their impulses.

15 to 25 will become ill enough to require treatment in a mental hospital.

5 to 20 will attempt suicide, of whom one or more will succeed.

Recognition of the debilitating emotional stress of many students and the need for colleges and universities to take affirmative measures to cope effectively with that stress was expressed by President William A. Stearns of Amherst over 100 years ago.

The breaking down of the health of students, especially in the spring of the year, which is exceedingly common, involving the necessity of leaving college in many instances, and crippling the energies and destroying the prospects of not a few who remain is in my opinion wholly unnecessary if proper measures could be taken to prevent it.

—(Stearns, 1869, in Farnsworth, 1957)

Although the rationales commonly adduced in the advocacy of college mental health services tend to dramatize the psychopathology and morbidity of students, such one-sided championing is rather outmoded and potentially insulting to students. As indicated by Binger (1961), the fact that about 10 per cent of students may require professional assistance during their college careers, does not mean that:

... those who seek help are necessarily sicker than those who do not. They may simply recognize and acknowledge difficulties which others try to deny.

Certainly a campus mental health service must be amply prepared to respond to students who suffer from severe psychological stresses and vicissitudes. It must be a dependable and useful refuge for those students who have chronic personality disorders, including those of the psychotic variety. On the other hand, a mental health service should not be instituted on the basis of a spurious and self-defeating notion that it is a facility which will be beneficial solely or even primarily to "sick" students. To identify the utility of a psychological service in such a tendinous manner might seriously discourage the utilization of such a program even by those students who truly suffer from serious psychiatric disorders and would certainly dissuade the more well functioning students who periodically require help with transient psychological difficulties from seeking assistance.

The experience of higher education has been recognized by Freedman as one which has the potential for animating an:

... appreciation of the complexity of people and social events, openness to new experiences, flexibility in thinking, compassion in judgment of people, and the like. These changes are large in some students, small in others. But few go through college without acquiring at least a tinge of this liberalization and the social consequences of such changes are enormous. (Freedman, 1967)

Jade Snow Wong, an alumna of City College of San Francisco, in her poignant autobiographical book, *Fifth Chinese Daughter*, states in personal terms how two years of college critically reorganized her personality.

Hand in hand with a growing awareness of herself and her personal world (Wong writes of herself in the third person), there was developing in her an awareness of and a feeling for the larger world beyond the familiar pattern. The two years had made her a little wiser in the ways of the world, a little more realistic, less of a dreamer, and she hoped more of a personality. (Wong, 1945)

If the experience of learning in college is dynamic and serves as a catalyst to further personal growth and understanding for many students, a college mental health program can legitimately be predicated upon the rightful aspirations of such students to further experiment and self-discover, in a credible psychological milieu within the educational institution itself.

THE CITY COLLEGE MENTAL HEALTH PROGRAM

The Mental Health Program had its obscure genesis in the Student Health Service of City College. In 1968, the Student Health Service was staffed by only one health practitioner, a public health nurse (PHN). Although her official responsibilities were to provide medical-nursing services exclusively, the PHN was continually besieged by students who were plagued with a wide variety of complex psychological difficulties. Her plaint, at the time, was that the only available means of assisting students was by means of referring them to community psychiatric clinics, a procedure which was frequently undesirable and abortive. In her own words, referring students in psychological crises to off-campus agencies too often meant:

... time-consuming searches for proper assistance, long waiting lists, endless red-tape and financial hassles. In addition, many students have found the process of applying for services elsewhere an awesomely formidable challenge, due to feelings of self-stigma, which they would prefer to avoid. Usually, by the time adequate assistance has materialized, it has been too late, and the student's whole semester is at stake; one factor which accounts for the unusually high rates of leaves of absence each semester.

Based upon the PHN's own findings, which were solidly substantiated by available epidemiological research of college students on other campuses, a pilot project was conducted in the Spring of 1969. The objectives of the pilot project were: (1) to centralize psychological services on campus; and (2) to determine the extent of potential utilization of such a program. To implement this study, a third-year psychiatric resident with the San Francisco Mental Health Services was assigned to the Student Health Service for the Spring Semester. His responsibilities included: (a) direct psychological services to the PHN, faculty and administration, in dealing with the emotional problems of students; and (3) psychiatric liaison services to community agencies to facilitate mutual referrals of students for psychotherapy.

The Student Health Service maintained an open intake policy, seeing all students who applied and seeing them soon after application. The psychiatric resident spent the majority of his time in direct psychotherapeutic work with students. He also spent a generous amount of time in consultation with college personnel. Deliberately, minimal time was allotted to activities such as processing applications, history-taking, psychological assessment and record-keeping. At the end of the Spring semester, 98 different students had been served by the program. This group received a total of 253 sessions. Although these 98 students comprised only a minuscule proportion of the total number of 14,000 day students enrolled in 1969, these figures are impressive for several reasons: (1) the program was new and, therefore, the student body initially had little knowledge of its availability or whereabouts; (2) the psychiatric resident, who was the sole provider of psychological services, was new to the campus himself and had had little time to familiarize himself with those programs and personnel which could serve as effective sources of student referrals to the Student Health Service (as was pointed out in subsequent years, vast numbers of college personnel knew virtually nothing of the pilot study which was conducted in 1969); and (3) as Farnsworth (1964) suggests, the extent to which students utilize the Student Health Service will depend in part on the manner in which they perceive the service and its usefulness to them.

Since one semester was clearly a too abbreviated period of time in which to engender student trust in the usefulness of the program, the intake figures for the Spring semester of 1969 were not regarded as a valid index of future utilization of the psychological services.

Based upon the relative success of the demonstration project, the PHN next proceeded to contact major community hospitals and psychiatric clinics, hoping to enlist their support in organizing and staffing a formal mental health clinic on campus. The earliest responses from personnel of these organizations were friendly to the concept of an on-campus psychological service at City College but quite unreceptive to bearing certain practical sacrifices in order to bring such a program to fruition. At best, those agencies intimated that they could provide consultation services to college personnel, if such a bilateral arrangement were practicable.

In 1969, the PHN submitted grant requests to local foundations for funding of a "demonstration" Mental Health Program at City College. The Zellerbach Family Fund of San Francisco awarded a grant which was supplemented by funding from the National Institute of Mental Health. This supplemental grant was provided under the auspices of the Westside Mental Health Services (a local consortium of mental health agencies) which assumed, with a community psychiatric clinic, co-sponsorship of the Mental Health Program. The Mental Health Program began serving students in January, 1970.

With the advent of the Mental Health Program, several service priorities were established.

1. To deal effectively and rapidly with basically well functioning students in psychological crisis.

2. To refer those students in need of services that were not available at the college to other community resources.

3. To provide supportive services on an ongoing basis to some severely disturbed students needing such assistance.

4. To help students learn as much as possible about the maintenance of mental health and the minimization of emotional stress.

5. To make consultation services readily available to all college personnel, with respect to their concerns about the mental health needs of students.

In order to implement these service goals, the following guidelines and policies were adopted: there would be no charge for services and intake was to be entirely voluntary; i.e., no student would be seen against his or her wishes. All information was to be held in strict confidence within the Student Health Service, kept separate from all other student records. The importance of the preservation of confidentiality applied also to the question of whether or not a particular student had come to the clinic at all. The program would maintain an "open" intake seeing any regularly enrolled student who applied as soon as possible after application. Waiting periods and waiting lists would be kept to a minimum.

The general goal of psychological services was to promote personal growth by giving students an opportunity to explore problems which interfered with studies, work, and relationships with family and friends. Those clinical staff recruited to the program were specially sought for their proven skills, sensitivity and experience in handling acute problems. The ethnic composition of the staff would approximate the composition of the multiethnic student body (Carey, Swartz and Leavitt, 1971). This practice would hopefully encourage minority students to utilize the psychological services in numbers proportionate to their percentages in the student body as a whole.

The mainstay of the program was to be short-term crisis-oriented services to insure the availability of immediate appointments for a maximum number of students. Although it was expected that most students would receive individual psychotherapeutic services, provisions were made for group therapy as well. Group services were developed to assist students whose problems were largely in the area of interpersonal relations. Also, consultation services were developed with the goals of fostering a campus-wide atmosphere and attitude which allowed for students who received mental health services, if they were at all identifiable, to be treated no differently from other students. Because the clinical cornerstone of the program was to be short-term psychotherapy, procedures for inter-agency referrals were immediately instituted.

Although the proportional representation of specific ethnic groups who have worked in the program has shifted throughout subsequent years, the program's commitment to maintaining a genuinely multi-ethnic staff has never been challenged or jeopardized. For example, during the academic year 1976-77, there were four senior staff and four trainees, three of whom were Asian, three of whom were White, one of whom was Black, and one of whom was Filipino.

The goal of extending immediate or early appointments to students was consistently met. Rarely did it take more than two days for a student to see a therapist. Emergencies were always given the highest priority and were responded to immediately.

The leave of absence rate for students who have received psychological services has regularly been approximately half the rate of leaves of absence for the general student population. This figure is particularly impressive since students who receive psychological services for the purpose of dealing with personal crises might logically be regarded as having a high-risk potential for dropping out of college, as compared with those students who manage without such services.

The goal of encouraging minority students to utilize psychological services on a proportional basis has been met effectively, with the possible exception of Asian students. Although the intake figures differ from month to month, Black and Hispanic-American students have utilized the program in numbers proportionate to their representation in the student body.

From January 1970 to 1977, over ten thousand individual treatment hours had been provided to almost 4,000 different students.

Based upon the evident success of the "demonstration" project, there was unreserved support for the continuance of the Mental Health Program from students, faculty and administrative staff. Because the "demonstration" purpose of the program had been fulfilled, the Zellerbach Family Fund substantially reduced its funding in 1972. These funds were partially replenished by the Bothin Helping Fund of San Francisco, but in order to restore the program to an adequate level of subsidization, it was necessary to receive subvention from the Community College District.

Although the college administration had originally made no firm commitments to allocate funds to the Mental Health Program, the former President of City College, in 1969, expressed in a letter to prospective funding agencies, his confidence that the college could financially support the program through its regular budget, in the event that other sources of funding became unavailable. That confidence proved to be collectible, for, in 1972, the Community College District allocated $30,000 to insure the continuity of the program. With this allocation, the college became the principal source of funding for the Mental Health Program.

In 1973, the sponsorship of the Mental Health Program was transferred to Progress Foundation, a private non-profit organization which specialized in the administration of half-way facilities for the emotionally disturbed in San Francisco. Each year, from 1973 through 1976, one-year contracts were negotiated between the college district and Progress Foundation, under which the latter organization would provide accountant services, administrative sponsorship, program evaluation and regular psychiatric consultation to the clinical staff by the Medical Director of Progress Foundation.

The end of the academic year 1975-76 marked the culmination and resolution of an impasse which had existed between the Mental Health Program and the college administration. Despite the generous financial support which the program received from the college, the administrative policy of funding the program on a one-year, contractual basis under the auspices of private agencies, was a source of deep insecurity to the staff of the program.

Under that administrative arrangement the staff had no assurance, from one year to the next, that they would return to work in September of the forthcoming academic year. Each Spring the staff would anxiously await a resolution from the City College Board of Governors to refund and renegotiate a contract to continue the program. Because of the perennial tenuousness of the program, the staff recommended to the college administration and Board of Governors that the college permanently integrate the Mental Health Program by allocating funds for two certificated mental health counselor positions. The college administration initially proposed and advocated an alternative measure which would indefinitely integrate the Mental Health Program into the system of the San Francisco Community Mental Health Services (SFCMHS).

The college administration had long regarded SFCMHS as the logical inheritor of the Mental Health Program, since there had been a close and harmonious relationship between that agency and the college. The staff of the Mental Health Program, however, considered the college administration's proposal to be fraught with serious pitfalls which would imperil the future of the program.

Basically, the staff regarded the proposal as a measure which would serve to reinforce the status of the program as an impermanent service administered by "outsiders." (SFCMHS could make no financial commitments to the Mental Health Program; therefore, it was offering only the administrative umbrella of yet another community agency.) The staff believed that permanent integration of the Mental Health Program into the Student Health Service was an absolute requisite to the legitimization of the program as an integral part of the college.

In the Spring of 1976, the college administration agreed to support the principle of a permanently integrated, college administered

Mental Health Program. Two full-time college certificated mental health counselor positions were ratified by the Board of Governors in the Summer of 1976. Currently (1985), there are four salaried clinical positions assigned to the Mental Health Program. The evolution of the program, from a rather tenuous pilot project to a permanent and integral component of the college, has been uneven, struggle-ridden and, at times, painfully slow. However, in an era when mental health services were generally being defunded and retrenched, the growth and achievements of the Mental Health Program, made often against great odds, were truly remarkable.

The process of integrating a mental health program into the institution of a college might be likened to the transplantation of a vital organ into the human organism. As in the case of a dramatic surgical procedure, the expected social responses to a new mental health service may range from delirious hopes for a miraculous cure of all systemic disorders to a morbid dread that the new component will spell death to other components of the host organism (institution). Very likely, the initial "organismic" response of the host institution to the introduction of a mental health program will, at times, be rather allergic or rejective.

The college mental health service, as it is being newly incorporated into the institutional system, will perhaps be tainted with a good degree of controversy. Those who work in such programs should expect that their unconventional presence will arouse both realistic and unrealistic hopes and suspicions, in administrators, faculty members and students. These expectations, whether realistic or not, must be acknowledged with sensitivity, compassion and respect.

References

Allen, N. *Physical Culture in Amherst College.* Massachusetts: Stone and Huse, 1869.

Binger, C. A. L. Emotional Disturbances Among College Women. *Emotional Problems of the Student.* Edited by G. B. Blaine, Jr., and C. C. McArthur. New York: Appleton-Century-Crofts Inc., 1961.

Carey, J., and Rogers, E. L. Health Status and Health Knowledge of the Student in the Changing Community College. *American Journal of Public Health.* Vol. 62, No. 2, 1973, 126-133.

Carey, J., Swartz, J., and Leavitt, A. Developing a Mental Health Program at an Urban Community College. *Journal of the American College Health Association.* 19:200, June 1971, 289

Farnsworth, D. (Ed.) *Mental Health in College and University.* Cambridge, Mass.: Harvard University Press, 1957.

Farnsworth, D. *Psychiatry, Education, and the Young Adult.* Illinois: Charles C. Thomas, 1966.

Farnsworth, D. *College and Health Administration.* New York: Inc., Appleton-Century-Crofts, Inc., 1964.

Freedman, M. *The College Experience.* San Francisco, CA: Jossey-Bass, Inc., 1967.

Wong, J.S. *Fifth Chinese Daughter.* New York: Harper and Row, 1945.

Overcoming the Problem of Face-Saving: Outreach Services to Chinese Students

There is an underutilization of mental health services by Chinese students at City College of San Francisco which parallels the general patterns of Chinese underutilization of community psychiatric resources in San Francisco. This article will first attempt to describe and explain some of the cultural factors which deter many Chinese students from utilizing college psychological services. This discussion will be followed by a delineation of the conceptual and pragmatic approaches which have been used by the City College Mental Health Program to overcome the cultural resistances of Chinese students to the utilization of psychological services.

CULTURAL RESISTANCES TO THE UTILIZATION OF MENTAL HEALTH SERVICES

For the Chinese, the idiomatic expression for mental illness or "nerves" is *sun ging*. Vernacularly translated, this means "spirit infested." It originates from a primitive view of the world. According to this view, man is controlled by external, mystical forces of fate; the spirits of good and evil prevail. He can attempt to ward off these evil spirits by means of ancestral worship and the close observance of a vast array of superstitious beliefs and rituals. Among those observances which are related to the maintenance of mental health is the avoidance of strong affects such as anger. Thus, one strives to ignore angry feelings, remain patient and sacrificial, turn the other cheek, and give the appearance of equanimity. Such behavior is particularly important when a person is dealing with his elders or authority figures.

Since there is little tolerance for uncontrolled emotions, there develops a social aversion to the psychologically disturbed, who are viewed as persons who have inordinately lost control of themselves.

51

Those who suffer from *sun ging* are threatening to one's family and society because they are incitive reminders of each person's fear of losing control of his own feelings. For those who already have doubts about their own ability to control impulses, there is a dread of any association with the possessors of *sun ging*.

Unfortunately, the services of the college mental health program are sometimes avoided due to the fear of "guilt by association" with those who suffer from *sun ging*. The resistance to seeking help can be extreme. Going to a mental health clinic is, for many, an admission of being "out of one's mind." Students then tend to wait until a crisis overwhelms them before they seek help or are brought in for assistance. In this dysfunctional state they often find it extremely difficult to maintain a sense of self-worth with which to offset their tremendous feelings of shame.

The age-old Chinese concern with "saving face" (*mean gee mun tie*) is a primary reason for avoiding mental health services and a critical impediment to successful psychotherapy. Historically, saving face originated 2,000 years ago with the Confucian tenet of social propriety. All of man's social behavior, according to this tenet, can be organized around and based upon one's social position. Rulers behave like rulers, subjects like subjects. Families are headed by fathers; the wives and children must obey. The lines of authority are well defined and include all positions.

Children learn their social behavior through child-rearing practices and group pressures of the family which induce shame and guilt. When a child errs—for example, fails in his academic work—the teacher blames the parents. The parents become ashamed and, to avoid any future loss of face, they shame and punish the child, according to his role and position in the family. For example, a common reprimand for an eldest son would be: "Since you are the eldest, you should be a model for your younger brothers and sisters; and since you are a son, you carry on our surname and should know better than to disgrace the family (including his ancestors)."

The problem of saving face is taught very early and manifests itself outside of the home as well, particularly in the schools. The child's foremost responsibility (one is a child until one's formal education is completed and one is married) is to do well in school since he obviously is not yet ready to prove himself worthy by means of assuming adult responsibilities, such as working for a living. If the child fails to fulfill his academic responsibilities, there results a loss of face for him and his family. Thus, academic failure must be avoided at all costs.

An additional dimension to the problem of saving face is the great emphasis placed upon psychological independence and self-reliance in the Chinese family, as demonstrated by the following example.

A nurse in the Student Health Service was called to answer an emergency in a classroom where she found a young, foreign-born Chinese man bent over with complaints of stomach pain, nausea and headache. He initially refused her assistance. The instructor had earlier noticed the student appearing ill and had unsuccessfully referred him to the Student Health Service. The student finally agreed to accept help from the nurse and compliantly followed her to the health center. Upon examination, he readily felt better and offered information regarding his history of drug abuse and the recent loss of a girlfriend. It surprised the nurse that he was so "open" and "recovered" so rapidly. She cleared him medically and referred him to the Mental Health Program in order to "talk about his problems."

The student was resistive to the referral. As he put it, the psychological approach would not work. Furthermore, the "White counselors would not understand." With much coaxing and a promise that a Chinese counselor was available, he accepted. During the therapeutic session, the student was cooperative but suspicious of being labeled mentally ill. The psychotherapist was careful to respect his autonomy and engaged the student in a mutual attempt to understand his crisis so that he could remain in control of his life.

Although he was relieved to be able to speak with another Asian who could "understand what I have been through" and felt that talking was helpful, the student did not return for subsequent appointments. After the initial confusion and anxiety were alleviated, he could not tolerate the shame and embarrassment which were engendered by his psychological dependency upon the psychotherapist.

Teachers of foreign-born Chinese students frequently have considerable difficulty in encouraging their verbal participation in a classroom situation. These students are often embarrassed and awkward over their difficulty speaking English. In addition, traditional Chinese teachings admonish the student to be sensitive to the needs of the group, as opposed to his own needs; thus, he seeks to avoid drawing attention to himself by withholding his personal thoughts and feelings.

The foreign-born Chinese student is more receptive to dealing with matters which are concrete and unambiguous (such as those which commonly arise in physical science and mathematics courses). These students have particular difficulty responding to situations which require the expression of personal feelings or controversial thoughts (such as commonly occur in social science courses or psychotherapeutic sessions). Their reticence to discuss personal feelings and thoughts is not due to a lack of interest, but rather is the consequence of cultural taboos which discourage psychological and social spontaneity.

Typical concerns which affect the Chinese student are whether others are genuinely interested in what he has to say and whether they might be offended by his comments. The historical origins of such self-abnegation can be discovered, for example, in ancient Chinese art. In landscape paintings, a human figure, such as a tiny fisherman, is overshadowed by vast mountains. Man is depicted as a minute part of the universe and his role is to find his humble place and live harmoniously with the world around him. The ancient cultural value placed upon humility and self effacement often carries dilemmas for the foreign-born Chinese student who attempts to adapt to the rigors of the American college or university.

The American college as an institution values the expression of individual thoughts and feelings, much as the dominant cultural mode in this society values "free" expression of personal opinion in practically any circumstances. This, coupled with the overall societal emphasis upon individualism, presents quite a conflict for the Chinese student who has learned to devalue his personal thoughts and feelings. The Chinese student is almost "preprogrammed" to do poorly in class participation and psychotherapeutic encounters. Some do struggle to change their values and behavior in the process of assimilation and in the face of academic and economic necessity.

As the Chinese student undergoes the process of assimilation from the traditional home to Western institutions and the mass media, there is a gradual learning of new values and norms. This transition can be a source of acute conflict and turmoil. Such values as assertiveness and spontaneity clash with traditional Chinese values. This explains, to a great extent, why Chinese students, both foreign-born and American-born, tend to avoid mental health services. Mental health programs are recognized as agencies which enhance the potential for assertiveness and spontaneity, and, therefore, are shunned as threats to the Chinese student's sense of cultural pride and integrity.

THE SOCIAL AND ECONOMIC STRESSES
OF THE CHINESE COMMUNITY

The Chinese word for America is *gum san*, literally, gold mountain, a conception which harks back to the gold rush days when the first Chinese emigrated to the United States. The dream then and now, is for economic wealth. It is the undisputed goal of the Chinese student in our contemporary colleges and universities to acquire material wealth. Formal education leads to "better" jobs and "better" jobs beget improvements in one's economic status. Since the Chinese student's family frequently counts upon him to improve their own social and economic standing, he is driven by a cultural preoccupation to survive and succeed academically. Thus, academic failures such as a poor grade or nonadmission to a college or university stigmatizes and undermines not only the student, but his entire family as well.

The low standard of living of recent Hong Kong immigrants who reside in San Francisco's Chinatown has been well documented. The cycle is perpetual and demoralizing. Low formal education and inadequate English-speaking abilities lead to low-income employment, substandard housing conditions and mental and physical illness. Alarmingly high rates of tuberculosis and suicide render public health officials helpless. For many of these families, poverty is an inescapable way of life; it serves only to foster even greater family and individual disorganization.

Despite this deadly spiral, almost all Chinese families believe that hard work and formal education can lead to rapid social and economic mobility. It is the American dream of rags to riches that some immigrants have realized. Those who are fortunate, have the opportunity to attend a college or university . However, many learn, all too quickly, that the goal of economic success is very far away. The demand for selective academic programs, exemplary grades and lucrative jobs exceeds the supply. To the dismay of many, the unwavering pursuit of academic and vocational goals does not solve all of one's social and emotional needs.

The single-minded pursuit of academic success is sometimes observed in certain students who force themselves to fulfill their customary scholastic responsibilities despite a recent tragic death in the family. Other students, for example, those with severe physical or psychological handicaps, develop unrealistic expectations of themselves. For example, a young Chinese male who has had a serious physical disability since childhood and a history of schizophrenia, has been enrolled in City College for five years with aspirations of becoming a physician. Despite consistently failing grades and very little aptitude for a career in medicine, he persists in his very futile academic endeavors, primarily to please his parents.

OUTREACH SERVICES: CLASSROOM PRESENTATIONS

Each year, increasing numbers of students, including the Chinese foreign-born, become aware of the availability of the Mental Health Program at City College of San Francisco. Generally, Chinese students tend to use the program's services only during a crisis and only after they have exhausted their personal resources, such as family, friends, etc. As indicated earlier, the number of Chinese students who receive mental health services is not representative of the number of Chinese students who attend City College. Caught between a traditional and an industrial culture while experiencing tremendous pressure to succeed and, at the same time, cope with ghetto conditions, the foreign-born Chinese are particularly susceptible to mental illness and particularly resistant to psychological help, as indicated by their low rate of utilization of mental health services.

To reach a greater proportion of the student population, particularly the "resistant" Chinese student, the Mental Health Program has relied heavily upon educational and preventative measures. The program has made extensive use of outreach services such as film workshops and student discussion groups which deal with a variety of mental health subjects, such as aggression, depression, guilt, etc.

The presentations which staff members made to classes were carried out with the prior authorization of the department chairperson and the permission of the instructor. These administrative clearances tended to give the program an "official" sanction from respected authority figures which promoted a greater acceptability for the speaker. For the Chinese student, the Mental Health Program seems less alien and less formidable when the speaker is himself Chinese. Using a variety of techniques (which will be discussed in detail later in this article), the speaker seeks to make the subject of mental health less fearful and less shameful. The classroom setting itself affords the student a sense of anonymity which protects him against feelings of self-exposure and enables him to identify with other persons in the class who are "OK" and yet express interest in the services of the Mental Health Program.

CONCEPTUAL APPROACHES TO
REACHING THE CHINESE STUDENT

Based upon our clinical experience, we assume that all students have life problems or potential life problems. The more aware and informed the students are of themselves and life stresses, the more prepared they are to fend for themselves. In order to assist students in gaining self-awareness, the speaker attempts to present his facts and points of view in the most persuasive manner possible. The basic approach and attitude used are those which have also been found to be effective in brief psychotherapeutic encounters. Thomas Rusk (1971) refers to five facets of an effective therapeutic stance in crisis-oriented psychological services: calm confidence, hopefulness, active leadership, intrusiveness, and explicit empathy. These factors have been of considerable practical value to the Mental Health Program staff as they extend their services to students throughout the campus.

The importance of calm confidence is clear when one realizes that students are quick to judge whether or not a staff person is acceptable as a helping person. A role model who demonstrates genuine interest and competence can improve a student's own sense of resourcefulness and independence. The expressed confidence of the staff member in the capacity of students to develop new and exciting perspectives of themselves and the external world is often an important inspiration to many students.

When the staff representative enters the classroom or the therapeutic session, he seeks to effect psychological change by honestly conveying his sense of hope. His expectation that there can be positive results from his work can be contagious. He often must explicitly counteract the student's feelings of hopelessness which, heretofore, had been formidable obstacles to change.

Similarly, in crisis-oriented psychotherapy or in classroom presentations, there is no room for a shy, passive approach. During a classroom presentation, the psychotherapist is showing his "wares;" giving a sample of his active therapeutic style. Students want to know if they will be actively assisted. They do not want to be abandoned to a wandering, aimless struggle for self-understanding. They want and need active leadership in learning how to live their lives more creatively and assertively.

The fourth of Rusk's factors, intrusiveness, may have negative connotations for those who, like the authors, value psychological autonomy. However, when students are in crisis, they tend to develop rigid and maladaptive psychological patterns and are unable to focus clearly upon discrete aspects of their problems. This is precisely the time when the staff person must be willing to intervene in order to elicit the attention needed to exert influence upon the student. When dealing with a student who is confused or conflicted by a psychological crisis, the psychotherapist explicitly indicates that both he and the student count and that he refuses to accept a hopeless view of the student's emotional difficulties.

Students frequently hope that the psychotherapist not only intellectually grasps their psychological concerns, but also has the capacity to empathize with their emotional distress. The psychotherapist fosters a working alliance with the student based upon his readiness to reach out and acknowledge the student's emotional pain and burden. By means of his empathic acknowledgements, the psychotherapist enables the student to overcome a sense of isolation and despair.

TECHNIQUES USED TO REACH THE
FOREIGN-BORN CHINESE STUDENT

How does one present mental health concepts in the most interesting and palatable manner to a class of foreign-born Chinese students? One technique which has been effective is the use of a few basic Chinese characters as "object lessons." Given the fact that most of the foreign-born Chinese students at City College have received some formal education in Hong Kong, this group, for the most part, reads and writes the Chinese language proficiently.

The staff member who speaks to a class of foreign-born Chinese students in their native tongue is able to establish rapport with them almost immediately. Students are pleased to be able to demonstrate their command of the Chinese language, especially when their linguistic and writing skills surpass those of the guest speaker from the Mental Health Program. The speaker's imprecise pronunciations give the students a chance to teach him something important; thus, a give-and-take relationship is initiated. The speaker is then given a significant opportunity to demonstrate how to overcome a personal deficiency. Without embarrassment he asks about the impreciseness of his pronunciations and freely and gladly welcomes the students' advice and corrections of his speech. His manner and verbal replies indicate that there has been no "loss of face." The students can quickly infer that they need not be threatened by his presence and that he and the students can fruitfully learn from one another.

Their literacy in the Chinese language enables these students to understand the etymology, meanings and usages of many Chinese characters, some of which beautifully demonstrate mental health principles. For example, the Chinese characters which denote a "crisis" are (gui gay). The first character signifies "danger" and the second character (gay) symbolizes "opportunity." These two characters, used in combination with each other, contain a good degree of psychological wisdom. They illustrate the sound principle that psychological crisis is a state provoked when a person faces a threat or *danger* to important life goals; however, this same state of disequilibrium is also an *opportunity* to learn more adaptive methods of coping with personal change and stress. This useful illustration enables the student to better understand the nature of psychological crises and to appreciate the potential for recovery and growth which is inherent in personal states of crisis.

Another psychological concern which can be graphically illustrated with the use of a Chinese character is that of suicide. Originally, most characters portrayed a literal picture of the phenomena which they represented. In the case of suicide, the character which denotes danger, (gui), is again significant. When one looks at segments of this character, it is possible to first perceive a cliff, and then a man on the edge of a cliff, who appears to be dangerously close to jumping or falling off (Gorden Lew, Eileen Meehan). The dramatic quality of this character tends to evoke strong emotional reactions in students. By using the metaphor of the "person on the edge of a precipice," the speaker attempts, in a general way, to discuss the students' reactions to the character and to place those reactions within the framework of what he knows about frightening or self-destructive feelings. He takes this opportunity to offer students his theoretical understanding of the dynamics of suicidal emotions. He also imparts his hopeful attitude that such feelings can be effectively managed and transformed into positive strivings, with the benefit of self-awareness (and perhaps psychotherapy).

Mental health services that work with Chinese students must be sensitive to their cultural resistances to psychological interventions. Chinese students who perceive such programs as respectful of their cultural concerns and values will utilize these services more willingly. Educational activities such as classroom presentations by Chinese staff members is one method which has proven effective in enabling many Chinese students to perceive the City College Mental Health Program as a nonthreatening and beneficial psychological resource.

References

Rusk, T. Opportunity and Technique in Crisis Psychiatry. *Comprehensive Psychiatry*, Vol. 12, No. 3 (May, 1971), 249-263.

Special thanks to Gordon Lew and Eileen Meehan for their assistance in the preparation of this paper.

Why People Distrust Psychotherapists

A character in one of George Bernard Shaw's plays wittily remarked that all professions were conspiracies against the laity. Psychotherapy as a profession is sometimes seen in this unseemly light by the public.

There are many rational and valid reasons for the widespread distrust of the psychotherapy profession. First, many therapists are poorly trained and, therefore, lack the requisite skills and knowledge to perform their professional duties well. Second, it is hardly a secret that psychotherapists as a group are apparently as prone as the rest of the population to personality defects and mental illness. When the emotional conflicts of psychotherapists remain unresolved, their objectivity and judgment become impaired and the quality of their clinical work of course suffers as a consequence.

Finally, the rich smorgasbord of diverse and contending psychotherapies that have proliferated in this country must give even the most unsuspecting observer cause for concern and skepticism. After all, if one therapy emphasizes the importance of self-insight; another, behavioral change; and yet another, emotional catharsis—each laying claim to irrefutable success with its methods and objectives—how is it possible to accredit one without discrediting the others?

In addition to these rather obvious reasons for mistrust, the profession of psychotherapy arouses suspicions due to a number of other, more subtle, factors, some of which involve attitudes that are not altogether rational or conscious.

POLARIZED PERCEPTIONS OF PSYCHOTHERAPISTS

Two quite polarized perceptions of therapists may sometimes serenely cohabit the mind of a single individual. One perception is that therapists are providing clandestine services which are designed to subvert the status quo of the individual and society. At this end of the perceptual spectrum therapists are viewed as champions of sexual libertinism, irreligiosity and indiscriminate nonconformity. The policy of confidentiality which therapists maintain about their work is seen as further evidence of nefarious goings-on.

At the other end of the perceptual spectrum the psychotherapist is viewed as a rich font of miraculous cures. Therapists are endowed with the godlike qualities of omniscience, infallibility and an imperviousness to the ordinary hardships of life. A frequent offshoot of these attitudes is the expectation that therapists have "all the answers" to the human condition and can, if they would only apply their omnipotent talents, completely eliminate human suffering.

What accounts for these polarized attitudes? One explanation is that therapists are readily perceived as parental figures and, thereby, arouse strong transference or infantile reactions in others. Thus, they tend to represent either the "good," flawless parent of early infancy who succors and heals, or the "bad" parent who rejects, abandons or secretly plots mischief (sexual and otherwise).

The perception of the therapist as a "bad," conspiring parent understandably arouses distrust and suspicion. It is important to recognize, however, that the perception of the therapist as the personification of all that is good also arouses feelings of distrust. Unquestionably, a belief in the perfection of others can never be realistically fulfilled or trusted and when it is irrationally embraced as a conviction, it inevitably leads to disappointment, disillusionment and even greater distrust.

THE NEED FOR PERFECTION:
THE "EMPEROR'S CLOTHES" SYNDROME

In certain respects, the mere existence of psychotherapists is an incitive reminder of the imperfections of society and of the human personality. Since most people prefer to minimize or conceal their imperfections, psychotherapists, by dint of their dedication to the uncovering (and understanding) of personal imperfections, are commonly viewed as relentless adversaries. They are the symbolic counterparts of the child in the fable, "The Emperor's Clothes," who ingenuously betrays the emperor's nakedness. Psychotherapists, as seekers and revealers of naked personal truths, threaten the very fabric of those human strivings which seek to cover and disguise imperfections.

This perception of psychotherapists leads to the fallacious belief that professional involvement with a psychotherapist is an unavoidable indication of one's lack of personal success and wholeness. If one happens to be the parent of a person who enters psychotherapy, the therapist may very well be viewed as a foe who will expose and blame the parent for his imperfections as child-rearer. In short, the quest for personal perfection can become a powerful source of distrust toward psychotherapists who, in accord with their avowed professional objectives, quest to uncover and learn about personal imperfection.

PSYCHOLOGICAL DEPRIVATION AS A SOURCE OF DISTRUST

Those persons who do not receive psychotherapy may develop intense ambivalent emotions toward those who do, especially if the recipient of treatment is a close friend or relative. When a member of a family enters psychotherapy, for example, other family members may react with strong feelings of deprivation as a result.

There are at least two explanations for this reaction. First, family members may experience a sense of loss and envy over the patient's willingness to share deep personal concerns with someone other than themselves. They may interpret the patient's actions, perhaps with a fair degree of accuracy, as a criticism or indictment of the quality and character of family life. In this instance it is the therapist who is envied for being the principal repository of personal information about the family.

Second, when one person hears about another entering therapy, he may quite involuntarily compare himself unfavorably to the patient. Realistically or not, he may entertain thoughts of the patient in therapy engaging in an enriching personal experience. From such thoughts may evolve feelings of deprivation, loss and rivalry toward the so-called "privileged" patient. In this instance it is the patient who is envied for being regarded as the fortunate beneficiary of a nurturing relationship. Viewed from this perspective, the therapist is unavoidably cast in the role of the "bad" parent who plays favorites, i.e., nurtures "undeserving siblings," while depriving others. This image of psychotherapists as favorers of the fortunate few and deprivers of the neglected many, easily leads to feelings of distrust toward them and their profession.

ECONOMIC CONSIDERATIONS AS A SOURCE OF DISTRUST

Economic considerations sometimes play a curious role in arousing distrust of psychotherapists. When we purchase most commodities or services, whether they are refrigerators or new doors, we have a tangible idea of what such items should cost. We also have certain concrete yardsticks for measuring the quality of the work or commodity purchased. If the carpenter's door falls off the hinges or the refrigerator breaks down in a week, we can quickly and correctly decide that we have not gotten our money's worth.

How can a person effectively apply economic principles to the experience of psychotherapy. If, for instance, a patient spends thirty dollars a week in psychotherapy, what does he have to give up in order to incur this ongoing expense? If it is an occasional dinner out or a vacation, the patient must weigh the loss of these psychologically beneficial treats against what he may gain from psychotherapy. How is this done? How will the patient evaluate in monetary terms how much increased self-esteem, greater insight, bolstered self-confidence and improved social relationships—the potential rewards of therapy—are worth to him?

Self-esteem, confidence, insight and self-respect are intangible qualities. Since it is impossible to put a price on or quantify these personal qualities, it is enormously difficult for most people to precisely determine, in financial terms, the potential value of therapy.

Another factor which makes it extremely difficult to precisely determine the economic value of therapy is the vagueness of the term "value." The effects of psychotherapy are multidimensional; that is, people can improve in more than one direction at a time. If, for example, a person feels more confidence as a result of therapy, but uses the self-confidence to bully others, can we truly regard the therapy as having value?

Finally, the cost-effectiveness of psychotherapy is torturously difficult to determine for the following reasons: (1) It is never possible to prove with exactitude a causal relationship between a therapist's interventions and a patient's psychological gains. For example, a therapist may over a period of several months encouragingly explain and reveal to a patient the many (past and current) sources of his psychological stress, Over this time the patient becomes more self-aware, confident and hopeful. Although patient and therapist alike may for good reason agree that the therapy is beneficial, realistically it will not be possible for them to identify: (a) what exactly occurred in the therapy to produce such positive results; and (b) to what extent outside influences (e.g., a new love relationship) also contributed to the psychological progress of the patient.

(2) A perpetually elusive issue in assessing the (cost) effectiveness of psychotherapy is the matter of deciding *when* to evaluate psychological change. Let us take the hypothetical example of a nineteen-year-old woman who has been treated successfully for depression over a period of ten months. Should we study her progress after five months? Or, would it be better to do this at the point of termination of therapy? Perhaps, instead, it would be more valid to assess her improvement after a lapse of ten years, at which time she may be pursuing a career and/or raising children.

In a society which has become pervasively technological and computerized, there is an increasingly widespread intolerance and suspicion of ambiguity, particularly with respect to the economic costs of human services. Since psychotherapy is an inherently ambiguous human enterprise, with a cost-effectiveness which can only approximately be estimated, economic considerations can play a major role in generating attitudes of distrust toward the professional psychotherapist.

IDEALIZATION AS A SOURCE OF DISTRUST

As indicated earlier, the mere presence of a psychotherapist can induce powerful transference reactions in others. The psychotherapist can activate those strong infantile wishes and longings which were originally harbored in relation to one's parents. For example, it is not unusual to detect indications in many persons of a genuine conviction that psychotherapists have omniscient and omnipotent powers. A corollary of this conviction is the magical belief that those who practice psychotherapy can actually "see through" others. Naturally, such beliefs cause one to feel psychologically transparent and vulnerable in relation to therapists.

The transference attitudes which therapists animate in others sometimes cause them to be approached on an interpersonal basis as if they were larger-than-life, bounteous personages. All too often, as a result, they are treated with adulation and obsequiousness in social situations. Such treatment occasionally places social hardships upon psychotherapists who, in order to demonstrate their humanness, may feel it necessary to ostentatiously give evidence to others of their own personal doubts and weaknesses.

The tendency to idealize psychotherapists readily leads to distorted perceptions of how they lead their personal lives. For example, therapists are often thought of as having perfectly integrated personalities which are impervious to the human conflicts of everyday life. They are expected to always work and relate harmoniously with others and to respond only in an unemotional, self-controlled and ascetic manner. In other words, they are expected to conduct themselves in their personal lives very much as they commonly do in their psychotherapeutic encounters with patients.

As clinical observation has clearly established, underlying and paralleling attitudes of idealization and awe are usually equally powerful feelings of (largely unconscious) contempt. The combined attitudes of lofty admiration and devaluing contempt produce interesting social reactions to the disclosure of unsettling events in the personal lives of therapists. Thus, the discovery that a therapist has committed suicide or is the parent of an emotionally disturbed child frequently causes the lay person to initially react with shock and disappointment (loss of the ideal). This reaction is soon followed by a kind of self-righteous indignation (the surfacing of the underlying contempt) verbalized by such comments as: "Therapists think they are so smart and perfect. They have as many problems as other people, Actually, they have more problems than others. So what makes them think they can help others when they can't straighten out their own lives?"

Idealization of therapists engenders unrealistic expectations of their human capabilities and qualities. The envy that awe inspires and the inevitable disappointment which results from the discovery of a therapist's human limitations combine as strong catalysts of distrust.

The realistic and unrealistic causes for distrust of the psychotherapy profession are legion and complex. Considering the complexity and universality of these causes, it is indeed a remarkable fact that an estimated thirty-four million Americans are currently receiving psychotherapy.

Dealing With the Disruptive College Student: Some Theoretical and Practical Considerations

The increased number of disruptive students attending colleges and universities has reached alarming proportions. In order to deal effectively and humanely with such students, schools must establish a systematic and legally acceptable set of procedures for dealing with disruptive behavior. An on-campus mental health program can be an invaluable asset in assisting college staff in developing and implementing such procedures.

SETTING

The findings presented in this article are based upon clinical experience over the past 15 years in the City College of San Francisco Mental Health Program. The Mental Health Program is an on-campus psychological service which provides short-term (i.e., 10-12 sessions) psychotherapy to community college students.

City College, like other urban community colleges, has a student population which reflects the diversity of the city itself. More than one-half of the students are from ethnic minorities. The majority of the students are between the ages of 18 and 29, an age group particularly susceptible to a variety of medical, social, and personal problems including venereal disease, substance abuse, and unwanted pregnancy.

THE INCREASING NUMBER OF
DISRUPTIVE COLLEGE STUDENTS

Over the last several years, college personnel throughout the nation have found themselves faced with an increasing number of disruptive students. These are students who, through their behavior or attitude, persistently interfere with the academic and administrative activities of the campus. Some of these students actively hamper the ability of other students to learn and of instructors to teach. Some even threaten the physical safety of themselves and others.

Predictably, a disproportionately large number of disruptive students are seriously emotionally disturbed; their emotional disturbance being either a cause or effect of their disruptive behavior. There are several reasons for the burgeoning numbers of such students now attending colleges and universities:

1. Recent legislative changes have occasioned the release from state mental hospitals of more emotionally disturbed patients in the local communities. For example, in California during the past 20 years, the state's mental hospitals have depopulated from a patient caseload of 37,000 to 3,000.

2. Advances in the use of psychotropic medications have helped to maintain psychiatric patients in their local communities, thus allowing many such persons to avail themselves of an education in a nearby college or university.

3. Many mental health practitioners, often with good reason, regard the college campus as a desirable and enriching resource for their patients. Occasionally, however, some emotionally disturbed students are ill prepared to cope with the rigors of college life and, in response to their own acute anxiety and confusion, will behave disruptively in order to enlist the assistance and support of others. This problem is frequently exacerbated by a lack of collaboration and planning between the college and the referring mental health practitioner, causing some emotionally disturbed students to feel defenseless and abandoned when they arrive on campus.

FIVE PRINCIPLES

The disruptive student, whether emotionally disturbed or not, often angers, baffles, alarms, and immobilizes those instructors and administrators who must cope directly and immediately with the disruptive behavior. In some cases the disruptive behavior clearly warrants disciplinary action on the part of the instructor or administrator.

According to Close and Merchat,[1] there are five principles relating to discipline which emerge from case law.

1. The law does *not* expressly prohibit a college from disciplining a student for misconduct, even when that misconduct is directly related to his/her physical or mental handicap.

2. Each college *is required to provide* "reasonable accommodation" to the physically/mentally handicapped. That is, major disruptions to the educational process may be met with disciplinary action, but minor disruptions need to be tolerated under the "reasonable accommodation" principle.

3. Each college is required to adopt rules and regulations regarding appropriate student behavior, spell out penalties for violation of these regulations, and clearly describe due process procedures for students who wish to appeal these penalties. The formal policy statement of the college should, therefore, provide *a wide range of sanctions* so that there is a *series of alternatives* to deal with the disruptive behavior of students. Alternatives for minor disruptions should include efforts to provide assistance to the student, for example, by referring him to a mental health professional on campus if available.

4. The sole basis for imposing disciplinary sanctions on a student is that student's behavior, regardless of the etiology of that behavior. A college may not discipline a student for being "mentally ill"— only for explicit behavior prohibited by the Student Code of Conduct. For this reason, it is extremely important that the student's exact behavior be *documented in writing in accurate detail.* All procedures and recommendations relating to the disciplinary process also need to be clearly documented.

5. Although mental health professionals must follow legally defined obligations to maintain confidentiality regarding client communications and records, all persons employed by a community college must report serious threats or risks of harm to self or others, as well as known instances of child abuse. (This principle is based upon a section of the California education code which applies only to community colleges in California. My own survey of six other populous states—New York, Ohio, Michigan, Illinois, Massachusetts, and Pennsylvania—revealed that no such education code exists in those states, suggesting that this fifth principle and the code upon which it is based are perhaps peculiar to California.)

THE COMPLEXITIES OF COPING WITH THE DISRUPTIVE STUDENT

Colleges have sometimes been hampered in their attempts to cope with disruptive students because of an inability or unwillingness to clearly define what they mean by the term "disruptive." In addressing itself to this issue, the California Community College Chancellor's Ad Hoc Committee on Disruptive Student Affairs[2] defined the "disruptive" student as a person who: verbally threatens or abuses college personnel, physically threatens or assaults others, willfully damages college property, misuses drugs or alcohol on college premises, habitually interferes with the learning environment by disruptive verbal or behavioral expressions, or persistently makes inordinate demands for time and attention from faculty and staff.

Szasz[3] states that the college psychotherapist is duplicitous and ineffectual in handling disruptive students because he is in actuality a "double agent," serving both administrators and students, but owing real loyalty to neither.

Blain and McArthur[4] declare that, in dealing with the disruptive student, the college psychotherapist should not have any authority for discipline but instead should play an important role in delivering professional opinions regarding a student's personality in order to assist the institution in making the correct disposition of a disruptive incident.

Pavela[5] points out that the role of the college mental health professional is severely limited in handling cases involving discipline because college therapists cannot adequately fulfill an expectation that they can determine which students experiencing "emotional problems" will actually engage in violent behavior.

The rapid and judicious resolution of disruptive behavior is often impeded or undermined by the very nature of the disruption itself. Orleans and Steimer[6] suggest that very difficult human judgments are at stake in such instances. They state, "Too severe a view of the situation may 'unfairly penalize' the student; reluctance to make a judgment (or follow well-grounded intuition) may yield disaster."

Finally, the ambiguity or absence of college policies and regulations which govern student conduct can inflame an already serious disruptive crisis. Pavela[5] states, "Most schools now face a greater risk of being hauled into court for running afoul of their own convoluted regulations than for violating the simple standards of 'basic fairness' which the judiciary required."

THE NEED FOR DISCIPLINARY PROCEDURES

When the disruptive behavior of a student threatens the welfare of other individuals and the educational institution itself, it may be necessary for the college to institute disciplinary measures. The range of disciplinary measures may include warnings, reprimands, and, in the more serious cases of disruption, exclusion from certain classes or from the college as a whole. Residential colleges may also prohibit students from residing on campus as a form of discipline.

Although most colleges have adopted a set of rules and regulations regarding student conduct, as Wagener et al.[7] point out, relatively few schools have adopted detailed procedures to be followed when considering restricting the enrollment of students for disruptive behavior. Some schools do not intervene until the state laws on civil commitment or criminal behavior apply. Others regard disruptive behavior as strictly a disciplinary matter to be dealt with solely on an administrative basis.

THE ROLE OF THE MENTAL HEALTH PROGRAM

At City College of San Francisco, the mental health program is utilized extensively by instructional, administrative, and classified staff in trouble-shooting and resolving incidents involving disruptive students. The utilization of a crisis-intervention model that makes use of the expertise of mental health practitioners has several weighty advantages.

First, college staff who are confronted by disruptive students are frequently frightened, diffident, and unclear about their rights and prerogatives. The mental health professional can provide staff not only with vital emotional support and empathy throughout the disruptive crisis, but can also be helpful by informing staff of their legal and administrative rights and limitations.

Second, the alarming nature of many disruptive incidents frequently causes college staff to be either overly permissive or inordinately punitive in their attempts to resolve crises. A mental health professional can be invaluable in assisting college staff to develop effective strategies and the requisite objectivity to carry out disciplinary action (if such is necessary) in an efficient and humane manner.

Third, because instructors and administrators sometimes have widely different and conflicting viewpoints regarding the causes and degree of seriousness of disruptive crises, they may each tend to favor and pursue disparate courses of action to resolve them. This can result in an acrimonious and dangerous impasse that serves to protract and aggravate the crisis. In instances of this nature, a mental health professional can be essential in identifying the areas of disagreement, in serving as a mediator for the contending principals, and in making recommendations as to how their differences and the crisis can best be resolved.

REPORTING AND DOCUMENTATION

When staff consults the mental health program for assistance with a disruptive student, they are usually advised to carefully document their observations and concerns. The documentation should be devoid of psychological jargon or speculation (e.g., This person seems to be a "paranoid schizophrenic" or "I think he's on drugs"). Documentation should be specific and concise, describing exactly the disruptive and objectionable behavior that has been observed. The documentation should be immediately transmitted to the department chairperson and to the appropriate administrator.

Depending on the gravity of the disruption, the staff member may receive recommendations from the mental health professional ranging from issuing a warning to the student to desist from further disruptions to, in very serious or dangerous cases, immediate exclusion from class or the college. If the disruptive student seems to pose a serious and imminent danger to the staff member, the latter is given extensive advice and information regarding which administrative and/or law enforcement authorities must immediately be informed of the matter and advised also as to what precautions must be taken in order to insure his/her own personal safety and the safety of others.

When the disruptive student's behavior warrants administrative intervention, the mental health professional and the staff member, individually or jointly, immediately contact the appropriate administrator in order to report the incident and to share their interpretations and recommendations regarding the matter. If the endangered staff member is an administrator, there would perhaps be little need to include anyone other than the mental health professional in the consultation, unless the seriousness of the danger required enlisting the services of higher level administrators or law enforcement authorities.

If the disruptive incident has been resolved at the administrative level, it is essential that the staff person who originally reported it be informed of its disposition or resolution. Without the benefit of this information, the reporting staff person is unnecessarily left on tenterhooks to wonder and worry about whether the crisis will actually be resolved.

REFERRALS FOR PSYCHOTHERAPY

It is understandable that staff who report disruptive students to the mental health program frequently expect to resolve the crisis by referring such students for psychological treatment in the program. Although such referrals are frequently appropriate and beneficial, in most instances they are abortive and unnecessary. There are several reasons why such referrals are often unsuccessful.

First, students who are referred for psychological treatment on the basis of their disruptive behavior ordinarily (and usually quite correctly) consider the referral and the therapy to be a punitive measure and, therefore, want no part of it. Second, based upon the hundreds of incidents of disruptive student behavior which I have evaluated and helped to resolve at City College of San Francisco, it is my clear impression that the vast majority of seriously disruptive students have already received (and may still be receiving!) psychotherapy. Since the therapy they have already received has not yet prevented them from manifesting disruptive behavior, they surely are entitled to take less than a sanguine view of seeing yet another therapist about their "problems."

Thus, in most instances, joint consultation between the mental health professional, the staff member who is reporting the disruptive student, and the appropriate administrator—without the direct involvement of the student himself/herself—is initially the preferred course of action. Naturally, the student who is alleged to be disruptive has every right to rebut and appeal the ultimate administrative decision and to have full and direct involvement in an administrative review of the decision should he/she so choose.

MANDATORY PSYCHOTHERAPY AS A FORM OF DISCIPLINE

In my role as a mental health consultant to some of California's community colleges and to the California Community Colleges' Chancellor's Office, I have discovered that many, if not most, community colleges require that the disruptive student receive psychiatric or personal counseling as a condition of either continued enrollment or reenrollment in the college. Although this practice may, in part, be motivated by a humane recognition that the disruptive student is a victim of emotional stress (as either a cause or effect of his disruptive behavior) and, therefore, could conceivably benefit from psychotherapy, there are several reasons why this practice should be discontinued and prohibited.

1. Requiring the disruptive student to receive psychotherapy distorts and undermines the basis for corrective disciplinary action. The focus and impetus for disciplinary action is the disruptive behavior of the student, not the student's putative mental illness or disorder. When college administrators require the disruptive student to undertake psychotherapy, they are perforce making a *psychiatric* judgment using psychiatric criteria. Even if they were doing this with the benefit of having first consulted a mental health professional, the requirement is being carried out by means of the administrators' authority and, therefore, is unavoidably a psychiatric determination.

Administrators do not possess the legal right to make psychiatric evaluations and determinations of this nature. On the other hand, they most certainly do have the legal right and prerogative to determine what is and is not acceptable student behavior on their respective campuses and to carry out nonpsychiatric discipline in cases of student misconduct (e.g., reprimands, suspensions, etc.).

2. The requirement of psychotherapy for the disruptive student is often motivated by fanciful and naive notions about psychotherapy itself. One such notion, for example, is the belief that once students receive psychotherapy, their disruptive behavior will abate or cease. Although this is sometimes true, it is also true that many persons who receive psychotherapy remain socially disruptive and at times actually become violent, despite their psychiatric treatment.

An analogous belief is that psychotherapists have the omnipotence not only to prevent disruptive behavior, but to accurately predict disruptive recidivism. Numerous research studies as well as common sense indicate that the ability of the mental health professional to predict disruptive or violent behavior is admittedly quite limited.

Monahan,[8] for example, cites five studies which capably demonstrated that clinical predictions of violent behavior among institutionalized mentally disordered people are accurate at best about one-third of the time. He further quotes the American Civil Liberties Union

(ACLU) which has expressed a very dim (and, in my view, extremist) view of the lack of predictive prowess among mental health professionals. The ACLU has flatly stated that "it now seems beyond dispute that mental health professionals have no expertise in predicting future dangerous behavior to self or others. In fact, predictions of dangerous behavior are wrong about 95% of the time."

Rofman, Askinazi, and Fant,[9] based on their study of emergency involuntary psychiatric hospitalizations, have concluded that "predictions of dangerous behavior have validity *when the time of prediction and the time of validation are relatively close together*" (italics added). Monahan, who has himself extensively researched the subject of the clinical predictability of violence, suggests that there is perhaps a ceiling of 50% on the level of accuracy that can ever be expected of the clinical prediction of violent behavior. If this estimate is correct, mental health professionals are probably not very much more adept than lay persons at predicting violence.[8]

There are at least two reasons why mental health professionals will be limited in predicting the disruptive behavior of students: (1) The way in which psychiatric patients think and behave in the consultation room often has little relationship or carry-over to how they will behave and think elsewhere. Thus, therapists, especially if they do not understand well their patients' states of mind, may have an unrealistic view of their social functioning and their potential for behaving disruptively outside an office. (2) No psychotherapist, no matter how sensitive or astute, can anticipate the myriad stressful circumstances which a patient may encounter on the college campus. Thus, patients may be well fortified by their therapy to enter college; however, once there, a poor grade, a humiliating academic evaluation, or a long delay on the registration line can cause the fragile patient to regress and become disruptive.

For these reasons, the common practice of requiring psychiatric agencies and practitioners to submit reports to administrators indicating their patients' readiness to reenroll is suspect and should be eliminated. This should be replaced simply with an administrative requirement that the disruptive student who is petitioning for continued enrollment or reenrollment meet with designated administrator(s) who will inform the student that a repetition of the disruptive behavior (assuming the student is allowed to continue) will result in further disciplinary action. If a referral to an on- or off-campus mental health agency seems appropriate, the administrator can tactfully assist with such a referral without making it a *requirement*.

3. Requiring a disruptive student to receive psychotherapy is unequivocally a coercive measure that serves to instill in the student resentment toward potential sources of help, i.e., the therapist and the

therapy. If such students conform to this requirement, they will agree to see a therapist but frequently will invest no personal involvement in the treatment process itself; consequently, they typically derive little from the therapy other than the impression that psychotherapy is a form of punishment which must be stoically endured. It may reasonably be argued that some of these students eventually overcome their hostility and resistance and thereby receive some benefit from therapy that they would otherwise not have received had they not been required to be in treatment. If this is indeed true, I would argue that, considering the resentment and distrust which so frequently ensues from compulsory therapy, the price is much too high.

4. Ordinarily, for psychotherapy to work effectively, it must be conducted on a confidential basis. This is the cornerstone of psychotherapeutic treatment and is maintained in order to instill in the patient a trust of the therapist which is essential to the patient's welfare. A requirement that the disruptive student receive psychotherapy naturally implies that the college will be informed of the student's therapeutic activities, including perhaps his progress and prognosis. Thus, this requirement serves to contaminate and undermine the confidential therapeutic relationship and, consequently, limits the potential for success.

5. The administrative requirement of psychotherapy as a condition of continued enrollment tends to divide the authority over the student's status in the college between the college and the mental health community. In practical terms, what frequently happens is that a therapist will recommend reenrollment, and the administrator will feel protected and reassured by that authoritative recommendation. In reality, that recommendation affords no protection to the administrator or the college, insofar as that student's future behavior is concerned.

6. The requirement that students receive psychotherapy as a condition of continued enrollment is clearly tantamount to excluding them on the basis of a mental or psychiatric handicap. That being the case, such a requirement is, in my view, a violation of Section 504 of the Rehabilitation Act of 1973 which reads, in part: "No otherwise qualified handicapped individual shall, solely by reason of his handicap, be excluded from participation in, be denied the benefits of, or be subjected to discrimination under any program or activity receiving Federal financial assistance."

SUMMARY

The increased numbers of disruptive students attending colleges and universities has reached alarming proportions. In order to deal effectively and humanely with such students, schools must establish a systematic and legally acceptable set of procedures for dealing with disruptive behavior, An on-campus mental health program can be an invaluable asset in assisting college staff in developing and implementing such procedures.[10]

References

1. Close CA, Merchat MM. *Emotionally Disturbed Students: Legal Guidelines.* Chancellor's Office, California Community Colleges, 1982.
2. California Community Colleges Chancellor's Ad Hoc Committee on Disruptive Student Affairs. *Dealing with Disruptive Behavior in California Community Colleges.* J. Lynne Boylan (ed.). Chancellor's Office, California Community Colleges, 1983.
3. Szasz T. The psychiatrist as double agent, in *Where Medicine Fails*, Strauss L (ed.). New Brunswick, N.J., Transaction Books, 1973.
4. Blain G, McArthur CC (eds.). *Emotional Problems of the Student.* New York, Appleton-Century-Crofts, 1961.
5. Pavela G. Therapeutic paternalism and the misuse of mandatory psychiatric withdrawals on campus. *Journal of College and University Law* 1982-83;9(2).
6. Orleans J, Steimer W. *"Psychiatric" Withdrawals and Readmissions.* Paper presented at the National Association of College and University Attorneys 24th Annual Conference, June 21, 1984.
7. Wagener JM et al. Reacting to the uncooperative, severely disturbed student: A survey of health center policies. *J Am Coll Health* 1983 April;31(5)
8. Monahan J. The predictions of violent behavior: Toward a second generation of theory and policy. *Am J Psychiat* 1984 January; 141(1)
9. Rofman E, Askinazi C, Fant E. The prediction of dangerous behavior in emergency civil commitment. *Am J Psychiat* 1980 September; 137(9).
10. Amada G. Mental health consultation on the college campus. *J Am Coll Health* 1983 April; 31 (5).

by Gerald Amada and Paul A. Grayson

Anxiety

Anxiety is one of the themes, like relationship problems, family concerns, and developmental issues, that intersects every other problem area in this book. We expect every student who voluntarily consults us to be anxious about something, at least unconsciously, or else what is the reason for an appointment? Anxiety plays a part as both a cause and a consequence of students' problems.

For example, students who are anxious about academics may avoid studies through procrastination, which in the end damages their performance and aggravates their anxiety. A woman who is anxious about her attractiveness and lovability may eat compulsively to quell her fears, but the weight she gains will damage her self-concept further and increase her anxiety. A male's anxiety about his sexual adequacy will impair his performance and thus reinforce his anxiety. With each of these problems, the therapeutic approach requires understanding the role of anxiety and finding constructive ways to cope with it.

The remarks in this chapter therefore bear on virtually every case that comes to the college counseling center. The following sections present causes of anxiety in college students, principles of therapy, and two case examples.

CAUSES OF ANXIETY

Anxiety is defined as "apprehension, tension, or uneasiness that stems from the anticipation of danger, which may be internal or external"; it is characterized by "motor tension, autonomic hyperactivity, apprehensive expectation, and vigilance and scanning" (American Psychiatric Association, 1987, p. 392). In college students it may seize attention suddenly in the form of incapacitating panic attacks, or may reside in the background of consciousness, like noise from the street.

Its existence may be known to students, who insistently want it to go away, or it may be so familiar as to go unnoticed and have to be inferred from students' accounts. It may be, or at least appear to be, situation-specific.

One graduating senior, for example, was obsessed with what was to him the terrifying prospect of landing a prestigious postgraduate job. His sleep, diet, studies, mood, and relationships deteriorated as he tortured himself with single-minded apprehension about his qualifications and performance on interviews. The more usual pattern, however, is for anxious students to be anxious across the board. Fears expressed in last week's session about taking a test are supplanted this week by fears about going home for Thanksgiving and next week by fears about asking a roommate to pay a phone bill. The details change, but the plot remains familiar.

The causes of human anxiety are as much a subject for social critics and philosophers as for psychologists and psychiatrists. Blame has been attributed to society's over emphasis on competition and individual achievement, the breakdown of ties to the extended family and community, the erosion of traditional values and norms of behavior, and the insidious threat of global nuclear disaster. But even though our era may be particularly an age of anxiety, as W. H. Auden's poem styles us, the human condition has always been shadowed by anxiety.

According to psychoanalytic doctrine, every member of our race struggles with the irreducible and inescapable fears of object loss, loss of love, castration, and super ego demands and prohibitions (Brenner, 1982). Also within the psychoanalytic tradition, Fenichel (1945) points out that adults never entirely put behind them the helplessness they experienced as infants when bombarded by stimuli they could neither differentiate nor master. Existential theory postulates that none of us is immune from anxiety caused by awareness of death, helplessness against chance, the responsibility to find meaning in our lives, and the recognition that we are ultimately alone (Tillich, 1952).

When we wish to compare and understand the anxiety of specific individuals, it is essential, of course, to make broad diagnostic differentiations. Establishing whether a person's anxiety is associated with incipient psychosis, personality disorder, neurotic conflict, developmental issues, or unusually severe current stressors illuminates its origin and informs the process of treatment. However, very often within the college population, anxiety cannot be assigned to a particular diagnostic pigeonhole; rather, it betokens some combination of environmental, developmental, and psychopathological factors.

Thus, a young man in his first semester may have a fear of final examinations (an objectively stressful experience); this may be heightened by underlying ambivalence about separating from his family through succeeding at college (a developmental issue), and also the unconscious wish to fail in order to confirm his deeply held sense of being a misfit (a pathological issue). Ignoring any of these aspects would mean oversimplifying the cause of his distress.

If the broad diagnostic groupings often do not tell the full story, the same can be said for the finer distinctions among anxiety disorders drawn by the revised third edition of the *Diagnostic and Statistical Manual of Mental Disorders* (DSM-III-R; American Psychiatric Association, 1987). In our experience, college students' anxiety problems tend to cross over the boundaries drawn by DSM-III-R among Social Phobia, Generalized Anxiety Disorder, Obsessive-Compulsive Disorder, and Panic Disorder. That is, often the same individuals evidence, concurrently or at different times, signs of fear of scrutiny by others, excessive anxiety and worry about life experiences, persistent unwanted thoughts, and even attacks of panic.

However, full-fledged Agoraphobia as defined in DSM-III-R is rarely seen at college counseling centers. The most common, DSM-III-R Post-Traumatic Stress Disorder, at most counseling centers concerns the aftermath of rape ... although the Mental Health Program at the City College of San Francisco, where one of us (Gerald Amada) worked, contains a concentration of international students, some of whom have been traumatized by war and torture.

Let us briefly catalog areas that engender anxiety in college students. One of the most familiar problems at college counseling centers is a generalized social phobia—commonly known as shyness—which involves a fear of and compelling desire to avoid social situations. P. G. Zimbardo (personal communication, 1988), director of the Stanford University Shyness Clinic, conducted a randomly distributed survey in which 40% of college students identified themselves as generally shy, another 15% as shy in particular situations, and another 40% as shy in the past-leaving only 5%, by their own account, free from the problem. Shy students have trouble initiating and maintaining conversations (Peritonea, 1977).

Though they are at times able to form one or two sustaining relationships, their fear of other persons typically causes them difficulty in making friends and forming romantic attachments. For some, the therapist may be their only nonthreatening association. One young man, who was intensely though ambivalently attached to his parents, had been an outsider among peers for his entire life. His only "friends" outside of family were the therapists he had seen since childhood. Leading the same solitary existence at college, he now came to the counseling center to establish in therapy his customary lifeline to another human being.

But shy students are shy in therapy, too. They may avoid eye contact, squirm and fidget, and manifest inappropriate affect such as giggling while discussing painful subjects. They may withhold information or at least not take the initiative in disclosure, or they may speak vaguely or obliquely. Though they frequently complain about receiving too little recognition and respect from others, their low self-esteem makes them acutely uncomfortable if they are commended by the therapist, whom they then view as patronizing or as a poor judge of accomplishment.

The academic arena can rouse social anxiety as well. Many students never raise their hands in class and sit in dread that they will be called on by the instructor. Delivering a speech or exposing their writing to scrutiny can be a traumatic event. A female student of above-average intelligence became panicky and blocked whenever she was confronted with written assignments that required creative expression. She submitted her essays late and displayed a tendency to hedge and underplay her viewpoint, as if she wanted to eliminate herself from her writing.

In addition to these public aspects of academic performance, such private aspects as concentration, memorization, and assimilation of written materials can be impaired by anxiety. Test anxiety, often reaching phobic proportions, afflicts vast numbers of students. Often co-existing with test anxiety is procrastination (Rothblum, Solomon, & Murakami, 1986), which involves the self-defeating cycle of fear, avoidance, impaired performance, lowered self-esteem, and renewed fear.

Another focus of social anxiety deserving mention is anxiety and shyness about the body, which is quite common among even attractive, well-formed students. At a developmental stage where many are uncertain about their lovability and appeal, college students naturally focus worried attention on their physical selves. It is not unusual for them to come to therapy dressed in loose-fitting sweaters or coats that disguise rather than reveal their shapes. In fact, a student's arriving bundled up to a session may be taken as a sign of self-repudiation. "I am afraid to show myself," the outfit declares, "because I am inadequate and you will reject me."

Concerns about the body also may be expressed in morbid worries about health (hypochondriasis). Many such students are referred to the counseling center after first seeking medical treatment at the health center. They are sometimes not good candidates for therapy, preferring to monitor and detail their symptoms rather than unearth the causes. Related to these concerns are fears of external danger and death. One student reported fears of choking on food, flying on airplanes, driving a car, riding in a train, and walking on city streets.

On a deeper psychodynamic level, students fear their own impulses. Some fear their tender side—it makes them appear needy or weak. Some fear sexual impulses; perhaps they are attracted to the "wrong" gender or sex act. Many are afraid of hidden hostile impulses, which, according to Horney (1937), are a wellspring of human anxiety. These are the students who lend money to persons they dislike or who keep silent when someone plays an electric guitar at 2 a.m. They are afraid that if they assert themselves they will provoke a retaliatory attack, and they are also afraid of losing control once the genie of self-assertion is let out of the bottle. Outwardly nice and obliging, these students tend to be haunted by daydreams and nightmares of violence, or they may keep hostile impulses at bay through obsessive-compulsive defenses.

Another familiar source of anxiety is the process of change, and particularly the changes associated with the major transitions of college. Every year a handful of shell-shocked first-year students and panic-stricken graduating students find their way to counseling centers. Part of what makes these transitions so frightening is the belief of many students that they are crossing the Rubicon, with no turning back. Though this idea is partly grounded in reality (growing up does mean leaving part of one's past behind), its absolutism can be dispelled by therapists' giving encouragement to first-year students to live at home or go home during weekends and to graduating students to spend an extra semester at college. When allowed to proceed at a slower pace, these frightened students tend to reconcile themselves to moving ahead.

This overview of what makes college students anxious is far from complete. Bright persons who turn their ingenuity to finding justifications for worry can always detect new dangers that a therapist has not yet discerned. If should also be stressed that students sometimes can not name what they are anxious about—their anxiety is free-floating and almost always they are ignorant of the deeper psychodynamic issues lurking beneath the proximate sources of worry. External dangers are easier to recognize than internal dangers; environmental stressors are more identifiable than developmental and psychopathological issues. Bringing the hidden causes of anxiety to light is one of the purposes of psychotherapy.

PRINCIPLES OF TREATMENT

In theory, diagnostic considerations should determine the disposition of anxiety problems. Psychotic episodes require hospitalization and/or major tranquilizers; entrenched neurotic patterns and personality disorders require long-term psychotherapy; developmental issues (e.g., separation/individuation and identity formation) respond well to short term, insight-oriented psychotherapy; and environmentally induced anxiety usually warrants only a few sessions, But for the majority of anxious students, whose fears are neither psychotic nor strictly situational but instead stem from a combination of environmental, developmental, and psychopathological sources, this neat scheme breaks down. They generally come to the counseling center because they are anxious about an immediate situation. Whether they then continue in therapy to explore deeper developmental and psychopathological issues has less to do with the existence of these issues than with their rapport with the therapist, their interest and faith in the therapeutic process, the number of sessions the counseling center offers, and so forth.

A modified short-term psychodynamic model fits the needs of most of these students. The City College of San Francisco Mental Health Program, where Amada has worked for 18 years, applies this model to a diverse urban population of community college students. Grayson has employed the model at both a small liberal arts and arts-oriented public college and a small liberal arts private college. Though ideally suited to developmental issues, the short-term psychodynamic model also can be geared to environmental or psychopathological emphases. Students who define their problems as strictly environmental can benefit from the model's accent on finding parallels across situations. By learning how their particular coping mechanisms consistently fail them, they become better prepared to respond to current and future stressors.

Meanwhile, college students who are prepared to delve into psychopathological issues may find, thanks to their remarkable capacity for growth, that they can make substantial inroads with this model. At the very least, they can get the ball rolling; they may then continue the process in long-term treatment on or off campus.

The goal of psychodynamically oriented therapy is to unearth the core fears and motives, the central conflicts, with which the anxiety is associated. The assumption is made that beneath the dangers that may be obvious to students lie deeper dangers of which they are incompletely aware. For example, the process of leaving home may be frightening because it is unconsciously equated with the threat of being abandoned by parents, or conversely with the threat of being accused by dependent parents of abandoning them. The prospect of failing a test may unconsciously evoke fears of being chastised by a critical parent, or it may mean that one is doomed to follow in an unsuccessful parent's footsteps.

The therapist searches for these underlying meanings by collecting evidence of parallels within and among students' childhood relationships, current dealings with others, and reactions within the therapeutic relationship (cf. Angola, 1965; Malawi, 1976; Schafer, 1983). Thus, if a student was frightened of her father's anger and acts now as if afraid of the therapist's anger, then one can hypothesize that her current anxiety about dating stems from a generalized fear of angering men.

Of course, short-term work never yields a complete explanation of students' anxiety. Though certain motifs become clear, every student's story contains complications, distortions, and omissions. But complete explanations are not necessary for anxious students to derive relief. It helps merely to bring dark fears and hidden motives out into the open; perhaps they are being admitted for the first time to anyone, maybe even to the student himself or herself. Discussing them with a supportive, understanding adult counteracts one of the darkest fears of all—that one's innermost nature is too strange and reprehensible to reveal to another person.

It helps students also to learn that their anxiety is at least potentially understandable; they are not in the grip of quirky, inexplicable forces. And whatever tentative explanations do emerge tend to encourage students to confront their fears. The knowledge a woman gains that her anxiety stems from childhood fears of her father may hearten her to break the pattern. She realizes that perhaps as a young girl she needed to draw back, but she need not do so as a young woman.

This is the essence of the short-term psychodynamic model for treating anxiety problems. In addition to these general principles, there are certain theoretical considerations and practical modifications that must be taken into account when one uses this model with anxious students. These are detailed below.

Deciding When to Take Strong Measures

Students who suffer from acute anxiety often feel and convey a sense of urgency. Wanting to be relieved of anxiety right away, they subtly or overtly demand, "Save me." A key therapeutic task, accordingly, is to decide whether to take strong or even emergency measures to bring them relief. Complicating this task is the possibility of countertransference feelings. When students are desperate, therapists are susceptible to feelings of inadequacy and the concomitant temptation to prove their competence by taking dramatic action. Such countertransference reactions, if not understood and controlled by therapists, obviously may work against students' best interests.

The legitimate reason to institute strong or emergency measures is because students are unable to function without them. Their studies, living situation, or emotional stability is in jeopardy. In these cases therapists may choose to increase the length or frequency of sessions, offer direct advice ("Maybe you should drop the course"), act as agents for the students (arranging housing changes, speaking to instructors), ask the campus physician to prescribe a tranquilizer, or—at the extreme—arrange for hospitalization or a medical leave of absence. When these measures succeed, they reduce students' anxiety to a manageable level, restoring their capacity to function and enabling the regular business of therapy to proceed. At the least, they convey the comforting message that someone cares, is taking charge, and is trying to do something about the problem. Provision of advice, in particular, is often necessary to extricate students from harmful situations or relationships. An anxious young woman may ask, regarding a destructive relationship, "How do I leave him?" Sometimes it is appropriate to tell her.

There are risks, however, in departing from usual therapeutic practice and employing strong interventions. Such measures may reinforce students' belief that anxiety is unacceptable and unbearable, that they should be afraid of their anxiety (cf. Beck & Emery, 1985). If these steps fail to bring relief, then students may conclude that nothing can help, and their despair will intensify. These measures may also teach students that outside intervention is necessary, that they themselves cannot manage their problems.

The best rule of thumb, then, is to withhold extra sessions, advice, medications, and the like unless and until it is clear that such measures are necessary. Whenever possible, therapists should be calm and patient in their approach; this suggests that students themselves have the resources to ride out and eventually overcome their anxiety. When therapists explain in words and show by example that anxiety is a part of life, not a cause for panic, often students' anxiety will diminish accordingly.

Maintaining Empathy

It is a truism that empathy is essential to all forms of therapy, with all clients, and with all problems. Anxious students can tax therapists' empathy, however. Those who demand relief, as we have seen, can instill in therapists feelings of inadequacy and the incentive to play rescuer. Acutely anxious students also may cause therapists to back away because of the intensity of their need. Those who remain anxious may evoke in therapists an inwardly critical or angry reaction, as if to say, "Enough already!" If students sense any of these countertransference responses, their despair and sense of isolation may be heightened.

A key therapeutic task, therefore, is to retain the capacity to enter into, accept, and mirror anxious students' subjective worlds. Comments such as "I know it must be frustrating to be feeling so bad week after week, even after coming to therapy," demonstrate that someone understands and cares even if he or she is unable to provide a panacea. The interpersonal climate that empathy creates helps ultimately to shake the foundations of students' anxiety.

Encouraging Activity and Assertiveness

Anxious students often perpetuate their problems because of their withdrawal and unassertive behavior. The result is that they do not acquire skills or achieve successes, thereby diminishing their self-esteem and heightening their anxiety. One way to break this vicious cycle is to encourage students to do the very things that frighten them—to assume an active and assertive rather than a passive stance. Doing so initiates a positive chain of events in which students gain skills and successes, bolster self-esteem, and accordingly reduce their anxiety. In pursuing this strategy, therapists may want to employ or even assign the reading of a manual on assertiveness training (e.g., Alberti & Emmons, 1970).

There are dangers inherent in this approach, however. One must not push students toward actions they presently cannot perform. It is also essential that students define success in terms of trying, not achieving perfection. The goal is to ask a question in class, not to make a brilliant comment. It is to ask someone out on a date, not necessarily (though it would be nice) to be accepted.

Helping Students to Express Themselves

Anxious students display all manner of difficulties in self-expression, They may be vague, halting, discursive, disjointed, or tangential as they try to explain themselves in therapy, These problems in communication are both a consequence and a cause of anxiety. On the one hand, they reflect both the confusion of anxious students, who often do not know what is happening to them or how it started, and also their fears concerning self-disclosure. On the other hand, problems in communication perpetuate anxiety by suggesting that the causes of suffering are too overwhelming, mysterious, or awful to capture in words. The inexplicable is *ipso facto* a cause of dread.

Therapists should not be impatient with anxious students, who are communicating as well as they can or dare. The task is to be understanding and gentle, yet active in helping them to express themselves more clearly. When students are vague, clarifying questions are recommended, such as "What exactly happened yesterday when you felt upset?" or "In what particular situations are you nervous?" When they fail to complete their thoughts, it helps to ask questions (P; "Yesterday was ..." T: "How was yesterday?"), or even, if necessary, to finish the thought for them (T: "Yesterday was a bad day, wasn't it?"). When they skip from one problem to another, it is useful to steer them back to the topic under discussion. When they become distracted by a minor point, it helps to direct them to a more pivotal issue ("I notice we haven't talked today about that course that's been worrying you").

Provided they are used with tact and empathy, such structuring questions and comments can help reduce anxiety by conveying that students' problematic situations can be spoken about and understood. In particular, structuring questions and comments can illuminate for students, who often have only a foggy notion of what led up to their present crisis, the events that brought it to pass. Discovering the sequence that preceded an outburst of anxiety contributes to making anxiety understandable, and hence to reducing it.

Identifying Anxiety-Producing Beliefs

Anxious students characteristically entertain irrational, exaggerated, and self-defeating views of themselves, their world, and their efforts. They tend to consider themselves inferior, unable to master challenges. They perceive the world as threatening and hostile, its challenges as frightening. And they believe that it is unacceptable and devastating to fail at these challenges. Such core beliefs engender anxiety. A sound therapeutic strategy is to identify these beliefs, which may be either obvious to students or outside their conscious awareness, and to trace them from their origin to their current manifestations. In this way, the psychodynamic approach we follow dovetails with the cognitive approaches articulated in Beck's (Beck & Emery, 1985) cognitive therapy and Ellis's (Ellis & Grieger, 1977) rational-emotive therapy. Both the psychodynamic and cognitive approaches examine these pivotal cognitive components of subjective experience.

In contrast to Ellis's method, however, we do not advise a strategy of confronting or attacking anxiety-producing beliefs. Doing so may be interpreted as a failure in empathy-proof that therapists do not understand students' feelings of unworthiness and perception of the world as menacing. Furthermore, an attack on beliefs may be perceived as an attack on the self. A better strategy is simply to increase students' awareness of their thinking. What exactly is their opinion of themselves and their world? When do they think this way? What evidence do they use to confirm their beliefs? A related tactic is to have students put down on paper, either during therapy or between sessions, all the negative ideas they entertain. When students' irrational, exaggerated, and self-defeating beliefs are transferred from the private domain of personal thoughts to the more public arena of speech and writings, they themselves may question and gradually modify their beliefs.

Using Relaxation Methods

Though we do not usually employ relaxation methods in our own practice, some anxious students apparently benefit from learning progressive muscle relaxation or deep breathing exercises. Benson's *The Relaxation Response* (1975) may be assigned as supplemental reading. A simple technique is to recommend taking a few deep breaths, perhaps while inwardly reciting the word "relax." Minimal though it is, this method may give students a sense of having some control over their anxiety, which in itself alleviates their mental state.

Applications of the psychodynamic model of therapy and these special modifications are illustrated in the following case examples, which have been altered in certain details.

ANNA: A PSYCHODYNAMIC EXPLORATION

Anna was a 21-year-old student who enrolled at City College soon after emigrating from an Asian country 2 years ago. Her primary expressed concern was a relationship with a man that was causing her acute states of anxiety, which undermined her concentration and lowered her academic standing. Although she was not initially receptive to exploring her motivations, probably because reserve is valued in her culture, her case demonstrates the effectiveness of a patiently applied psychodynamic approach.

In her first session, Anna spoke in a highly self-conscious and rambling manner, discussing the symptoms of her anxiety rather than the actual events that led up to them. It was necessary to ask gently but repeatedly for clarifications; her communications had to be facilitated step by step. Thus, the therapist encouraged her to recount when and under what circumstances she began to experience an increase in anxiety. In response, she vaguely alluded to "boyfriend" problems. He asked what specifically disturbed her about this boyfriend. She said he treated her badly but didn't mean to. The therapist asked in what way he treated her badly. She dodged the question and brought up a neutral topic. Later, sensing from certain clues that she really did want to discuss the relationship, the therapist tried again: 'Anna, in what way does this man treat you badly?" Through many questions of this nature, the therapist gradually helped her to express herself and supply the details of her current situation.

The story she told was that a man whom she had dated for only a short time was drunkenly calling her on the telephone and heaping verbal abuse upon her. She said that she tolerated his actions because he was a good person and did not mean to hurt her. As a Christian, she could not justify being angry at him. However, she admitted that worrying about his actions was causing her to neglect schoolwork and was inducing considerable anxiety.

Concluding that Anna's wish to tell about herself outweighed her natural reticence, the therapist proceeded in this first session and in subsequent sessions to employ the basic treatment strategy of searching for parallels among her childhood experiences, her current relationship with the man, and her transferential relationship with the therapist. The investigation disclosed the salience of fear of abandonment, which in turn fueled a fear of her own anger and assertiveness. Anna related that as a child her parents had failed to understand her and responded to her requests for emotional support by recoiling and accusing her of being a crybaby. Fearful of expressing her rage and thereby incurring more disapproval, she withdrew from them and instead sought support by rather indiscriminately attempting to rescue other people from their problems. In her view, if she could somehow help others, they would appreciate and nurture her. It was essential that she please them and withhold any signs of anger, lest she lose them too.

When at the end of her fourth session Anna expressed bitterness at her parents for neglecting her, her display of hostility caused her to be overcome with anxiety. The same dynamics were obviously at the core of her difficulty with her "boyfriend." She was so afraid to confront him and risk losing him that she behaved in an obsequious and fawning manner, which of course only led to an escalation of his abusive behavior. Meanwhile, she also acted indecisively and dependently with the therapist, asking repeatedly what she should do. Though his refusing to give her a solution obviously made her angry, she predictably found it difficult to express these feelings toward him as well.

As the therapist pointed out the common theme in all these relationships, Anna initially reacted with denial and an effort to change the subject, instead asking for advice about what she should do. Later on, the cumulative weight of many interpretations started to have an effect. She began to recognize that her powerful fear of abandonment had led to a lifelong pattern of unassertive behavior and suppression of anger. At first her acknowledgments had a mechanical quality, as if to say, "Yes, that's true, but it doesn't make any difference." Eventually, the insights started to sink in. In one session devoted to her childhood deprivations, she let herself cry intensely and recognize the depth of her unfulfilled need for closeness.

Still, insights alone were not enough; Anna obviously had to take steps to end her relationship with this man. Yet despite her burgeoning self-understanding and his continued harassment, she insisted for some time that she would continue to help him. It is no small matter, of course, to turn one's back on a lifelong pattern of behavior. The therapist here had to walk a tightrope. To give direct advice to drop the relationship—perhaps a good idea with another client—would mean to Anna being assigned to her familiar submissive, dependent role, which would perpetuate her fear of assertiveness.

Anna herself had to initiate the break. Yet, at the same time, it was essential that she not be allowed to evade the issue of her self-destructive relationship. The therapist's tack, therefore, was to question her frequently about her thoughts and wishes regarding the man. What did her best judgment suggest she should do? This line of questioning had the effect of encouraging assertiveness while respecting her autonomy. The behavioral move, when it came, happened suddenly. At the beginning of the fifth session she reported, her voice loud with anger, that she had stopped the man when he tried to taunt her during a chance meeting on campus. She announced then that she wanted nothing more to do with him. When he later tried to call, she immediately hung up.

Having finally jettisoned the anxiety-producing relationship and proved to herself that she could act assertively without catastrophe, Anna was rewarded with reduced anxiety. The remaining seven sessions were devoted to a deeper exploration of her long-standing difficulties with her family and her fears of abandonment and self-assertion. At the termination of therapy, her studies had improved and she was determined to carry on more constructive relationships in the future.

BRENDA: A MODIFIED APPROACH

Brenda's therapy resembled Anna's in important respects. Her current anxiety was traced to its roots through an insight-oriented investigation, and the insights she gained were coupled with encouragement of activity and assertiveness. However, because of the compelling nature of her presenting complaint, the therapist chose to depart more than in Anna's case from the orthodox psychodynamic blueprint, Brenda's case illustrates the flexible approach college therapists sometimes must employ in responding to a student's particular needs.

Brenda's chief concern was mounting dread of delivering a speech in one of her classes. This fear, like Anna's worry about her "boyfriend," could be readily traced to its origins. Indeed, though she spoke in a halting, self-deprecatory manner and rarely established eye contact, Brenda was eager from the start to tell her story. She explained that as a child she had been sadistically ridiculed and teased by her father. Her mother, apparently afraid to intervene, told the girl that the father acted this way only because he wanted the best from her.

As a result, Brenda grew up believing that not only would she be subjected to ridicule, but she was wrong to get upset about it; she deserved castigation for her shortcomings. She became a frightened child who cowered when spoken to by adults and hid behind her mother. Later on in school, she felt terrified and self-conscious about speaking in groups, especially among strangers. Determined now to conquer her fear, she had enrolled in a public speaking class. As the week approached for her to deliver a brief speech, however, she was becoming increasingly apprehensive and was seriously considering withdrawing from the class.

The search for parallels among past, present, and transference relationships was for Brenda a tonic experience. She came to understand that the thread of fear of ridicule ran through all her relationships, even patently safe ones, as with the therapist. She had generalized her experience with her father and now expected ridicule from everyone. Though Brenda already suspected as much, having this theme corroborated and illustrated in detail increased her awareness and re-enforced her resolve to overcome it. Meanwhile, speaking openly to the supportive therapist provided at least a partial "corrective emotional experience" (Alexander & French, 1946; see also Guntrip, 1971), proving that not everyone, in fact, would demean her. As the sessions progressed, Brenda grew more comfortable and more confident with the therapist.

Had the speech not loomed ahead, this standard psychodynamic approach might well have been sufficient. However, Brenda was still experiencing severe anxiety in anticipation of delivering the talk and was still tempted to drop the course. Since she saw the speech as the acid test of her ability to change, the therapist decided to concentrate on improving her chances for success. Focusing on her anxiety-producing beliefs, he questioned her about her expectations of the event. What images and thoughts came to mind? What exactly did she tell herself about the speech? She responded that speaking before the class would be a catastrophic experience. Her ideas would be poorly formed and jumbled further because of her anxiety; the class would be scornful (if only in silence); and she would end up in tears. At the same time, reason told her that her fears were perhaps irrational or exaggerated. "I know this is silly, " she kept saying, as if her fears were shameful.

The therapist's task with this material was delicate. He had to be careful not to join in her denigration of her fears; which would have confirmed her belief that she was ridiculous. Therefore he remarked that her background gave her good reason to expect the worst; furthermore, her fears, far from being silly, were a concern that they both needed to take seriously. But the therapist also wanted to shake the foundations of her anxiety-producing beliefs. Perhaps, he suggested, she was right that her fears were exaggerated. Could she imagine outcomes other than the disaster she predicted? What were more constructive thoughts she might entertain about her performance and the reactions of the class? Through such questions, he invited her to challenge her fears in a nonjudgmental way.

In addition to examining Brenda's cognitions, the therapist decided to teach her methods of relaxation and stressed the importance of breathing deeply before and during the speech. He had her role-play the talk in his office and suggested that she also try it out with her roommate He instructed her that people can perform in spite of anxiety; indeed, she should expect to be anxious on the day of the talk. Most of all, he encouraged assertiveness—and essentially gave advice—by urging her to follow through on her intentions. The anxiety she was suffering now in anticipation of the speech, he said, was the short-term price to pay for permanent psychological and social rewards. Delivering the talk could be a watershed for her self-confidence and ability to take risks.

It is impossible to say which technique or combination of techniques turned the tide. Perhaps the willingness of the therapist to try different methods in her behalf communicated an involvement that was in itself anxiety-reducing. Whatever the reason, the session after her scheduled speech Brenda came in aglow with triumphant enthusiasm. Despite butterflies from beginning to end, she not only had got through it, but was commended by her classmates and instructor. That session and one other were spent consolidating the lessons she had learned, after which Brenda terminated therapy with a considerable sense of accomplishment.

SUMMARY

Anxiety is a common denominator for virtually every college student who comes to the counseling center. It has many causes, both proximate and psychodynamic; it manifests itself in social situations, academic performance, bodily concerns, and indeed, every aspect of students' college adjustment. A modified short-term psychodynamic approach is recommended for treating the anxiety problems of college students. This approach aims to unearth core fears, motives, and conflicts by searching for parallels among students' past, current, and therapeutic relationships. The insight students gain into the unconscious sources of their anxiety then brings them relief. Working with anxious students calls for certain special therapeutic considerations and modifications within the psychodynamic model. Therapists may decide to take strong measures, encourage activities and assertiveness, help students to express themselves, identify anxiety-producing beliefs, or use relaxation measures. Maintaining empathy can be a particular challenge with anxious clients. The importance of taking a flexible approach within the psychodynamic model is illustrated by the two case studies.

References

Alberti, R., & Emmons, M. (1970). *Your perfect right*. San Luis Obispo, CA: Impact.

Alexander, R., & French, T. (1946). *Psychoanalytic therapy*. New York: Ronald Press.

American Psychiatric Association. (1987). *Diagnostic and statistical manual of mental disorders* (3rd ed., rev.) Washington, DC: Author.

Angyal, A. (1965). *Neurosis and treatment*. New York: Wiley.

Beck, A.T., & Emery, G. (1985). *Anxiety disorders and phobias*. New York: Basic Books.

Benson, H. (1975). *The relaxation response*. New York: Avon Books.

Brenner, C. (1982). *The mind in conflict*. New York: International Universities Press.

Ellis, A., & Grieger, T. (1977). *Handbook of rational-emotive therapy*. New York: Springer.

Fenichel, O. (1945). *The psychoanalytic theory of neurosis.* New York: Norton.

Guntrip, H. (1971). *Psychoanalytic theory, therapy, and the self.* New York: Basic Books.

Horney, K. (1937). *The neurotic personality of our time.* New York: Norton.

Malan, D. H. (1976). *The frontier of brief psychotherapy.* New York: Plenum.

Pilkonis, P.A. (1977). The behavioral consequences of shyness. *Journal of Personality,* 45, 596-611.

Rothblum, E. D., Solomon, L. J., & Murakami, J. (1986). Affective, cognitive, and behavioral differences between high and low procrastinators. *Journal of Counseling Psychology,* 33, 387-394.

Schafer, R. (1983). *The analytic attitude.* New York: Basic Books.

Tillich, P. (1952). *The courage to be.* New Haven, CT: Yale University Press.

Date Rape on the College Campus: The College Psychotherapist as Activist

*Cases of rape, particularly date rape, have reached almost epidemic pro-
portions on college campuses throughout the country. In this article the
author describes how he extended his role as a college psychotherapist in
order to undertake activism in behalf of college date rape victims generally.
The author as activist undertook two major courses of action: (1) Testified
to the California State Legislature in support of Assemblyman Tom Hayden's
bill dealing with college date rape; and (2) Appeared on a television news
program that investigated the crime of college date rape. The author later
utilized a video recording of the program in conjunction with a series of
lectures he conducted on his campus regarding the subject of college date rape.*

At the time that I was assisting two victims of acquaintance rape
on my own campus I learned that California Assemblyman Tom
Hayden was sponsoring a bill to deal with the problem of college date
rape. The bill would request all institutions of higher education in California to take specified action with respect to sexual assaults that occur on college and university campuses.

I called Assemblyman Hayden's office, described to a member
of his staff the cases of rape in which I was intervening at my college
(taking strict precautions to protect the confidentiality of the victims),
and volunteered to speak to the legislature in behalf of the Hayden
bill. The response to my offer was enthusiastic and I was urged to
testify when the bill came before the Sub-Committee on Higher Education.

Assemblyman Hayden's bill was fortified by some rather horri-
fying statistics. A 1985 national survey of 7,000 students on 35 campuses revealed the following findings (Koss, Gidycz, and Wisniewsky,
1987):
1. One in eight women have been raped; and

2. Eighty-five percent of these incidents occurred among students who knew one another and 5% of the attacks involved more than one assailant; and

3. Three-quarters of the victims of acquaintance rape did not identify their experience as rape and none of the males involved believed they had committed a crime; and

4. Forty-five percent of the males who committed acquaintance rape said they would repeat the experience; and

5. More than one-third of the women raped did not discuss the experience with anyone and more than 90 percent of them did not report the incident to the police.

Several persons, including myself, all of whom either attended or were employed by California colleges and universities, testified in behalf of Assemblyman Hayden's bill (Hayden, 1987). Somewhere in the legislative process the bill was converted to a resolution and ultimately passed by the state legislature.

Essentially, Assemblyman Hayden's resolution calls upon colleges and universities to: educate all incoming students about date rape; investigate, report and record rapes on campus; take disciplinary action against student attackers. The fundamental purpose of the resolution is to prevent rape victims from having to endlessly struggle and humiliate themselves in order to receive adequate help from their respective colleges.

Assemblyman Hayden also indicated that if the resolution does not yield satisfactory results, he will push to have it enacted into law, thus making the provisions of the current resolution mandatory rather than permissive, as they are presently constituted. At this writing, it appears that many, if not most, of the colleges and universities have been dilatory in adopting and implementing the provisions of the resolution. Therefore, Assemblyman Hayden's avowed readiness to sponsor a bill with mandatory provisions will very likely be tested within the next year.

Because of my collaboration with Assemblyman Hayden's office, a member of his staff recommended me to KCBS-TV, Los Angeles, which was in the process of producing a four-part series on the subject of date rape on the college campus. I went to Los Angeles in order to appear on this program, which included interviews with rape victims, rape-victim counselors, non-victim children and college students (some of whom had never been oriented by their schools to the risks of rape victimization), and a convicted rapist. Assemblyman Hayden also appeared on this program in order to underscore the "sorry situation" that exists on today's college campuses with respect to the problem of date rape.

Because I considered this newscast to be of excellent quality and far-reaching importance, I arranged to have it videotaped for use on my own campus. (Unfortunately, due to copyright restrictions, it is not generally available.) During the past year I had volunteered to present the film to classes in several subject areas: English, Behavioral Sciences, Health Education and Human Sexuality. The showing of the film is followed by a brief lecture and the students are encouraged to comment upon and discuss the problems connected with date rape.

Thus far, the responses of students to these presentations have been overwhelmingly positive. Many students have indicated that this is the first time, in any setting, that they have heard a formal presentation on the subject of date rape. Many women students in these classes have openly acknowledged that they have had firsthand experiences as victims of date rape or attempted date rape. Consequently, they have vigorously attested to the vital need for educating students about the subject. A large number of male students have also expressed concerns about where to "draw the line" on their dates and about not knowing precisely what is sexually legal or illegal behavior toward a woman. They have felt especially assisted by these presentations in making such legal and socially essential distinctions.

Recently, a health education instructor has reproduced the videotape and will herself be conducting lectures on date rape as a regular component of her future courses. In the coming months I will be attempting to encourage other instructors, especially those in the health and social sciences, to do likewise.

CONCLUSION

Since academic institutions have a legal and moral responsibility to protect the safety of members of their college communities, what should they do to prevent and intervene in cases of acquaintance rape? If, as the aforementioned survey of college student rape victims indicated, over 90 percent of the victims do not report the crime to the police, the onus perforce falls upon the colleges and universities to educate their students about the immorality and viciousness of date rape, and to carry out decisive disciplinary measures against student rapists.

It is common knowledge that the values and attitudes that predispose some men to view women as sexual objects to be ravished against their will are formed in early childhood. Thus, the time is long overdue for our elementary and secondary schools to also address and enlighten the sexual attitudes and values of their students so that future generations of men do not need to rape women in order to feel manly. Perhaps those personnel in college and university mental health programs who can skillfully teach about the complex causes and traumatic effects of date rape should consider extending their professional services to the faculties and children of the grade and high schools in their communities. (I myself have recently given several guest lectures on date rape at a local high school. Several students thought the issues I had discussed with them were so important that they planned to ask their principal to have me lecture to the entire student body in the high school auditorium.) In my view, such efforts would have the highly positive, ultimate effect of markedly reducing the incidence of date rapes at the college level.

As Susan Estrich has noted in *Real Rape* (1987), her landmark study of date rape.

> It is time—long past time—to announce to society our condemnation of simple (date) rape, and to enforce that condemnation "to secure that fewer of them are done." The message of the law to men, and to women, should be made clear. Simple rape is real rape.

References

Estrich, S. (1987). *Real Rape*. Cambridge: Harvard University Press.

Hayden, T. (1987) *Assembly Bill No. 2017*. California State Assembly.

Koss, M., Gidycz, C. and Wisniewski, N. (1987). The Scope of Rape: Incidence and Prevalence of Sexual Aggression and Victimization in a National Sample of Higher Education Students. *Journal of Consulting and Clinical Psychology* 2, (2), 162-170.

Coping With the Disruptive College Student: A Practical Model

This article offers some practical suggestions for college faculty and administrators who must deal with disruptive students. It emphasizes the need for well-defined codes of student conduct and clear procedures for dealing with disruptive behavior, and considers why university officials may be reluctant to deal with disciplinary problems related to psychiatric disturbances. The author discusses the distinction between disruptive and dangerous behavior, looks at the use of mandatory psychiatric withdrawals, makes recommendations for conditions of re-enrollment, and suggests how a campus mental health service can be useful in dealing with the problem.

The findings in this article are based upon my clinical experience over the past 20 years in the mental health program at the City College of San Francisco. This program is an on-campus psychological service that provides short-term psychotherapy (i.e., 10-12 sessions) to community college students. In addition to my role as an administrator of this program, I have also served as a consultant on the problem of the disruptive college student at many other colleges and universities in California. Thus, I believe the conclusions and recommendations outlined in the following discussion generally reflect the intense concerns of a great many college personnel in California and, most likely, throughout the nation.

As I indicated in an earlier article,[1] the number of disruptive incidents reported on college campuses has risen sharply in recent years. Many of these incidents (fighting, alcohol abuse, plagiarism, and date rape) appear to involve students who are quite diverse diagnostically. There is little doubt, however, that a significant number of the disruptive incidents reported by college employees involve students with such serious psychological disabilities as manic depression and schizophrenia, as well as some of the serious character disorders, particularly the antisocial personality disorder and the borderline personality disorder (acting out).

Several explanations have been advanced to account for the large increase in the numbers of seriously emotionally disturbed students attending colleges: legislative changes that have helped to retain and treat psychiatric patients in their local communities; advances in the use of psychotropic medications to stabilize psychiatric patients in local, noninstitutional settings; and the well-structured, culturally rich, and hospitable qualities of the college campus itself, which are surely inviting to most students, including those with psychological disabilities.

In my contacts with college and university employees throughout the country, I have noted an appreciable increase in complaints that, as the community mental health system over the past decade or so has deteriorated as a result of severe funding cutbacks, larger numbers of seriously disturbed individuals are being admitted to colleges, especially community colleges. Many of these students are not receiving or, in many instances, even asking for, the full benefit of the local psychological and social services they desperately need if they are to succeed.

This article, although undoubtedly of theoretical or heuristic interest, is intended to be primarily of practical value to those who will be encountering and attempting to resolve disruptive incidents on campus.

THE NEED FOR A WELL-DEFINED AND PUBLICIZED SET OF CODES AND PROCEDURES GOVERNING STUDENT CONDUCT

As obvious and simplistic as this recommendation may seem, it is imperative that colleges periodically review their codes of student conduct for the following: Are the codes clear, coherent, comprehensive, mutually compatible, and enforceable? Will they withstand legal scrutiny and challenge? In a random survey of about 12 community colleges in California, I found, under the section dealing with student conduct in the college catalogues, that 8 schools had rather clear and explicit codes of student conduct, 3 had vague, ambiguous references to the need for general conformity to the social and moral standards of the campus community, and astonishingly, that one college had no written statement at all regarding student conduct. Clearly, this latter college unnecessarily places itself in potential legal jeopardy.

In reviewing the comprehensiveness of their student conduct codes, colleges should attempt to determine whether the codes will cover those forms of disruptive behavior that will arise most often on their campuses. Because obvious forms of disruptive behavior, that is, conduct that is physically violent or overtly menacing, are likely to be readily identified and included in the student conduct codes, colleges should also acknowledge in the codes, at least implicitly, that certain forms of passive and covert behavior may also be regarded as quite disruptive. These behaviors, although perhaps less urgent than more violent actions, may be equally disruptive of the academic process.

Examples of passive, yet disruptive, behavior are those students whose poor personal hygiene so seriously offends the sensibilities of classmates and instructors that the classroom becomes an academic environment that is no longer tenable. Or, to use another example, the student who each day conspicuously falls asleep in a class in which oral participation is a clearly established academic requirement.

To determine accurately the fairness, comprehensibility, and applicability of its codes of student conduct, administrators responsible for formulating and ultimately enforcing the codes should review them regularly with the administrative, instructional, and classified staff of the college and with representative groups of students. In determining the legality of those codes, the designated administrators must review them carefully with the college's legal advisors.

At the same time it makes its periodic review of codes of student conduct, the institution should evaluate those procedures that are to be used to implement the codes, taking care that each employee of the college understands what constitutes disruptive behavior, to whom reports of disruptive behavior are to be transmitted sequentially, and the range of options and prerogatives available to those reporting incidents of disruption. If, because of the passage of time, the staff's recollection of these procedures becomes fuzzy, it probably behooves the designated administrator either to have them occasionally reviewed in departmental meetings or to develop and disseminate a procedural handbook that can be readily used to handle troublesome or disruptive incidents.

DISCIPLINARY SANCTIONS

Establishment of codes and procedures that govern student conduct must be predicated upon a college administration's readiness to impose disciplinary sanctions for disruptive behavior. It is advantageous, therefore, that administrators who are responsible for carrying out disciplinary action endeavor to formulate and enforce a set of specified penalties for particular acts of disruption. Such a codified set of disciplinary sanctions need not be Hammurabian either in spirit or substance, but should be reasonably and gradationally commensurate with the seriousness of each act of disruption. In other words, the punishment should reasonably fit the "crime." For example, in developing such a hierarchy of disciplinary sanctions, a first-time case of plagiarism could perhaps result in a temporary suspension, whereas physical assault on an instructor or on-campus drug trafficking could conceivably result in expulsion.

In the interest of fairness and justice, a hierarchy that couples specific disruptive behaviors with proportionate sanctions should allow for extenuating circumstances that might mitigate disciplinary measures. Thus, a student who had just learned that a parent was diagnosed with a fatal illness and soon afterward "unprovokedly" defaced college property might, taking into account his grief-stricken state, receive a milder form of discipline than would otherwise be the case. Nevertheless, an administration that has in hand a ready-made set of reasonably proportionate and legally enforceable sanctions that specifically match a broad spectrum of potentially disruptive behaviors will reduce its own likelihood of administering discipline in a precipitate, muddled, or discriminatory manner.

Many incidents of disruptive behavior are quite ambiguous. It is often extremely difficult to unravel the truth about who, college employee or student, originally provoked or perpetuated a particular act of disruptiveness. As a result, the extent of a student's culpability, if any, may be extremely difficult to determine. Important questions may also arise regarding cultural differences that manifest themselves in atypical (for the college) styles and standards of dress, hygiene, speech, and behavior that can be too easily misconstrued as willful acts of misconduct.

On the one hand, it is important to understand and respect cultural differences as much as possible to prevent ethnocentric biases from being used to punish those who are simply different. On the other hand, colleges must also be alert to the possibility that some students will use their cultural differences, whether contrived or real, as a pretext for conducting themselves in a genuinely abusive or disruptive manner.

In any case, when confronted with highly ambiguous disruptive situations that require consideration of extenuating circumstances, administrators often discover that a too-rigid adherence to the codes of student conduct may cause more harm than good. Often, an infusion of common sense and good judgment will provide a better resolution of the problem than the automatic invocation of a conduct code.

A DEFINITION OF DISRUPTION

In its broadest and most generic sense, the term disruption applies to behavior that persistently interferes with academic and administrative activities on campus. Ordinarily, such behavior actively hampers the ability of the other students to learn and of instructors to teach. Extreme forms of this behavior may even threaten the physical safety of students and staff. The following are some specific examples of disruptive behavior that commonly result in the administrative imposition of discipline: verbal abuse of college personnel, physical threats or assaults upon others, willful damage to college property, and misuse of drugs or alcohol on college premises.

Another form of disruptive behavior that has been included in the codes of student conduct of certain colleges, including my own, is the inordinate and inappropriate demands of students for time and attention from faculty and staff. Based upon my own observations, I would suggest that this particular kind of disruptive behavior—loud, incessant, prolonged, or belligerent insistence from students that they be accorded more time, attention, and respect from certain college personnel—constitutes the majority of reported cases of student disruptiveness.

The more passive and covert, albeit sometimes serious, forms of disruptive behavior, such as a student's offensive personal hygiene, are ordinarily either overlooked or minimized until they arouse widespread and vocal concern.

RECOMMENDED GUIDELINES AND CONSIDERATIONS FOR REPORTING INCIDENTS OF DISRUPTION

The most common sources of reported incidents of disruption are college faculty members who, by dint of their instructional duties, have the most extensive and, quite often, nerve-racking contact with disruption-prone students. Typically, by the time a faculty member reports an incident of disruption, the situation has reached quite serious, if not dire, proportions. There are several explanations for this.

First, faculty are often reluctant to report a disruptive student because they hope that benign inaction will lead to some form of spontaneous resolution. In other words, the instructor hopes that such students will somehow see the error of their ways and eventually shape up on their own.

Second, instructors worry about the possibility that they will not be adequately supported by the administration if they report a disruptive student. Worse, they sometimes exaggeratedly fear that the problem will be seen as a reflection of their own professional inadequacies and that a resultant investigation will only lead to the discovery of their own blameworthiness in the matter.

Third, some instructors feel that most forms of discipline, no matter how mild and warranted, are excessively harmful to the disruptive student, who is seen as too fragile psychologically to withstand the pressure of any disciplinary measure. Finally, some instructors hesitate to complain about a disruptive student because they feel unprotected from reprisals from that student. Such fears, unfortunately, are not always unfounded.

By the time the disruptive student is finally reported to the administration, therefore, the behavior is usually recurrent, flagrant, and fairly insusceptible to change by any means other than a disciplinary measure. For this reason, if an administrator determines that a given student has been disruptive and deserves to be penalized, it is ordinarily important to consider the fairness and proportionality of the disciplinary sanction and also which form of discipline would best help the disruptive student take positive steps to correct his or her behavior.

Essential Prerogatives

Faculty under pressure of coping with a disruptive student may forget that they, as instructors, have two essential prerogatives. The first is to establish and implement academic standards, the second is to establish and enforce reasonable behavioral standards for each class. In carrying out this latter prerogative, the principle of reasonable accommodation should be followed—minor disruptions should be tolerated as well as possible, but major disruptions to the educational process should be met with disciplinary action. It is normally very reassuring to faculty to know that they do have rights and prerogatives and can insist upon conformity to reasonable codes of conduct within the jurisdiction of their own classes and offices.

A quite prevalent concern of faculty who report disruptive incidents relates to the potential dangerousness of the disruptive student. Although this concern is sometimes disproportionate and groundless, it should never be dismissed out of hand. After all, many disruptive students are bigger, younger, and more vigorous than the instructor, and may, in extreme cases, have little compunction about using a weapon.

Even when there is no clear-cut evidence of a particular student's potential for violence or mayhem, no administrator or mental health practitioner can ever state with absolute certainty that the instructor is completely safe from harm. Instead, in disruptive situations that appear relatively innocuous, the instructor can be told that the student is probably not a potential threat to him or her. Should there be any doubt or apprehension on this score, however, he or she should take whatever precautions are necessary to avoid the possibility of being endangered. One example of such a precaution would be to arrange to meet with the disruptive student only in the company of other staff. Another would be to call upon the assistance of campus law enforcement officers to deal immediately with the student who demands to continue, unrelentingly, a rancorous discussion with the instructor.

When it appears there is a definite and imminent risk of physical harm to the instructor, the student should be reported at once to the designated administrator and to the campus police. If the campus does not have a law enforcement unit, the assistance of the city police or sheriff's office may be enlisted. In such cases, an administrative investigation and assessment should be undertaken immediately to determine the advisability of allowing the student to remain in the instructor's class. In California, based upon a relatively recent education code, instructors may unilaterally (that is, without administrative approval) remove a disruptive student from two consecutive classes. This is often a handy intervention because it buys time until the matter can be more thoroughly and safely reviewed at the administrative level.

In cases that involve recurrent, blatant, and clearly unresolvable disruptive behavior but are not truly dangerous (except, possibly, to the morale and sanity of the instructor and the other students), a somewhat different tack may be necessary. Many of the students who fall into this category are demonstrably psychologically disabled and are simply unable to modify their disruptive behavior, even with the benefit of constant reminders, blandishments, or warnings. In such cases, it may be best for an administrator to meet privately with these students, apprise them that they are at an unfortunate and insoluble impasse and that it is decidedly in their interest to withdraw from the class (or college) as soon as possible.

It may also be necessary to tell the student that, although no disciplinary action is currently under consideration, any further repetition of the disruptive behavior would probably lead to some form of penalty. To avoid the stigma of having that personally tarnishing outcome recorded in their academic records and to relieve themselves of the burden of having to struggle further with a clearly irremediable situation, such students would find it to their great advantage to withdraw immediately.

In my own experience, when such students are approached in this way—especially when the administrator's manner is empathic but firm—they generally and gladly accept the offer to withdraw without penalty. When they do not do so, the administrator must be prepared to carry through on the threat to initiate a disciplinary procedure if the student continues to be disruptive. The alternative and common practice of referring psychologically disabled students who have been disruptive to counselors or psychotherapists will be discussed later. Suffice to say here, however, that when mental health referrals are deemed appropriate, they should ordinarily be conducted on a voluntary and confidential basis and kept quite separate from disciplinary procedures.

Documentation

In formally transmitting information about disruptive student behavior, instructors are advised to accompany their oral reports with written documentation of their observations. The documentation should be devoid of psychological jargon or speculation (e.g., "This person appears to be a paranoid schizophrenic" or "I think he's on drugs"). With as little editorializing as possible, the instructor should provide information that is specific and concrete, stressing only the student's unacceptable *behavior*. Finally, if instructors hold strong preferences regarding the ultimate disposition of their complaints, they should specify these preferences in their reports. This helps to remove some of the guesswork on the part of administrators who, in attempting to determine a proper course of action, will probably want to take the complainant's wishes into account. Upon completion, the documentation should be accurately dated and transmitted to the appropriate administrative officer for investigation and resolution.

When a disruptive incident has already spiraled dangerously out of control and an instructor needs immediate assistance to deal with it, that assistance should be readily available. The administration of a college has a twofold responsibility in this regard. First, it should ensure that emergency services (city or campus police or a mental health or crisis intervention team) are well in place and immediately enlistable. Second, all staff should be informed, in writing, about the procedures and resources that are to be used in the event of a dangerous emergency.

Noninstructional Staff

Although this discussion has focused rather exclusively on the role of the instructor in handling disruptive students, instructional staff are obviously not the only college personnel who must deal with student disruptiveness. Counselors, support staff who work as secretaries and custodians, personnel who manage the bookstore, and administrative officers who are ultimately responsible for administering discipline are all, from time to time, involved in directly coping with disruptive student behavior.

The principles and procedures outlined above for instructors should therefore also be considered valid and useful for noninstructional staff. Each college employee, irrespective of his or her particular professional assignment or work area, has the right to be treated with respect and dignity by students (and vice versa, of course). As one college official pointedly phrased the matter, "Suffering abuse is in no one's job description. No staff member or instructor should ... have to put up with bullying, intimidation, or violence" (Suzanne Belson, Concordia University, Montreal, personal communication).

THE AVERSION TO ADMINISTERING DISCIPLINE

It is quite common to find that college instructors and administrators are averse to meting out discipline, even well-deserved discipline, to disruptive students. There are several explanations for this. First, discipline, especially admonitory discipline, tends to inflict psychic pain upon its recipients. Thus, unless the disciplinarian is an unregenerate sadist, he or she will administer discipline only with a degree of guilt, reluctance, and uneasiness. Second, many, if not most, college personnel easily lose sight of the potential positive value of discipline in coping with disruptive students. They often rather one-sidedly believe that discipline will necessarily serve only to exacerbate and escalate an already inflamed conflict, and may even hold to this position in the face of considerable evidence that their prolonged inaction has inadvertently led to a serious escalation of disruptiveness. Third, many academicians are drawn to academe by a desire to teach in a relatively disruption-free and untrammeled intellectual milieu and, therefore, react with dismay when they discover and then must deal with disciplinary situations.

It is important for those responsible for disciplining disruptive students to realize that discipline is not inherently cruel or immoral. Just and fair disciplinary measures, in providing a form of external control, may be exactly what a disruptive student needs to regain self-control. In some instances, decisive discipline may be the only anti-dote for dealing with an uncontrollably disruptive student. As Pavela[2] has pointed out, the imposition of a just punishment can affirm and enhance one's capacity to make moral choices. Keeping this in mind, administrators who must mete out discipline to disruptive students might find it helpful to understand that the correct use of discipline quite often serves the interests of both the disruptive student and the college. When the discipline is successful, the student regains self-control and, it is hoped, remains in college; the college benefits by having one less disruptive student.

Nonetheless, it would be the height of self-serving Pollyannaism to assume that those disciplinary measures deemed good and beneficial by the college will necessarily be regarded favorably by the disruptive students themselves. It is, perhaps, more realistic to assume that many disruptive students will feel that the disciplinary sanctions imposed upon them are unwarranted, unfair, and unhelpful, even though they may change their behavior as a result. Because the college is seeking and requiring nothing more than a positive behavioral change, there is no particular reason for it to expect, demand, or attempt to engender in disruptive students a friendly attitude toward the discipline they have received.

The Special Burdens Carried by Administrators

Administrators, in particular, have several additional burdens to deal with when confronted with reports of disruptive behavior. To carry out discipline properly, they must first carefully evaluate the report they have received. Ordinarily, they must ask themselves, "Is this report credible? Is the instructor who has reported the disruptive student perhaps exaggerating or manufacturing the gravity of the circumstances?" When there is doubt about the credibility or accuracy of the allegations, it may be necessary to hold a formal hearing rather than, for example, meeting informally only with the student—in which witnesses can be questioned and allegedly disruptive students can fully defend themselves against the charges. Based upon my own experience with the reports of such incidents, however, I would venture to say that in most cases of reported disruptiveness, the facts seem to speak for themselves. The complainant is normally a quite credible, reliable, and rational person, and the designated administrator needs to act immediately and decisively to resolve the problem.

Some cases of reported disruptiveness, by their sheer complexity, will confound and discomfit even the most knowledgeable, astute, and self-assured administrator. There are college employees who, for whatever reasons, develop an unwavering animus for particular students and use their complaints against them to carry out personal vendettas. Sadistic and mendacious college personnel may deliberately lie and distort the facts when submitting complaints against students. Other college employees—racists, ageists, sexists, homophobes—may use their xenophobic prejudices to denounce and punish students who are different from themselves.

To complicate matters further, there are students who enter college with a seemingly personal agenda to make life miserable for everyone they happen to encounter. They are, regrettably, quite adroit in accomplishing their objective. At the first hint of an administrative investigation of their misconduct, they become litigious, threatening to file an expensive law suit against the college for the supposed injustices about to be inflicted upon them.

In short, the enormously complex personal idiosyncrasies of staff and students alike, when considered during an administrative investigation of a complicated case of alleged disruptiveness, might lead one to conclude that the administrator best suited to this Olympian task is an individual who is doubly endowed with the patience of a Job and the wisdom of a Solomon.

Administrators often feel stymied and thwarted because some instructors who report disruptive students have not followed due process. In other words, those instructors who are petitioning for administrative intervention with disruptive students have not given sufficient warning to the offending students about their behavior or have not adequately documented their observations since the inception of the objectionable behavior. Administrators rightly consider themselves hamstrung when there has been little adherence to due process. If they proceed with the disciplinary procedure under these circumstances, they may be professionally and personally vulnerable during a judicial investigation or hearing.

Two courses of action are available to help obviate this dilemma somewhat. First, if administrators discover that their staffs are too regularly overlooking the need to follow due process, administrators must develop written materials and in-service training activities so that all employees can become familiar with the need and procedures for fulfilling these requirements. Second, when immediate intervention is necessary and due process has not heretofore been followed, administrators, if necessary, can accelerate, condense, and streamline the entire investigative/administrative process. They may first request that instructors quickly and retroactively document the course of disruptive events and promptly transmit their written reports to the administration, then suggest that the instructor refer the student to the appropriate administrator for an immediate interview and official review of the matter. If necessary, administrators may consider imposing an immediate "interim suspension" upon the student who poses an acute and imminent danger to the campus community in order to defuse the element of risk quickly and to allow more time to resolve the disruptive crisis.

A further complication that fosters an aversion for and delay in administering discipline is that most college administrators who serve as disciplinarians are middle management executives—often the deans of students. They do not possess the ultimate authority for resolving certain cases of disruptive behavior in a way that is commensurate with their official responsibilities for meting out discipline. When faced with complicated disciplinary cases, administrators will often turn to their administrative superiors for help. The latter may, in turn, consult the college attorney for a more authoritative legal opinion. Implementing these multiple consultations will sometimes cause protracted and frustrating delays in resolving the disruptive crisis.

To complicate matters further, the final opinions and recommendations of the legal staff or of the highest ranking administrative officers of the college may be inimical to the interests or desires of the college employee who originally reported the disruptive student. For example, instructors who have been confronted with highly disruptive and possibly dangerous students and are virtually at the end of their emotional tether will probably want such students removed and barred from their classes at once. The college attorney or a high-ranking administrator, however, may recommend that the college delay action until the instructors more adequately fulfill the requirements of documentation and due process.

Administrators who are at the center of this crossfire of conflicting demands and perspectives are on the horns of a rather nasty dilemma. If, in deference to a legal opinion, they refuse to fulfill the terms of the instructor's petition for help, they can be subject to accusations of moral spinelessness and dereliction of duty. If they opt to grant the instructor's request immediately by intervening despite an inadequate adherence to due process, they may later find themselves rather far out on a legal limb, with few institutional allies or safeguards to protect them from students who might seek legal retribution.

An Institutional Anomaly

One method of escape that has been commonly used by administrators who face this dilemma is to refer disruptive students to counselors and mental health practitioners for evaluation and/or therapy in hopes that this will somehow ameliorate or resolve the crisis. Although many administrative referrals of students to counselors and psychotherapists are quite appropriate, especially when the students themselves indicate a desire to receive psychological services, referrals of students who have been disruptive (and are being referred *because* they have been disruptive) are usually inadvisable and of little value. Depending on the degree of force and coercion employed in carrying out such a referral, this particular strategy may also be of questionable legality as well.

It is common for administrators to refer disruptive students to counselors and therapists, not simply to escape a legal dilemma, but because they think it is somehow kinder, and perhaps less damaging, to students to have their difficulties viewed as mental health, rather than disciplinary, problems.

This particular strategy usually results in an institutional anomaly: Therapists and counselors (whose job it is to guide and heal) are asked or required, under administrative pressure, to assume quasi-disciplinary functions and responsibilities; and administrators (whose job, among others, is to administer discipline) are, instead, counseling disruptive students about their need for mental health services.

This anomaly is especially apparent when the evident purpose and expectation of the administrative referral is to have the therapist or counselor, by any means available, "stop" the student from being disruptive. Although there may be nothing wrong with an administrator's recommending psychotherapy to a student, it is ordinarily inappropriate and counterproductive to use such recommendations as a handy substitute for appropriate disciplinary action.

To appreciate better the implications of such institutional anomalies, I believe it helpful to consider a few trenchant caveats proffered by Halleck:[3] (1) When society decides that a person is behaving unreasonably enough to be a psychiatric patient, it simply makes a judgment, which must be sanctioned by professionals, about the maladaptive basis of that person's conduct and assumes that the person who behaves in such a manner is troubled or unhappy.

In some instances, the individual may not feel troubled; therefore, he may be placed in the patient role involuntarily (R. L. Arnstein, MD, in a 1991 personal communication, notes that it is also true that in most states "society" supports the idea that mental health professionals sometimes may need to "place someone in the patient role involuntarily," at least briefly). (2) The judgment of unreasonable suffering or behavior is always a value judgment, frequently based on arbitrary and shifting criteria. (3) The psychiatric profession has often loaned its talents to perpetuate unsubstantiated belief systems or myths. Inadvertently, therapists and counselors sometimes use their positions to deter society from confronting and dealing with inequities in the distribution of power.

A Few Alternatives

Instructors whose requests for immediate administrative intervention with a disruptive student are denied are normally faced with several unpalatable choices. They may simply accept the administrative decision and painfully bide their time with a disruptive student until the disruptiveness either subsides or further escalates. In the event that it persists or escalates, the ensuing escalation may provide the college with sufficient grounds for administrative action. Instructors will then be able to petition the college again with stronger evidence of the student's continuing disruptiveness and, the instructor hopes, provide a more convincing record of their adherence to due process.

A second choice. If instructors consider themselves extremely endangered by the retention of a disruptive student in their class and still cannot secure administrative support for removing that student, *and when the student's behavior seems to be in violation of the law (e.g., a misdemeanor or felony)*, instructors may certainly exercise their civil and constitutional rights by filing criminal charges against the student with the local police department. For example, in California a section of the state penal code makes it a crime willfully to threaten to commit a crime that will result in death or great bodily injury to another person. Another section of the penal code makes it a punishable public offense directly to threaten officers and employees of public or private educational institutions.[4]

Considering the unequivocal dangerousness of some acts of student misconduct it is imperative that college employees who are dealing with students whose disruptive behavior may be in violation of the law periodically review the penal codes of their own states and municipalities to determine the proper grounds for reporting potential crimes and to enlist the intervention of the judicial system in resolving on-campus acts of criminality.

Finally, in lieu of, or in addition to, filing criminal charges against students who appear to violate the law, college employees can— especially in cases that require the immediate imposition of security measures—seek the assistance of the courts in having a restraining order placed upon the endangering student.

A far more extreme and controversial step for college employees who believe they are unduly imperiled by the inaction of their own colleges in dealing with a particularly disruptive student is to threaten or actually carry out, in their own behalf, a legal action against the college. Such an action, if taken, would probably be based upon the charge that the student is seriously interfering with the civil or constitutional rights of the employee. Obviously, such an extreme measure can be fraught with considerable personal and professional risks and, therefore, should ordinarily not be undertaken without a good deal of circumspection and the benefit of expert legal advice.

Considering the many reasons that underlie a general aversion to discipline, it is understandable, as Pavela has stressed, that the administration of punishment often requires considerable moral courage.

MANDATORY PSYCHOTHERAPY AS A FORM OF DISCIPLINE

In an earlier article, I alluded to the following potential drawbacks of automatically or coercively referring disruptive students for psychotherapy.

1. Requiring disruptive students to receive psychotherapy distorts and undermines the basis for corrective disciplinary action, namely the students' disruptive *behavior*, not their putative mental illness.

2. The requirement of psychotherapy for the disruptive student is often motivated by the fanciful and naive notion that therapy, in itself, will eliminate or "cure" the disruptive behavior.

3. Requiring a disruptive student to receive psychotherapy is unequivocally a coercive measure that serves to instill in the student resentment toward the therapist and therapy. If such students conform to this requirement, they will agree to see a therapist but frequently will make no personal investment in the treatment process itself. As a consequence, the students typically derive little from the therapy other than the impression that psychotherapy is a form of punishment that must be stoically endured.

4. For psychotherapy to work effectively, it must ordinarily be conducted on a confidential basis. Requiring a disruptive student to receive psychotherapy often removes this cornerstone of therapy because someone, either the student or the therapist, will eventually be expected to report to the college administration that the student is, indeed, receiving psychotherapeutic services.

Several safeguards can generally serve to protect confidentiality in such cases. (a) Therapists may refuse to transmit substantive reports about students who have not given their voluntary, written consent to this procedure. (b) Students who have been referred for psychotherapy may willingly and, in writing, authorize their therapists to transmit certain information about them to specified college officials. (c) Students who are referred to therapists may be permitted explicitly to refuse, for whatever reason, the disclosure of therapists' reports about them to college officials without the threat of duress, penalty, or reprisal on the part of the college.

In this regard, it is probably worth mentioning that there are differences of opinion among both mental health professionals and college administrators regarding what constitutes "substantive" disclosures that violate the confidentiality of students who receive psychotherapy. In my own view, the simple fact that a student has entered psychotherapy is intrinsically substantive (and potentially inflammatory) information that should not be disclosed without the express voluntary and written consent of the student himself or herself. Although the disclosure of such limited information may seem quite innocuous, it can be used by the college, with or without intention, to embarrass, stigmatize, or manipulate students. I believe, therefore, that the student's decision to enter therapy should be given the same protections of confidentiality as that accorded the personal self-disclosures that later follow during the psychotherapy sessions themselves.

5. As suggested earlier, the administrative requirement of psychotherapy tends to transfer the responsibility and authority for administering discipline from where it rightfully belongs—the office of the designated administrator—to where it does not belongthe offices of counselors and therapists.

6. The requirement that disruptive students receive psychotherapy as a condition of continued enrollment is essentially predicated upon a policy that can exclude them because of their alleged mental or psychiatric disability. This is probably in violation of Section 504 of the Rehabilitation Act of 1973, which reads, in part: "No otherwise qualified handicapped individual shall, solely by reasons of his handicap, be excluded from participation in, be denied the benefits of, or be subjected to discrimination under any program or activity receiving Federal financial assistance."

In other words, the antiquated practice of requiring disruptive students to receive psychological evaluations and/or psychotherapy is probably illegal. Considering the many schools that still resort to its use and abuse (the prevailing attitude seems to be "I'll do it this way as long as I can get away with it"), it is truly extraordinary that college attorneys do not spend more time in courts defending those schools that regularly run afoul of the law in this manner.

Some college psychotherapists and counselors undertake mandatory or coercive psychotherapy with students even when they have ethical objections to this practice. Quite frequently, referrals for mandatory counseling or psychotherapy are made by an administrator who exercises some form of administrative authority and control over the mental health or counseling program. When this administrator authoritatively insists that students be seen for psychotherapy, the college psychotherapist who refuses to comply with these requests may be placing himself and his program in jeopardy. Conceivably, refusal to fulfill such requests may come back to haunt college psychotherapists or counselors in the form of funding cutbacks or unfriendly administrative policies and rulings vis-a-vis their programs. In any event, just imagining such a prospect could very well be a sufficient deterrent to many college psychotherapists and counselors who have ethical qualms about mandatory referrals.

An analogue to this dilemma that exists within the private sector applies to the role of private practitioners who accept mandatory referrals from colleges for psychological evaluations and treatment. Although these therapists, too, may have moral qualms about the legitimacy of this procedure, they may also realize that to refuse the college's request for such assistance may mean that they will cease to be used by the college as a community resource in the future. Obviously, it does not require an overabundance of venality on the part of private practitioners for them to have a distaste for and seek to avoid this unpleasant possibility. Thus, they may set aside their own ethical qualms about mandatory referrals from the college, at least for the time being.

In this regard, I have noticed that many therapists who are faced with this ethical quandary eventually transmit to colleges psychiatric reports that are so vague and so ambiguous as to be utterly indecipherable and of no practical value to the college. I suspect that many of these reports are deliberately written ambiguously, in part to assuage the guilt of the therapist for sending the report in the first place and also to minimize the potential harm the report eventually might cause the student in the college setting. Naturally, many college administrators who attempt to interpret and enlist these reports to carry out disciplinary decisions are frustrated and bewildered by them, perhaps without realizing that often they were written precisely to obfuscate the reader.

DISRUPTIVENESS VERSUS DANGEROUSNESS

Many well-documented studies, including those cited by Monahan,[5] have demonstrated that the ability of mental health professionals to predict dangerous or violent behavior is quite limited. The American Civil Liberties Union contends that "it now seems beyond dispute that mental health professionals have no expertise in predicting future dangerous behavior to self or others,"[5] an opinion that I consider too extreme.

The relative inability of psychotherapists to predict dangerousness is an important fact for lay and professional persons to recognize so that they can deal effectively and realistically with individuals who pose the risk of manifesting violent behavior. Nevertheless, this acknowledgment has only sporadic and peripheral relevance to most cases of disruptive student behavior. Specifically, if the prediction of dangerousness is at best precarious, the prediction of many forms of nondangerous but highly *disruptive* behavior on the college campus is not nearly so fraught with the risk of error, bias, or injustice. Most disruptive behavior that is ultimately reported to the administration by college personnel is blatant, publicly observable, and highly recurrent.

Because disruptive behavior that has already become chronic, flagrant, and publicly offensive ordinarily instigates an instructor to report the student, it is usually not difficult for an administrator to predict rather accurately whether the disruptive behavior will continue unabated without the intervention of discipline. For example, only common sense and logic would be necessary to predict that a student who, week after week, has been interrupting lectures with loud and raucous catcalls is, in all likelihood, going to continue doing so if he is not disciplined for this behavior. It should always be borne in mind that even the best predictions and most ingenious uses of discipline will not necessarily alter or rein in the disruptive behavior of some highly intractable students.

The potential for violence on the college campus is far more difficult to predict than the potential for nonviolent forms of disruptiveness for several reasons: (1) With some exceptions, violent acts of disruption committed by students fortunately tend to occur less frequently and are less likely to fall into a pattern than other, more innocuous, forms of disruption. Observable patterns of behavior, by their very nature, lend themselves to prediction far better than more sporadic forms of behavior. (2) In contrast to many nonviolent, disruptive acts on college campuses, most genuinely violent behavior—murder, rape, arson, or assault and battery—is carried out stealthily, often concealed behind closed doors, and, for lack of witnesses, shielded from detection.

Moreover, the locus of past violent crimes is likely to have been in the off-campus community, not on the college campus itself. Therefore, even if the perpetrator had been prosecuted and convicted of a prior violent crime, it is unlikely that the college would be privy to this violent history, given that the criminal record would probably be confidential.

In short, because prior patterns of violent behavior tend to be more sporadic and far less ascertainable than most patterns of nonviolent disruptive behavior—especially in those cases reported by college staff precisely because they have become chronic and public nuisances—violence and dangerousness are ordinarily much more difficult to predict than nondangerous disruptive behavior.

In sum, the conflagration of the terms *dangerousness* and *disruptiveness* is unfortunate and often misleading when applied to disruptive college students' behavior. Although dangerousness remains elusively unpredictable, most reported cases of student disruptiveness, given their generally recidivous and flagrant nature, lend themselves to fairly accurate predictions of future disruptiveness.

MENTAL ILLNESS AND DANGEROUSNESS

Many studies have commendably demonstrated that mental illness is not synonymous with either dangerousness or criminality.[6,7,8] These studies help to debunk and dispel public myths and prejudices about the mentally ill and are therefore of immense general importance. Yet, in assessing most college student disruptive behavior in particular, these studies are of limited value.

According to countless reports I have received from campuses across the United States and Canada, many, if not most, incidents of serious disruptions—save perhaps alcohol abuse, plagiarism, date rape, and fighting (serious forms of disruption that seem to involve students who are quite diverse diagnostically)—appear to involve students with serious psychological disabilities.

Although these diverse reports are anecdotal, impressionistic, and imprecise, they quite often suggest that the highly disruptive student is also, psychologically, a rather seriously disturbed individual. Particularly suggestive is the recurrent plaint one commonly hears or reads in these reports: The offending student is acting in a demonstrably bizarre manner, the student's behavior seems inspired by hallucinatory, delusional, or paranoiac psychological processes. When school authorities have been able to procure such information from the student or his family, an extensive history of severe psychological difficulties and psychiatric hospitalization is often revealed.

Such factors represent some of the generally reliable hallmarks of mental illness. Nevertheless, the contention that there is a high correlation between mental illness and many forms of on-campus disruptiveness remains largely inferential and, therefore, unproved and controversial at this time. Because of the paucity of good research studies in this area, our understanding of this problem remains murky. Future research studies, it is hoped, will be able to shed better light on the relationship between student disruptiveness and mental illness.

The importance of this is obviously not to stigmatize or establish the moral culpability of the disruptive or mentally ill student. Rather, it is to underscore one of the major points of this article: If it is fair and accurate to assume that significant numbers of disruptive incidents actually involve students with psychological disabilities, the simple, humanitarian values to which our colleges are avowedly committed should inspire them to develop effective and comprehensive programs for psychologically disabled students that integrate them better into the educational community and reduce their potential for manifesting disruptive behavior.

One example of such a program would be an on-campus mental health service that would provide treatment to the psychologically disabled student (and, presumably, to all other students) on a voluntary basis and in the early phases of a potentially disruptive crisis. Although not all potentially disruptive students would use such a service, an appreciable number undoubtedly would, thereby reducing the overall number of disruptive incidents on campus. A programmatic approach of this kind is certainly preferable to a plan that resorts to mandatory referrals for psychological treatment *after* a student has become disruptive.

Psychological services that are provided to disruption-prone students on a voluntary basis and at a time when the students have not already committed acts of disruption have a decided advantage. Generally, students who enter psychotherapy on their own volition, rather than as a result of a mandatory disciplinary process, are more highly motivated to make positive use of their psychotherapeutic experience and will be less likely to manifest disruptive behavior.

THE USE OF MANDATORY PSYCHIATRIC WITHDRAWALS

It is generally recommended that colleges avoid using "psychiatric" or "medical" withdrawals in order to suspend, expel, or simply remove disruptive students from their campuses. The use of a psychiatric withdrawal will probably require a (possibly involuntary) psychiatric evaluation and diagnosis, a measure that may not withstand legal scrutiny and challenge, partly because of the possibly coercive and involuntary nature of the evaluative procedure itself, and partly because of the imprecise and ambiguous nature of many such diagnoses.

At the risk of appearing to contradict myself, I should indicate that I regard the formulation and use of psychiatric diagnoses as highly useful guideposts in my own clinical practice. I would, however, argue that these same diagnoses, even when formulated and propounded by renowned authorities in the mental health field, should not be used for punitive or disciplinary purposes such as removing students from college. In addition to the questionable legality of such procedures, their enlistment in the context of carrying out disciplinary measures bastardizes, in my view, the primary and unassailable purpose and values of developing a diagnostic nosology in the first place—to improve psychotherapeutic treatment.

In addition to the possibility of inadvertently stigmatizing students with invidious labeling, the (mis)use of psychiatric diagnoses to effect withdrawals of disruptive students serves to undermine the college's efforts to impose just and proportionate discipline. The college has the legal right, assuming that due process has been followed and the student's constitutional rights have been adequately protected, to suspend or expel a student who has been seriously disruptive—for that student's *behavior*.

It should not, and need not, try to adduce superfluous, legally questionable, psychiatric rationales for removing the disruptive student from the campus, especially since these selfsame rationales may ultimately be used in later judicial proceedings by the disruptive student to challenge effectively the propriety of an expulsion based upon psychiatric criteria. My point is not to impugn the diagnostic skills of psychiatrists and psychologists but, rather, to caution against using psychiatric evaluations and diagnostic criteria, regardless of their scientific accuracy and validity, to carry out a procedure that is essentially disciplinary. As Steele has pointed out, "Colleges and universities considering any attempts to subject the mentally handicapped to mandatory psychiatric withdrawal should seek legal advice."[9]

Pavela[2] has suggested that mandatory psychiatric withdrawals might have possible use to remove from campus students who are suicidal or seriously anorectic. He also cautions that such practices not be adopted as policy because suicidal or anorectic persons are not necessarily "mentally ill." My own recommendation is as follows: Students who are either suicidal or suffer from severe anorexia should be immediately helped to receive in- or out-patient psychological and medical services as regularly and intensively as necessary. If the students' life-threatening behaviors persist, with or without the benefit of treatment, they should be regarded as disruptive conduct because the students' persistent self-imperiling behaviors are eventually likely to traumatize and victimize their roommates, classmates, and the college personnel who must deal with them throughout each crisis.

For example, the roommates of recurrently suicidal students sometimes engage in protracted and abortive rescue efforts that, in time, snuff out their ability to sustain academic work and can lead to their own scholastic failure and withdrawal from college. College authorities must consider the welfare of these students, as well, when dealing with the highly self-destructive student.

In my view, the college can justifiably impose a suspension or expulsion strictly based on the student's *disruptive behavior*, without resorting to the use of psychiatric diagnoses, if the following three conditions can be met: (1) the persistent self-destructive behavior of the suicidal or anorectic student is having a markedly deleterious effect upon other students and/or staff; (2) disciplinary sanctions have already been imposed upon the suicidal or anorectic student for the harm that has been inflicted upon others; (3) the suicidal or anorectic student flouts the disciplinary sanctions by continuing to pursue his or her self-destructive courses of action.

In brief, the suicidal or seriously anorectic student can be removed from the campus for repeatedly behaving in a manner that is dangerous to self and others, not because he or she suffers from a mental illness. If, however, the college believes it is in the student's interest to withdraw immediately but, for humanitarian reasons, does not wish to impose disciplinary sanctions, it can offer the student the opportunity to leave with impunity. If the student accepts this offer and leaves, the college, rather than refer to the student's departure as a "psychiatric" or "medical" withdrawal, can simply call it an "administrative" withdrawal—a term that is deliberately nebulous and non-stigmatizing.

Lest I be considered callous and indifferent to the suffering of suicidal or anorectic students, I think it apt to point out a common characteristic of these students. Quite frequently such students will rigidly refuse to enter psychotherapy or medical treatment to deal with their life-threatening behavior. Often, they display a gross indifference, contempt, or egocentricity toward the emotional rights and needs of those persons who may suffer acutely from being regularly exposed to their self-destructive behavior. Attempts by therapists to help them are often met by denial and pertinacity.

The use of discipline, perhaps in the form of threats of suspension or expulsion, may be necessary in cases in which the blandishments of psychological and medical assistance have failed. Such discipline is not to punish, but possibly to save a human life and to protect the emotional rights of those who must continually and inescapably witness the dangerous behavior of highly self-abusive individuals.

Before concluding, it may also be helpful to mention that those college staff who are responsible for dealing with the psychological and medical needs of students must be prepared to expedite the immediate hospitalization, perhaps on an involuntary basis, of students who are dangerously suicidal or anorectic.

Finally, colleges will probably find it useful to develop policies and guidelines for referring students to mental health professionals expressly to secure evaluations that provide a perspective about the degree of illness, self-control, dangerousness, and suicidal tendencies of disruptive students. Such evaluations might enable administrators to deal more confidently and effectively with disruptive students. My own recommendation regarding such policies is as follows: If a psychological or psychiatric evaluation is deemed helpful, the college should seek the student's voluntary, written consent for this procedure, including permission for the mental health professional to discuss the general findings of the evaluation with specified college officials. If the student refuses to undergo such an evaluation, his wishes must be respected and no penalty should be attached to this refusal.

College administrators may feel that they are being unduly foiled in carrying out an important duty by what appears to be an excessive adherence to the rules of confidentiality, but it is important for all college personnel, including mental health professionals, to respect students' rights to refuse psychiatric examinations and treatment. A single, but major, exception to this rule is the student who is demonstrably an imminent danger to himself or others. Obviously, this student must be examined on an involuntary basis and perhaps even hospitalized against his wishes.

I have found, in my consultations with administrators, that a member of the mental health staff can usually provide a useful perspective regarding the student's degree of self-control and readiness to conform to the codes of student conduct without actually interviewing the student. These perspectives are based upon careful interviews with the complainants and with the designated administrator to gain detailed descriptions of the disruptive student's behavior, from which quite reliable impressions and recommendations can be formulated by the mental health staff. In handling matters strictly by consulting with the complainant and the designated administrator rather than by attempting to cajole the disruptive student to undergo a psychiatric examination, mental health professionals gain two decided advantages: (1) They are not bound by rules of confidentiality because they have neither treated nor examined the disruptive student, and therefore, can speak quite freely about their impressions of the student, albeit on the basis of others' reports; (2) they do not have to contend with overly suspicious, resentful, and belligerent students who have a (perhaps quite realistic) notion that the data derived from the psychiatric examination ultimately will be used against them.

CONDITIONS OF RE-ENROLLMENT

Students who have been suspended or expelled for disciplinary reasons should be required to meet with the designated administrator if they wish to reenroll. That administrator should spell out the conditions that the student must meet to return to the campus. If considered advantageous, these may be in the form of a written contract. Generally, the conditions should be that the student must adequately conform to the codes of student conduct of the college. If the student is not familiar with the codes, they should be produced and explained simply and specifically. If the student was originally suspended for a particular form of disruptive behavior, the administrator can remind the student that a repetition of that behavior will probably result in additional and perhaps more severe disciplinary sanctions, including the possibility of yet another, more protracted suspension.

At one college I recently visited, students were interviewed and evaluated for re-enrollment by a panel consisting of a cross-section of the college staff. I learned about this panel because I was asked what the college should do about the many serious threats that were leveled at panel members by students who were denied readmission. As a result of these threats, panel members understandably had become reluctant to complete their tenure on the panel. My advice was to indicate in the student codes that all threats made to members of the readmission committee would be regarded as seriously disruptive and punishable behavior.

Finally, two other recommendations for administrators are in order. First, because many disruptive students are disruptive often and in the presence of many different college personnel, it is possible that a single disruptive student will be reported to the appropriate administrator many times during the student's career at the college. It is advisable, therefore, that the administrator keep accurate records of each incident, including the names of the student and the complainant as well as a detailed description of the disruptive behavior. This will enable the administrator to discipline students who are guilty of multiple or ongoing acts of disruption on the basis of their cumulative (and, therefore, more serious) disruptive history, rather than treating each incident as isolated from all others (and, therefore, less seriously than they probably should).

Second, whether a reported disruptive incident has been administratively resolved or not, it is essential that the designated administrator regularly apprise the complainant of the status of the investigation. Without the benefit of this information, the complainant is unnecessarily left to wonder and worry about whether the disruptive crisis will actually be resolved. Failure to follow this procedure will probably leave many administrators open to the criticism, warranted or not, that their failure to report their findings signifies that, alas, they have not done their job.

CONFLICTS OVER THE USE OF MEDICATION

It is quite common for college psychotherapists and administrators to become entangled in time-consuming and fruitless power struggles with disruptive students over the students' failure to use prescribed psychotropic medications. Frequently, in the course of advising or disciplining the disruptive student, it is discovered that the student is in psychiatric treatment and has been receiving a prescription from his therapist for medications. Because the student is manifesting disruptive behavior, it is often deemed advisable to question him about the regularity of his use of those medications. At this point, the discovery is sometimes made that the student has interrupted his use of the prescribed medications. This leads to the quite logical conclusion that it is this remissness on the student's part that is aggravating his psychiatric condition and causing him to be disruptive.

Even students who largely benefit from the use of prescribed medications may, from time to time, feel the need to abandon using the drug. For some students, the ongoing use of medications interferes with their sense of personal autonomy and is therefore a source of humiliation. For others, the side effects, both immediate (drowsiness) and potentially long-range (damage to internal organs), of the medications are a strong dissuasive factor. In some instances, students with paranoid disorders refuse to use prescribed medications because they consider them poisonous.

In my view, the therapists and administrators who engage in protracted disputes with such students are making an uncalled-for mistake. These professionals may spend many wasteful hours trying to convince the student that it is in his best interest to resume the use of medications. Underlying their arguments is the highly plausible assumption that the medications will help to stabilize the student and thereby quell his disruptiveness. Yet, too often, these students adamantly refuse to yield to the logic of such arguments, leaving the college staff perplexed and stymied in their search for a solution to the problem.

I would suggest the following solution: First, realize that the student's use or disuse of medications is secondary to the central issue of whether the student is conforming to the codes of student conduct. Clearly, the student has an inviolable right to refuse medications, but it is *not* the student's right to behave disruptively. Therefore, if the student has been allowed to remain on campus despite his disruptive behavior, I would recommend that he be advised in the following manner: "It is my impression that it is decidedly in your interest to resume your use of the medications since they seem to help you function better.

Nonetheless, whether or not you use medications is really your business and your decision to make. However, I must warn you that, whether you use medications or not, your disruptive behavior on this campus will not be tolerated and its recurrence will result in the imposition of disciplinary sanctions." To eliminate any ambiguity that might ensue from this discussion, those sanctions should be spelled out immediately.

The above statement takes into account the reasonable possibility that a given student might resume his use of prescribed medications and yet continue to behave in a disruptive manner. After all, these medications, like psychotherapy itself, are not panaceas for disruptiveness. As one can easily imagine, the prevalent practice on many college campuses of insisting that the disruptive student use prescribed medications might lead many such students to assume, mistakenly and conveniently, that once they have resumed their use of medications they have fulfilled all behavioral obligations. They must be reminded that the primary requirement is not their adjunctive use of medications but, rather, their reasonable conformity to the codes of student conduct.

One final caveat regarding the matter of medications: Quite often, a student's failure to use prescribed, stabilizing medications is experimental (to see how he might cope without them) and short-lived. If a student's disruptive behavior appears to be a direct result of his failure to use medications and he has heretofore been generally conducting himself nondisruptively on the campus, it might be well to regard these factors as extenuating circumstances that militate for a lesser sanction. Of course, a recurrence would probably bring a greater sanction.

THE ROLE OF THE MENTAL HEALTH PROGRAM

An on-campus psychological service can be invaluable in dealing with the problem of the disruptive student. First, it can intervene immediately in cases in which the disruptive student is considered acutely psychotic or a danger to himself or others. In such cases, the mental health team can facilitate the psychiatric hospitalization of the student in a timely, efficient, and humane manner. Second, it can assist instructors and other college staff who are confronted with disruptive students by offering emotional support and timely advice to them as they strive to resolve the disruptive crisis. Third, because instructors and administrators sometimes have widely different and conflicting viewpoints regarding the causes and the degree of the seriousness of disruptive crises, each may tend to favor and pursue disparate courses of action to resolve them. The mental health team can assist them by identifying areas of disagreement and, as mediators for the contending principals, offering recommendations about how their differences and the crisis, itself, can best be resolved.

CONCLUSION

Reports of disruptive incidents on the college campuses in the United States have risen sharply in the last few years. This article provides a practical guide with which administrators, instructors, and other college personnel may deal with disruptive student behavior.

Because I have dealt almost exclusively with principles, policies, and procedures for dealing with disruptive behavior in this article, I have said little about the profound need for colleges to develop preventive psychological and educational programs for students who are prone to behave disruptively. If, as I have suggested, a significant proportion of disruptive students are psychologically disabled, the time is overdue for colleges to recognize the special difficulties of these individuals by providing them with the help they so desperately need and deserve.

Sound and humane disciplinary procedures, as essential as they may be, are in themselves not enough. Because most seriously disruptive behavior seems to be a manifestation of anxiety and desperation and probably represents a disguised plea for emotional help, educational and psychological services that can identify, anticipate, and address the underlying causes of disruptive conduct early will ultimately serve as better deterrents to disruptiveness than even the most enlightened systems of discipline.

References

1. Amada G. Dealing with the disruptive college student: Some theoretical and practical considerations. *J Am Coll Health*. 1986; 34:221-225.
2. Pavela G. *The Dismissal of Students With Mental Disorders*. Asheville, NC: College Administration Publications; 1985.
3. Halleck S. *The Politics of Therapy*. New York: Science House; 1971.
4. Title 11, 5, Section 422 and Penal Code 71, *West's California Codes*, 1990 Compact Edition. St. Paul, MN: West Publishing; 1990.
5. Monahan J. *Predicting Violent Behavior*. Beverly Hills: Sage; 1981.
6. Phillips MR, Wolf AS, Coon DJ. Psychiatry and the criminal justice system: Testing the myths. *Am J Psychiatry*. 1988; 145:605610.
7. Steadman HJ. Predicting dangerousness among the mentally ill. *Int J Law Psychiatry*. 1983;6:381-390.
8. Teplin LA. The criminality of the mentally ill: A dangerous misconception. *Am J Psychiatry*. 1985;142: 593-599.
9. Steele BH, Johnson DH, Rickard ST. Managing the judicial function in student affairs. *J Coll Stud Pers*. July 1984;25:337342.

The Role of Humor In a
College Mental Health Program

Dr. Gerald Amada has devoted his professional career to working with students, as humorously as possible. During their turbulent identity-forming years, students undergo many crises that tend to make their lives difficult. Dr. Amada chooses to work with the resistance, often using humor to alleviate the sometimes volcanic rages experienced by students and helping them to remove their blockages and graduate into adulthood He simultaneously may turn the humor magic on Counseling Center staff and faculty journeymen working with students. And, behold, the whole Zeitgeist changes in the direction of productive interactions.

———

When I was approached by the editors of this book to write a chapter on the role of humor in a college psychotherapy program, my first thoughts harked back to a pivotal episode in my own college career. After spending two dreary years enrolled in a business administration program, I had become thoroughly disenchanted with my lack of academic purpose and progress. One day, late in the spring semester of my sophomore year, I wandered about the corridors, eavesdropping on some of the lectures that could be overheard through open classroom doors.

Glancing into one of the classrooms, I observed a very attractive psychology instructor begin her lecture with a joke. The students had evidently been accustomed to this instructor's rib-tickling pedagogical methods since they were all smiling and attentive. I can no longer recall the content of the joke, but I do recollect that it was quite witty, risque, and pregnant with psychological significance. At the conclusion of the joke, the class laughed uproariously. I went away somehow profoundly affected by this fleeting event.

The soul-searching that followed this episode raised important concerns and considerations in my mind. I was finding my pursuit

123

of a business career to be a monotonous and dismal treadmill. Suddenly I had been exposed to its delightful antithesis in the form of a psychology course that was being taught with humor.

Early on, toward the end of my freshman year, I had already become aware of a budding interest in psychological studies. But I was definitely further catalyzed in this direction by the not altogether warranted belief, based upon my brief eavesdropping experience, that psychology courses were generally taught with stimulating and engrossing humor. With that provocative thought in mind, I went to see the university psychologist about my academic quandary. He administered a battery of aptitude tests which, as I had anticipated, confirmed the fact that I was disastrously ill suited for a business career. Conversely, the tests revealed that I seemed to possess the requisite skills and interests to successfully pursue a career in the field of human services. On the strength of this discovery, I transferred into the university's department of arts and sciences in my junior year, majored in psychology, and, as the saying goes, the rest is history.

It would of course be facile and naive of me to suggest that the single positive experience of overhearing a good joke told in a psychology course could, in itself, affect the entire direction of my career. There were naturally far more overarching reasons for my decision to change majors and careers at that juncture of my life, such as, for example, my boredom and atrocious academic record while in business school. But, in retrospect, I view that brief but memorable experience outside the classroom of a jocose psychology instructor as one of the truly pivotal moments of my college years.

I have introduced this chapter with an autobiographical vignette in order to illustrate a point. If, as my story suggests, even an accidental encounter with humor can catalyze a student's academic and maturational growth, should we not reasonably expect that the timely, selective, and ongoing use of humor in psychotherapeutic work with college students could yield significant reparative results?

THEORETICAL PERSPECTIVE

There has been much written and said about both the psychological vulnerabilities and developmental opportunities of college students (Margolis, 1989). Because college students are at the developmental crossroads of embarking upon relative independence from their families and pursuing what is likely to be a lifelong professional career, they are beset by many demands and pressures for personal and scholarly success. As all college psychotherapists are well aware, the unique demands of college life often lead to a wide range of psychological and interpersonal difficulties. Depression, alcoholism, substance abuse, unwanted pregnancies, date rape, and an impulsive, live-for-the-moment orientation are problems that are endemic among contemporary American college students (Amada, 1985b).

On the positive side, students are generally eager and ripe for new or enriching experiences. They attend college to enhance their knowledge of both themselves and the complex world in which they will soon function as independent adults. Because students are accustomed to learning from instruction, they are apt to turn to a college psychotherapist to be educated about themselves and about life in general. Therapists can teach students about themselves through a wide variety of modalities, interventions, and orientations, including cognitive, behavioral, didactic, environmental, and psychoanalytic approaches.

My own orientation is psychoanalytic, and, consistent with this theoretical model, my clinical work emphasizes such factors as the students' psychogenetic history, diagnosis, unconscious motivations, fantasies, and the quality of the transference relationship that develops during the course of treatment. There seems to be a general agreement among mental health practitioners, regardless of their theoretical orientations, that the indispensable cornerstone of psychotherapy is the development of an empathetically connected, positive therapeutic relationship (Ducey, 1989). An integral component of my own psychotherapeutic perspective is humor. Humor as an adjunctive yet essential clinical tool can be invaluable in two comprehensive respects.

First, it can be used as a versatile and fairly reliable diagnostic instrument. The quality and vitality of a student's sense of humor will probably provide some measure of how well he or she will weather emotional storms (Amada, 1985a). Frequently, for example, the presence, availability, and quality of a student's sense of humor can be a dynamic index of the depth and potential reversibility of his or her state of depression or anxiety. On a deeper level, the presence or absence of a sense of humor can, when evaluated in conjunction with other relevant factors, illuminate much about a student's character structure, family dynamics, and the social milieu in which the student was raised.

For example, a therapist initially encountering a student whose life and personality are quite devoid of humor can usefully test several important hypotheses. Is the absence of humor in the student indicative of a reactive depression? Or, is it more a manifestation of a certain deficit, rigidity, or depressive feature in the student's character structure? Does the absence of humor perhaps reflect and befit a social norm and value that prevailed within the student's family and social culture? In other words, was humor simply neglected or unused by the student's family as a potential mode of healthy, problem-solving communication? Was it somehow considered socially unbecoming or offensive? These are some of the questions and hypotheses that can be investigated for important diagnostic purposes.

A second, and more important, purpose for utilizing humor in psychotherapy with college students is to foster and effect positive therapeutic change. As pointed out by Salameh (1987), humor is more than just a technical tool. It reflects an attitude and a way of being. Therefore, it has the potential, if used wisely by the therapist, to promote positive transformations both within the therapeutic relationship and in other realms of the student's academic and personal life.

The positive effect of humor has been extensively discussed in the literature. Klein (1989) has noted the power of humor to heal and to release afflicted persons from grief, sorrow, disappointment, and loss. Fine (1983) has discussed the potential of humor for enabling groups to deal with forces that might threaten or disrupt them. He has also alluded to the power of humor for building confidence in groups as humor helps group members realize that they are in the same situation. Humor can be especially effective in helping persecuted groups deal with tragedy by providing them with a vehicle with which to poke fun at their oppressors.

The power of humor to persuade others, when more serious means have been abortive, has also received attention (Blumenfeld & Alpern, 1986). Furthermore, humor can be especially helpful in conveying a therapist's humanness to a patient when other, more traditional, therapeutic methods have been unsuccessful (S. Edwards, personal communication, 1989). Fay (1978) has highlighted the therapeutic efficacy of humor for pointing out dysfunctional aspects in the behavior of psychiatric patients without putting them on the defensive. Humor has been credited with the power of enabling an individual to overcome adversity by acquiring a sense of mastery (Lefcourt & Martin, 1986). One researcher (Vaillant, 1977) has even "honored" humor by designating it as one of the "mature" defense mechanisms.

TECHNIQUE

In this chapter I will highlight two principal therapeutic uses of humor. The first is the rather specific, limited application of humor as a means of resolving therapeutic impasses. The second is the employment of humor as a general framework for conveying optimistic concern, goodwill, and respect for student patients.

Obviously, the use of humor to melt a therapeutic stalemate and its more general use as an effective means of conveying regard, non-hostility, and respect for the patient often go hand in hand. Most clinicians have had the experience of resolving an impasse or conflict with a patient by injecting appropriate humor into a session precisely because the therapist's use of humor was correctly perceived by the patient as a sensitive and respectful attempt to establish mutual goodwill and understanding. Because humor can be a potent vehicle for transmitting empathy and understanding, its judicious use in psychotherapy may certainly be expected to enhance the overall quality of the therapeutic relationship and play a vital part in the entire therapeutic enterprise.

The students who use the City College of San Francisco Mental Health Program represent a broad range of ethnic groups, ages, and personality types. Some are well-functioning, moderately depressed or anxious individuals who seek treatment for rather transient and easily resolvable crises. Others suffer from more serious and chronic conditions such as severe character disorders and schizophrenia. Despite the diagnostic diversity among the student population, it has been my experience that most students, irrespective of their particular personality types, are responsive to humor as a therapeutic technique when it is used in a timely, sensitive, and dynamic manner. In my view, humorous interventions are most effective when used to address and alleviate the patient's central concerns and fears.

In order to determine the patient's primary concerns, therapists are advised to formulate, at least tentatively, a diagnostic (or dynamic) impression of each patient's personality. Assuming that the therapist's diagnosis will be relatively accurate and valid, it can serve as an important dynamic instrument with which to determine when and how to strategically intervene with humor. For example, obsessive-compulsive patients who, to their own detriment typically ignore or repress recurrent forbidden thoughts, may at times benefit from humor that focuses on the "unacceptable" unconscious impulses or fantasies they have diligently sought to repress.

Paranoid clients, who tend to suffer from persecutory delusions and severe interpersonal conflicts, may favorably respond to humorous interventions that address and allay their fears of having their thoughts controlled or manipulated by others. Depressed patients, who are usually afflicted with feelings of low self-esteem and hopelessness, can appreciate and derive comfort from a therapist's humorous perspective of their exaggerated sense of gloom, provided of course that the therapist's lighthearted viewpoint is not intended or perceived as ridiculing or dismissive.

Therapists who are well attuned to their patients' core concerns can use their humorous interventions to illuminate and objectify those concerns. Naturally, all therapeutic interventions, whether humorous or deadly serious, have the potential for backfiring and producing unwanted and undesirable results. Sometimes, the undesirable effect of a humorous intervention can be attributed to the guarded and intractable mood of the patient. At other times, the failure of a humorous intervention can be ascribed to poor timing, clumsiness, or the denigrating quality of the therapist's humor.

In the next section of this chapter I will illustrate how I have therapeutically used humor with college students either to troubleshoot a difficult impasse in the therapy or to address and explore an acute concern manifested by the student patient. I will attempt to explain with each example of a humorous therapeutic intervention why it did or did not succeed as I had hoped. Following that discussion, I will illustrate other pertinent uses of humor with students, faculty, psychological interns, and support staff in order to demonstrate the varied and significant role that can be played by humor in the daily operation of a college mental health program.

CLINICAL PRESENTATIONS

Case 1

An extremely morose and volatile student was generally regarded as belligerent and intimidating by his college peers. This man came to therapy irregularly, but usually following an incident in which his hostile behavior strongly offended or frightened someone at the college, causing him to be warned or disciplined by one of the administrative staff. Because this unfortunate man had little control over his moods and behavior, I thought it necessary to be very sensitive to the terrible distress these campus predicaments caused him. Throughout our interviews he would rant lengthily about perceived violations of his moral rights. Although he seemed partially trustful toward me, he gave me little opportunity to share my point of view about his problems. Overall, he was largely impervious to my attempts to lighten his angry and depressed mood.

Toward the end of one of our sessions he angrily asserted that no one respected his intelligence or acknowledged his academic accomplishments. He was, after all, a geology major, and a damned good one. Upon hearing this news, I asked him, "Since you're a geology major, what would you say if I told you that's gneiss (a granite rock, and homophone of the word 'nice')?" A broad smile broke out upon his face, the first that I had ever seen, and he sprightfully responded, "I'd say, 'gee,' that's a good joke, since it (gneiss) starts with a gee." The two of us erupted with a good belly laugh and during the following moments, we shared a closeness that had not been there before. His mood, which I could not dent by other means, began to lift after it was reached through humor. I suspect that this humorous intervention succeeded because it reflected my respect for the patient's intelligence and accomplishments as a geology student while also conveying my willingness to respond to his anger with a gesture of unmistakable friendliness

Case 2

Humor played a crucial role in defusing a potentially explosive situation with a very disturbed and hotheaded student. The student entered my office loudly proclaiming that she had been grievously wronged by friends, co-workers, and several of her college instructors. As the student plunged forward with her tirade against a menacing and conspiratorial world, she began to decompensate even further. Watching her shout and leer at various objects in my room, I apprehensively expected that she would pick up some object and hurl it at me.

Just as I was making up my mind about how I would extricate myself from impending danger, the student suddenly looked up at the wall and, seeing a photograph of my three adorable Shar-Pei dogs, smiled and said, "Are those your children?" Surprised and delighted at this sudden but very friendly digression, I seized the opportunity by replying, "Not exactly. The big one is my daughter. The other two are my granddaughters." The student laughed heartily and the conversation then turned to the emotionally safe and neutral subject of raising dogs.

By the time the session was over, the student was relatively calm and rational. She even agreed to see me again, which she did on several subsequent occasions. As expected, she remained prone to rapid and dramatic regressions under stress, but she fortunately felt safe enough with me to return to the clinic for timely assistance. The humorous exchange that took place between us seemed to have a positive effect because it related to an emotionally neutral and pleasurable subject (pets) while also revealing an important aspect of our basic humanness through the discussion of our common fondness for dogs.

Case 3

By contrast, an attempt to enlist humor as a means of resolving a therapeutic impasse once resulted in abysmal failure. A nineteen-year-old student who was exasperated with her overbearing and hypercritical mother requested that I meet with the two of them in order to mediate their disputes. After a few sessions, it was evident that the disputants were unbudgeably committed to their respective positions and entirely lacked respect for each other's viewpoints. Each looked to me to invalidate her adversary's opinions.

Having been incapable of resolving their irreconcilable differences through interpretation, explanation, empathy, or even sheer exhortation, I decided to try humor. Taking into account that these patients were Jewish, I thought it apropos to tell them a Jewish folkloric tale of which I am extremely fond due to its wit and wisdom.

The story is about a disputatious married couple who went to see their esteemed rabbi for advice. The wife, who was the first to consult the rabbi, told a long tale of woe about an insensitive, selfish, and uncouth husband who was entirely to blame for their marital problems. The rabbi sagely and patiently listened to the woman's long harangue and then said, "You know, I think you're right." Feeling vindicated, the wife left. The husband, who next consulted with the rabbi, excoriated his wife by referring to her as an inconsiderate, unkempt, and half-witted shrew who was entirely at fault for their marital difficulties. The rabbi once again listened with forbearance and then replied, "You know, you're right." The husband then left the rabbi's office feeling quite satisfied. Soon after the couple had left, the rabbi's wife entered his study in a state of obvious distress. She said to the rabbi, "I overheard what happened when you spoke to that couple. When the wife blamed their unhappiness on her husband, you said she was right. When the husband blamed all their problems on his wife, you said he was right. You know, they both can't be right." To which the rabbi replied, "You know, you're right."

I had hoped that the forbearance and moral relativism displayed by the rabbi would provide a positive example through which my two patients could begin to examine their own intransigence toward one another. To my disappointment, however, they each looked at me as if I had just committed some terrible *faux pas.* Dismissing this wise tale as if it had not been told, they immediately resumed their useless and endless squabble.

I believe that this example illustrates an important point regarding the use of humor in psychotherapy. It is important to recognize that a humorous intervention may be perceived as irrelevant or insulting by certain patients, due to either their particular personality formations or their current life conflicts. Obviously, a therapist cannot always predict the eventual outcome of a humorous intervention. Therefore, it is generally advisable that therapists who are inclined to use humor with their patients philosophically accept the fact that certain individuals are simply not amenable to it. Therapists who are ordinarily empathically attuned to their patients are usually, although not always, able to determine when it is appropriate to use humorous interventions. In this regard, it is probably helpful to bear in mind that the therapeutic use of humor is a form of risk-taking behavior that, due to its potential to inflict psychic pain upon patients, can strongly test a therapist's empathy. However, the same could be said regarding any other potent therapeutic technique.

Case 4

A more positive example of the therapeutic use of humor occurred at the very outset of a session with a student. The student, a 35-year-old gay man who worked as a part-time librarian, came to me in crisis immediately following the breakup of a longstanding love relationship. Although he desperately wanted to tell me about his grief, he could not initially overcome the expectation that I would view a gay relationship with contempt. He thought I would discount the depth of his grief by regarding his mournful reactions to be less painful than those experienced by heterosexuals when their love relationships dissolve. He began his first session with an angry challenge. He said, "Look, before I can tell you anything about what I've been through, I've got to know—what do you think of homosexuals?"

I must admit that for a moment I had no idea how to answer such an accusatory challenge. I then collected myself and said, "You know, I guess how I feel about homosexuals is a bit like Mark Twain when he was asked how he felt about Jewish people. He said that Jews were human beings like everyone else. And he couldn't imagine anything worse that could be said about a person."

The student laughed easily and, disarmed of his hostility, soon proceeded to disclose the recent difficulties he was having with his lover. Although my use of this quotation was extemporaneous, it has always been a favorite because it effectively says that no group of people should be vilified, or for that matter, glorified, for its differences. I had hoped that the patient would accurately interpret my use of this quotation. Perhaps what was most telling was my eagerness to respond to this patient, not with anger or with an apologetic discourse on the plights and rights of gays, but with a humorous quotation from a great and compassionate author whose humane values would be well known to this librarian.

Case 5

A student recently entered therapy in a state of disorganizing confusion and panic. His gay lover had left the country for a few weeks on a business trip, saddling the student, who was 21, with the formidable responsibility of caring for the lover's 16-year-old daughter. The daughter was a very testy adolescent who was involved with a highly sadistic man. Her father and the student had done their utmost to remove the girl from this destructive relationship, but to no avail. She refused to heed their advice and repeatedly exposed herself to psychological and physical danger as a result. The student feared that, during his lover's absence, his rebellious young charge would either run away from home or be seriously injured by her boyfriend. To add to his woes, he dreadfully anticipated that, when his lover returned from his trip, he would be blamed for whatever catastrophe befell his lover's daughter.

While the student spoke about these matters, I noticed that his speech was sprinkled with a great many jocular asides accompanied by frequent nervous giggling. I also noticed that practically all of the student's attempts at humor were self-disparaging and not in the least amusing. Consequently, I neither laughed nor smiled at his joking remarks.

As the student disclosed his personal history it became apparent that his exaggerated sense of responsibility for the care and welfare of his lover's daughter had been an outgrowth of his lifelong tendency to please and appease others at his own expense. While discussing this topic, he alluded to the fact that he had managed to cope with a miserable childhood by acting clownishly with his parents and other adults, such as his teachers.

Toward the middle of the session, after having tried to amuse me with his self-deprecating humor for the umpteenth time, the student turned to me and said with evident annoyance, "Don't you ever smile? You make me anxious by being so serious." I replied by telling him that I often smiled but thus far it seemed to me that the brand of humor he used was rather defensive and self-victimizing. I asked him if he felt compelled to act comically as a means of covering up certain painful emotions. The student then began to cry without restraint. When he finally stopped, his manner became calmer and much more natural. He went on to acknowledge that he was often annoyed and frustrated with himself for constantly resorting to self-humiliating forms of humor when faced with personal adversity. Gradually, as he was able to reveal and accept the depth of his painful emotions, he once again spoke humorously about his predicament. His manner, however, had changed dramatically. It was no longer forced or self-deprecating. In response to this positive change, I became more openly responsive to and encouraging of his humorous comments.

This example illustrates the need for therapists to exercise care and discretion in response to a patient's use of humor. When patients castigate themselves through humor, it is generally unwise for therapists to deliberately encourage such behavior. By smiling or laughing with patients who ridicule and humiliate themselves, therapists are apt to reinforce this self-punishing form of behavior and therefore compound their patients' feelings of low self-esteem. Obviously, to do this would be contrary to the basic objectives of psychotherapy.

Case 6

There are many women students who have entered therapy with rather gruesome tales about the men with whom they live. Many of these men are described as neglectful, selfish, amoral, brutal, and parasitic. Clinical research (Wild, 1989) indicates that many of the women who tolerate and endure chronic and severe abuse from men suffer from a borderline personality disorder. An important characteristic of the borderline personality is the proclivity to use primitive defense mechanisms such as splitting and denial (Goldstein, 1985).

A clear example of the use of denial that I have observed in abused women students is their tendency to wait and hope for miraculous personality transformations in the men who have chronically mistreated them. After describing how their lovers or husbands have long betrayed and beaten them, spent their earnings on dangerous drugs, and punished their aspirations for success and fulfillment, these women often state in the next breath that their partners are not really harmful to them, and, after all, they just may one day change dramatically and become good partners.

Therapists who encounter such patients may experience intense countertransference feelings of frustration and anger toward them for putting up with such sadistic men. It may be clear to the therapist that such men are unlikely to change quickly or radically and that the patient's life, if she chooses to remain with the man, is likely to go from bad to worse. However, the borderline patient's intense fear of abandonment causes her to cling to the relationship despite chronic and even savage abuse. In my work with abused women students I have used a wide range of techniques including interpretation, confrontation, empathic support, environmental manipulation, and humor. One of the humorous interventions used aims at calling attention to the patient's denial of the immutable abusiveness of her relationship. The following vignette is a rather typical example of how this intervention is used:

Therapist: You've told me that he beats you, steals from you, cheats on you, uses the money he takes from you for drugs, and has even threatened to kill you. And, furthermore, this has been going on for five years. What's keeping you in this relationship? What are you waiting for?

Patient: Well, I love him. And I'm afraid of being on my own. Besides, he's promised to change. Every so often he does something nice, like bringing me flowers. I think to myself that if I am patient enough he will someday overcome his problems and treat me well. And I always think that I can make him change if I only try hard enough and stand by him. What do you think?

Therapist: I think I might have a solution to your problem.

Patient: You have! What is it?

Therapist: Well, its a magical potion. It will make you live to be 700 years old. You see, you're going to have to live at least that long in order to see your boyfriend change. (In response to this intervention, many clients smile or laugh. Others will wince or cry out of a sense of regret over my wry and pessimistic depiction of their plight.)

Patient: I don't think I'd even want to live that long, especially if he doesn't change.

My deliberate use of a humorous intervention referring to a magical potion that prolongs life touches upon two principal defenses of the borderline patient. First, it addresses the patient's rigid denial of the immutably destructive nature of her current relationship. Second, it exposes the omnipotent and magical thinking that is a common hallmark of the borderline patient (Searles, 1986). Often, the borderline patient's magical belief in his or her own omnipotence and superhuman powers can cause him or her to grandiosely and endlessly aspire to transform and rehabilitate abusive partners. A humorous intervention that calls attention to the patient's proclivity for denial and magical thinking can animate his or her interest in facing and understanding their inner thought processes as well as the outer reality of their social world. By using the silly example of a magical potion, the absurdity of magical thinking is brought to life in a safe and comical manner that enables the patient to integrate the significance of the intervention without excessive fear.

Of course, the defense mechanisms of denial and omnipotent thinking are not peculiar to the borderline personality disorder. Therefore, the previous example of the therapeutic use of humor to address these particular defense mechanisms can probably be applied with variation to many other types of personality disorders.

Case 7

In my work with college students, I naturally encounter a great many who cannot discuss their parents critically without inordinate guilt. One of their favorite ways of dealing with the guilt they experience over their angry and critical feelings for their parents is to say, "Well, how can I be angry with them? After all, they meant well." When I hear this oft-used, hackneyed expression, I will perhaps teasingly reply, "You know, saying that someone meant well is just about the worst thing you can say about them."

The astonished student will of course ask why I would say such an outrageous thing. "Because," I reply, "when you go out of your way to say that someone means well it suggests that you can hardly think of any other good thing to say about them." By joking about students' sugarcoated descriptions of their parents in this way, I am often able to uncover the compensatory, guilt-laden quality of their remarks. This quite commonly leads to a frank and essential discussion of the student's true feelings toward his or her parents.

Many students who have grown up in homes where severe family discord was an everyday phenomenon will glibly describe their parents and families as perfect and totally problem-free. In dealing with such students, I am apt to feign great astonishment and exhilaration while saying, "This is quite remarkable. I've worked for many years as a therapist and have talked with literally thousands of students. But you are the first one I have ever met who has been reared in a perfect family. Your family is definitely a rarity."

Because my remarks are generally spoken in a laughing, joking manner, students quickly grasp that I am joshing with them. At the same time, they hear me restate in literal, albeit very exaggerated, form what they have told me about their family's alleged perfection. As a result, the distortions that stem from their idealized views of their families are farcically exposed and then discussed in the benign atmosphere induced by the humorous intervention.

A great many students who have been severely traumatized during their childhoods will vehemently deny that their current psychological problems have even the slightest relationship to their pasts. As far as they are concerned, they have come away from their miserable upbringings largely unscathed. From their perspective, any problems they may presently encounter are simply the result of how their personality functions now, not how it developed over the course of many years.

When dealing with such students in therapy, I may be inclined to kid them in the following manner. "You say you've had problems studying for years, your personal relationships have never been especially satisfactory, and you've always lacked self-confidence. Yet, you claim that your current academic and social problems have nothing to do with your past. I think I understand what you mean."

The student replies, "You do?"

"Yes. From what I can tell, years ago you were hatched from an egg in some remote forest and grew up without any human contact. That explains why you have no recollection of your life being influenced by emotional experiences within a family environment."

This parodistic intervention usually arouses a laugh and, at first, a defensive reaction such as, "Well, I didn't exactly say I didn't have a family or that my family didn't affect me in some respect. I just meant that I'm pretty much responsible for the kind of person I am today."

With these slight admissions from students that early family life has indeed made some contribution to their current difficulties, the students and I are then able to begin exploring their rather grim past within the lighter therapeutic atmosphere that was just induced by the humorous intervention.

PERTINENT USES

Beyond the strictly clinical uses of humor, there are an infinite number of ways in which humor can be effectively used by the staff of a college mental health program outside the consulting room. For example, each semester I am requested to lecture to several health education classes on the subject of psychological defense mechanisms (Amada, 1983). The instructor assigns each class to read the textbook chapter dealing with this subject a week before my lecture so that the students can be relatively conversant with the material by the time I arrive.

I usually begin my lecture by mentioning that the instructor informed me about assigning the defense mechanisms chapter for the class to read. "Is that true?" I query the class. In unison, almost everyone nods their head with an agreeable smile. I then continue, "Then I suppose . . ." When I pause, the students usually begin nodding their heads even more vigorously, expecting that I will finish my sentence by saying, ". . . you've all read the chapter." Instead, I say, "Then I suppose *none* of you have read the chapter." Upon hearing this unexpected, incredulous statement, the students laugh knowingly.

As I well know from past experience with these classes, most students indeed do not read the chapter beforehand as assigned. To make sure of the accuracy and fairness of my surmise, I quickly and good-naturedly poll the students. A show of hands usually indicates that no more than 5 students out of a class of about 35 have actually read the assigned chapter before I have delivered my lecture. By taking this humorous tack I have discovered something that I can usefully incorporate into my lecture on defense mechanisms. I first remind the students that I will be further discussing their disinclination to do the assigned reading later in the lecture when we get to the topic of psychological repression.

When I subsequently describe and explain the defense mechanism of repression, I first talk about how people forget such things as doctors' appointments, the names of familiar persons, bringing their textbooks to school, their parents' requests to take out the garbage, their keys, and so on. The class usually finds these examples interesting and amusing. Then I remind the class that they "forgot" to do the assigned reading for today's lecture. Because we had already discussed some of the dynamics of repression, I ask them, "Why do you think you forgot to do today's assignment?"

Because this issue has been handled with levity, the students are psychologically open to discussing some of their heretofore hidden motivations and many, not surprisingly, admit without much embarrassment that they did not do the assignment because they simply did not like it and, therefore, unconsciously forgot to do it. Together, we laugh about the way repression is often connected to feelings of anger, defiance, and rebellion. The humorous and modulated tone of the discussion enables the class to grasp some important psychological concepts that might be difficult to emotionally assimilate in a more serious, untempered academic atmosphere.

As I am sure many lecturers have discovered, humor not only fosters the receptivity of listening audiences, but helps to relax the lecturer as well. Therefore, when I lecture to college classes I usually try to think of a few good jokes to bring along with me. If they turn out to be too corny and the class boos or hisses, I then make fun of myself for inflicting such cornball on them.

Occasionally, a student will ask a question that will prompt me to play an impromptu gag on the class. For example, I was once asked by a student if I practiced hypnosis. I replied with pretentious seriousness that I did (I did not) and that, as a matter of fact I had, without their knowledge, placed the entire class under a hypnotic trance about 20 minutes earlier. For a brief second, I could see several credulous students stare at me with expressions of fear. Then with a smile I added, "Now if you will all pass your wallets to the front of the room." Most of the students find this gag quite funny. However, if I become aware that someone in the class still does not seem to understand that I was merely joking (e.g., a paranoid student who was hypersensitive to the possibility of mind control), I then simply make my intention absolutely clear to everyone.

As a college psychotherapist I have countless contacts with faculty and support staff each day. With many of these individuals I will stop to have a brief chat and tell a joke. I have found this to be an excellent way to overcome the sometimes stilted and stuffy atmosphere of academia and a great medium for getting to know my colleagues. It has been a source of interest and pleasure to me to discover that many of my colleagues now seek me out whenever they hear a good new joke. Unquestionably, these humorous, pleasurable exchanges help to improve and cement important professional relationships between the Mental Health Program and other members of the college staff.

For example, a member of the faculty recently called me to seek assistance with a professional matter. We chatted several times on the phone that same week and then arranged to meet. She asked what I looked like and I told her that I bore a strong resemblance to Burt Reynolds. Since I have very little hair on my head, this was clearly a lie. Nonetheless, the instructor chuckled with enjoyment. The next time we spoke she said that she had seen a photograph of me and that I really looked like Paul Newman instead. This light banter made our conversations easy and pleasant. When we finally met in person at a faculty meeting I presented the instructor with a bagged gift. It was a jar of Paul Newman's salad dressing which I claimed to have prepared myself earlier in the day. This opened our meeting on a note of hilarity that was very conducive to the discussion that followed. The next day I received a lovely potted plant from the instructor. Attached was a picture of Jane Fonda and a note that said, "From Jane." The humor we shared throughout our interactions enabled us to form an excellent professional relationship that I am sure will be of significant future benefit to our respective programs.

Most colleges and universities employ large numbers of so-called classified personnel who work as telephone operators, gardeners, carpenters, janitors, and secretaries. For social and cultural reasons, this group of workers—who occupy positions on the lower rungs of the organizational hierarchy—may be ignored or disregarded by the instructional and administrative staffs of the college. This is extremely unfortunate since the work performed by these individuals is essential to the successful implementation of the educational services of the college and, therefore, those individuals are certainly entitled to respect and acknowledgment. After all, instructors cannot adequately teach in classrooms that are improperly cleaned, heated, or lighted.

Due to the nature of my assignment as administrator of a college mental health program, my own contacts with the college's classified staff are minimal. Therefore, when I have a passing encounter with a member of the classified staff, I often take the opportunity to tell a joke or pose a riddle to them. I think this is a marvelous way to convey my interest in and appreciation for them. Also, like many of my colleagues, because I often turn to the classified staff for professional favors, I think the personal touch of humor enables me to convey that I appreciate their assistance and do not somehow regard it as my due by virtue of my supposedly superordinate position.

The following represents a fairly typical encounter I have had with one of the college telephone operators just before I requested that she place a call for me.

Amada: What do Jack the Ripper and
Winnie-the-Pooh have in common?

Operator: I don't know. What?

Amada: They have the same middle name.

After a brief pause, the operator laughed raucously. For weeks after this brief exchange she mentioned how she and her husband repeated and enjoyed this riddle with their friends. In my view, humorous and pleasurable interactions of this kind can do much to bridge otherwise unbridgeable professional gaps between college employees whose contacts with one another are ordinarily very scant and impersonal.

In addition to providing high-quality clinical services, I think it is also essential that a college mental health service maintain a warm and inviting facility for staff and students alike. To some extent, the warm and welcoming quality of a clinic can be reflected in the decor and furnishings of the facility itself. However, the extent to which a college clinic will be seen in a favorable light will largely depend upon how well people are treated when they come in to utilize the clinic's services.

The City College of San Francisco Mental Health Program is located in the on-campus Student Health Services building. Student Health Services offer both medical-nursing as well as psychological services, primarily to students. However, many faculty members come to the clinic at the beginning of each semester to have a tuberculosis (TB) checkup. Normally, they have to wait several minutes before seeing a nurse, during which time they either read a magazine or twiddle their thumbs.

On occasion, when seeing a faculty member waiting for his or her TB test appointment, I walk over and have something like the following conversation:

Amada: Here for your TB test?
   I can help you with that.

Instructor: You can? I didn't know you handled
   things like that, Jerry.

Amada: Of course. Ready?

Instructor: Sure.

Amada: Okay. Who was the first person
   to contract TB?

Instructor: Huh? How the hell do I know?

Amada: Don't know, huh? Well, who was
   the physician who invented the cure for TB?

Instructor: I haven't the foggiest idea.

Amada: Don't know that either?
   Sorry, but you just failed your TB test.

Usually, this ridiculous gag evokes some derisive but friendly laughter and then serves to ignite a further exchange of jokes or some friendly conversation. I have repeatedly discovered that many faculty members will arrange to take time every now and then to come to the clinic, tell me a joke, and schmooze a bit. Evidently, a college clinic whose staff can display genuine humor is likely to be viewed as a warm and hospitable context within which to receive personal services.

By virtue of my administrative role, I am frequently confronted with the need to notify the clinical staff of changes in policy and practice. If disseminating information by word of mouth is too time-consuming, generally the handiest alternative is a quick memo to the staff. In sending and receiving such memos for many years, it has been my experience that they are usually written in boilerplate prose that is quite dry, overly serious, and disagreeably authoritative. In order to counteract some of the disagreeable aspects of transmitting memos to staff, I have recently begun to write them in a lampooning style. The following is an actual example of such a memo.

> To: The Metal Hearth Staff
>
> From: Dr. Amoeba
>
> Because the clinic secretaries' assignments have become increasingly hectic, please check the waiting room for your patients if you have not been notified of their scheduled arrival by Gloria or Wendy. Remember, a bird in the hand is worth two good scrubbings.

The following is a memo I sent to the staff soon after receiving complaints that some persons were inconsiderately leaving bread, fruit, and other foods on the sink and table of the lunch room, evidently expecting someone else to clean up after them.

> To: Student Health Staff
>
> From: Arnold (The Exterminator) Schwartzbagle
>
> The lunch room has begun to look pretty seedy lately, that is, from the human standpoint (it's beginning to arouse ant-ipathy and ant-agonism, and enc-roach upon the hygienic rights of the tidiness-minded among us). So please, if generosity has prompted you to bring in a refreshment for the staff, please remove it before it becomes moldy and attacks us.

It has been my impression that humorous memos of this kind generate wholesome amusement. They are also read with greater interest and willingness to comply with their stated directives than are serious or authoritative memos.

Each year the Mental Health Program provides psychological internships to doctoral students from nearby graduate schools. These interns, who usually serve in the program 3 days a week, provide direct psychotherapeutic services to City College students, for which they are supervised by the senior staff. Before accepting these interns into the program, their resumes are carefully reviewed and evaluated. Each intern is then invited to have a personal interview with the staff in order to allow us to more precisely evaluate his or her levels of clinical sophistication and interpersonal skills.

During the course of these personal interviews, I am often asked by the interviewees to explain what particular qualities or qualifications I deem most desirable in prospective interns. In response, I candidly allude to such qualities as personal warmth, a capacity for self-disclosure, introspectiveness, a genuine interest in psychodynamic theory and practice, sincerity, intellectual curiosity, and a capacity to cope with and learn from constructive criticism and adversity. What I do not tell these interviewees is that I am also highly interested in the depth and quality of their sense of humor and, to the extent that such a quality can be determined in the course of only one interview, their teasability.

My interest in an intern's teasability partly relates to the fact that during the course of supervising interns I will use a light and easygoing manner of teasing them, especially during times of excessive difficulty. Times of difficulty arise for interns when they report their technical mistakes and countertransferential overreactions to clients, often with guilt, anxiety, and embarrassment. My own teasing reflects my attitude that the commission of errors and blunders in performing clinical services is largely unavoidable and forgivable, especially among neophyte therapists.

If dynamically understood, errors and blunders can become a valuable wellspring of learning and growth. Additionally, by my teasing interns about some of their mistakes in judgment, technique, or conceptualization, I am giving them the opportunity to realize that, because their supervisor can be philosophically nonjudgmental about their fallibility, perhaps they too can forgive themselves for and learn from their mistakes. This would in turn help them to develop a tolerant attitude toward their own patients.

Obviously, gross errors in judgment, such as deliberately violating the confidentiality of a patient, may need to be dealt with in an entirely serious manner.

I value a sense of humor and a capacity for teasability in psychological interns because of my belief that interns who can appropriately laugh, joke, and be teased will develop a better coping ability than interns who approach their work with unrelieved seriousness. A sense of humor can ease the tensions, crises, setbacks, and disappointments that normally occur in a college mental health program. Having provided clinical supervision for more than 20 years at City College, I am fully convinced that a resilient and versatile sense of humor is a most desirable trait to identify and strengthen in the psychological intern.

Because of the inherent imbalance of power and the evaluative nature of the supervisory relationship, interns often approach their supervisory sessions with an appreciable degree of trepidation and guardedness, at least initially. For this reason, I sometimes like to start a supervisory hour by telling a joke that I have recently heard. Not infrequently interns will respond by telling me one themselves, and a mood of friendliness and humor is thereby immediately engendered. Frankly, this tack also helps me to relax because I, too, frequently approach my supervisory responsibilities in a mood of unease and hypervigilance.

Quite often, in my supervision of interns, I seize the opportunity to turn an overly serious discussion into a light and humorous one. I will illustrate this point with a recent example. At the beginning of our supervisory hour, I informed an intern that I would need to reschedule one of our supervisory sessions. Since the rescheduled time seemed to be even more convenient for her, the intern asked if we could always meet at the new hour. I replied, "Do you mean even after you have terminated your internship here?" We both laughed uninhibitedly over my deliberately literal interpretation of her question, a pleasurable interlude that set a very warm and positive tone for the remainder of our session.

In 1988, I was asked by the campus newspaper, *The Guardsman*, to write an advice column called "Ask Amada." Since that time the column has appeared regularly. According to the feedback I have received thus far, it enjoys a fairly wide and faithful readership among students and faculty alike. In answering the letters submitted to me by students, I have tried to mitigate the heaviness of the advice and information presented in the column by infusing my replies with humor.

For example, I received a letter from a student whose girlfriend's son was exhibiting sexual curiosity by poking at him in the area of his genitals. The student wrote that his girlfriend advised him to tell her son that this was his "pee-pee" and should be left alone. After suggesting certain guidelines for dealing with this situation, I wrote that it was perhaps okay to use the term "pee-pee," but "to paraphrase Gertrude Stein, a penis is a penis is a penis." Such light touches of humor appear to be appreciated by readers of the column who will sometimes requote them to me at a later time.

Finally, this chapter would not be complete without at least brief mention of my mutually teasing and bantering relationship with the two Student Health Services secretaries. These two fine individuals are responsible for greeting and scheduling students, answering the telephones, and generally keeping everyone on their toes. Although we, of course, have our very serious moments, our sense of teamwork and camaraderie is definitely enhanced by the opportunities we take each day to exchange amusing personal tales or play innocent jokes and tricks on each other. My favorites have been to shake hands with one of the secretaries with my middle finger folded into my palm and then apologize for the "wart." Or, I would walk over to the other secretary and ask if I could count on her. When she says "Yes," I begin drumming on her shoulder with my index finger while counting, "One, two, three, four." As indicated earlier, silly but meaningful interactions of this kind help to lighten the social atmosphere of the workplace. Such interactions break down the sense of separateness and tension that may exist among college mental health staff who are usually preoccupied with exigent assignments. In the end they undoubtedly work toward enhancing staff morale and improving the overall quality of clinical services to students.

SYNTHESIS

In this chapter, I have attempted to demonstrate the central role of humor in the daily administration of a college mental health program. As illustrated previously, humor has played a crucial role in my psychotherapeutic work with college students due to its capacity to transmit dynamic insights, defuse potentially explosive situations, and resolve therapeutic impasses. It also serves as an effective means of conveying empathy, understanding, goodwill, and optimism.

I have attempted to show how humor can play a very important role in the nonclinical activities of a college mental health program. Humor can help to bridge the social gap between the psychotherapy staff and other members of the campus community. Within the college psychological service itself, humor can engender camaraderie and teamwork. In the supervision of psychological interns, humor can be used as a counterweight to the anxiety producing imbalances of power that normally characterize a supervisory relationship. Among the clinical staff, humor helps to attenuate feelings of separateness and interpersonal tension. In short, humor, if used judiciously, can be an indispensable helpmate to college psychotherapists in carrying out almost any clinical or administrative function.

A caveat is in order before concluding this chapter. I would like to clarify that my strong emphasis upon the use of humor in this chapter does not mean that I advocate a one-sidedly playful or hedonic approach to the practice of psychotherapy with the college student. My colleagues and I take our work very seriously. During those times when we realize that the use of humor would be either inappropriate or offensive, we generally avoid using it. Nevertheless, I like to think of the wise and creative use of humor as a splendid leavening force that can raise the qualitative level of my clinical and administrative work, and, for that matter, my life. Finally, for those readers who may wish to write to me regarding this chapter, I would like to mention that I welcome all letters, provided, of course, that they are highly flattering.

References

Amada, G. (1983). Mental health consultation on the college campus. *Journal of American College Health*, 31, 222-223.

Amada, G. (1985). *A Guide to Psychotherapy*. Lanham, MD: Madison Books.

Amada, G. . (1985b). Organizing a community college mental health program. In G. Amada (Ed.), *Mental Health on the Community College Campus* (pp. 112). Lanham, MD: University Press of America.

Blumenfeld, E., & Alpern, L. (1986). *The Smile Connection*. Englewood Cliffs, NJ: Prentice-Hall.

Ducey, C. (1989). Academic underachievement. In P. Grayson & K. Cauley (Eds.), *College Psychotherapy* (pp. 166-192). New York: Guilford.

Fay, A. (1978). *Making Things Better by Making Them Worse*. New York: Hawthorn Books.

Fine, G. (1983). Sociological approaches to the study of humor. In P. McGhee & J. Goldstein (Eds.), *Handbook of Humor Research* (pp. 159-181). New York: Springer-Verlag.

Goldstein, W. (1985). *An Introduction to the Borderline Conditions*. Northvale, NJ: Jason Aronson.

Klein, A. (1989). *The Healing Power of Humor*. Los Angeles: Jeremy Tarcher, Inc.

Lefcourt, H., & Martin, R. (1986). *Humor and Life Stress*. New York: Springer-Verlag.

Margolis, G. (1989). Developmental opportunities. In P. Grayson & K. Cauley (Eds.), *College Psychotherapy* (pp. 71-91). New York: Guilford.

Salameh, W. A. (1987). Humor in integrative short-term psychotherapy (ISTP). In W. F. Fry, Jr. & W. A. Salameh (Eds.), *Handbook of Humor and Psychotherapy: Advances in the Clinical Use of Humor* (pp. 195-240). Sarasota, FL: Professional Resource Exchange.

Searles, H. F. (1986). *My Work with Borderline Patients*. Northvale, NJ: Jason Aronson.

Vaillant, G. (1977). *Adaptation to Life*. Boston: Little, Brown.

Wild, E. (1989). *Borderline Pathology in the Chronically and Severely Abused Woman*. Unpublished doctoral dissertation, California School for Professional Psychology, Berkeley, CA.

The Role of the Mental Health Consultant in Dealing with Disruptive College Students

Ordinarily, the primary purpose of a college mental health program is to provide direct psychological services to students who are in crisis, usually on a short-term basis. During the course of providing such services, the staff of the program will also be called upon to provide consultation to various employees of the college regarding students who are, allegedly, disruptive. This article will describe the role of the mental health consultant, highlighting the specific ways in which the consultant can contribute to the resolution of disruptive crises as well as describing some of the misunderstandings and disjunctions that may arise between complainants and the consultant.

Ordinarily, the mainstay of an on-campus psychological service is the provision of direct assistance to students who are in some form of emotional crisis. As well, the mental health program inevitably will be called upon by college staff to assist them in their efforts to deal with disruptive students. In those instances in which the disruptive student is deemed acutely psychotic or a danger to himself or others, the mental health team can facilitate the psychiatric hospitalization of the student in a timely, humane and efficient manner, albeit an often quite formidable procedure when the student is uncooperative.

When the disruptive student is not at the same time a person who is experiencing a psychiatric emergency that requires direct crisis intervention and, possibly, arrangements for hospitalization, the college psychotherapist can then appropriately serve in the alternative role of consultant to those staff who report complaints about student disruptiveness. This article will describe my own model for carrying out the role of a college mental health consultant in dealing with student disruptiveness, drawing particular attention to the unique value of this role as well as noting some of the occasional snags, misunderstan-

145

dings and disjunctions that occur between complainants and the consultant.

Before proceeding further, I wish to point out that my use of the masculine pronoun throughout this article reflects only the fact that most of the students who have been reported to me as disruptive are male.

College staff who are confronted by highly disruptive students are frequently frightened, diffident and unclear about their rights and prerogatives. Thus, the consultant can be helpful by offering vital emotional support and empathy to complainants throughout the crises such students cause. The alarming nature of many disruptive incidents may paralyze some college staff to the extent that they become inert, ineffectual and dangerously permissive in dealing with these crises. Other college staff, out of fear, anger or desperation, react with disproportionate severity and punitiveness toward the disruptive student. The consultant can intervene in such cases by pointing out some of the pitfalls and adverse consequences that could conceivably result from an inappropriate handling of the crisis, suggest alternative and more constructive modes of response, and empathize with the feelings of apprehension, doubt, and anger that often accompany encounters with highly disruptive students.

GUIDELINES FOR REPORTING
DISRUPTIVE INCIDENTS

It appears that instructors, more than any other college employees, have the most direct contact with disruptive students and therefore most often appeal to the mental health consultant for help. For a wide variety of reasons—including fear of legal or physical reprisals from the disruptive student or, perhaps, dread over the possibility that an administrator who learns of the incident will hold the instructor/complainant to blame for its occurrence—it is common for faculty to display a reluctance to report incidents of disruption.

Prerogatives

The mental health consultant is in an excellent position to ferret out some of the reasons for this reluctance, and then to help the complainants overcome their aversion to reporting acts of student disruptiveness, assuming, of course, that the complainant appears to have legitimate reasons for filing a complaint against a student. An initial step in this process is for the consultant to point out to instructors that they have two highly essential prerogatives (Amada, 1992). The first, and most obvious, is to establish and implement academic standards. The second is to establish and enforce in each class, behavioral standards, the latter taking into consideration: (1) minor disruptions (such as students who only occasionally and briefly chatter during lectures) should be tolerated as well as possible while major disruptions (such as students who have verbally or physically threatened an instructor) should immediately be reported and investigated; (2) behavioral standards may vary according to the particular expectations and sensibilities of the instructor, the nature of the course itself, and the physical ambience in which the course is taught.

To suggest one obvious example of such variations, it is likely that an instructor of physical education would tolerate a greater degree of physical activity and horseplay in a gymnasium than the instructor of history who lectures in a conventional classroom situation. In any case, it is normally very reassuring to faculty to be reminded that they do have rights to insist upon general conformity to reasonable codes of conduct.

Dangerousness

Considering the ubiquity of violence in contemporary America, it is not surprising that many faculty initiate their discussions with the consultant by raising questions about the disruptive student's potential dangerousness. If, after hearing the facts, the consultant believes that the student is not likely to behave in a retaliatory or dangerous manner, it is probably appropriate to share that opinion. However, no matter how innocuous a disruptive student may appear, it is usually unwise and even risky for the consultant to state with absolute certainty that the instructor is completely safe from harm.

Many well-documented studies (see esp. Monahan, 1981) have demonstrated that mental health professionals' ability to predict dangerous or violent behavior is quite limited. Therefore, it is ordinarily best for the consultant to advise the instructor to take whatever precautions are necessary to avoid the possibility of being endangered. One example of such a precaution would be to meet with the disruptive student only in the company of other staff. In California, an education code permits community college instructors to unilaterally (that is, without administrative approval) remove disruptive students from two consecutive classes.

As a consultant to the faculty, I have very often recommended this handy intervention in cases that involved highly disruptive and potentially dangerous students. Its value is twofold: it buys time that can be used for a thorough administrative investigation and resolution of the crisis, and it can immediately defuse a volatile, imperiling situation.

When instructors describe disruptive students who clearly pose no physical danger but are simply a chronic distraction and nuisance, the consultant may take a different tack. Many such students are, for one reason or another, incapable of controlling their behavior. No matter how many times they are warned or reminded about the need to curb their disruptiveness, they somehow cannot stop being disorderly. Quite commonly, the chronically disruptive student, who is evidently manifesting poor overall adjustment to his role as a student, is also having severe scholastic difficulties and may be failing the very course in which he is misbehaving.

In any case, when the consultant has determined that the instructor and the student have reached an unfortunate, insoluble impasse that can only become worse, it might be necessary to advise the instructor to tell the student that it is in his best interest immediately to withdraw from the class without penalty. Coupled with this advice could be a warning that if the student remains in the class and persists in behaving disruptively, he will be reported and a request for disciplinary measures will ensue. To avoid the stigma and pain of undergoing a disciplinary procedure, many such students, in my experience, opt to withdraw. If they do not, and the disruptive behavior continues, the instructor, obviously, must follow through on his earlier threat.

Documentation

The consultant can play an important role in assisting faculty and other college staff in developing the requisite technical skills for documenting cases of disruptive student behavior. These skills are not especially complicated and are therefore easily teachable (Amada, 1986). Instructors are advised to accompany their oral reports with written documentation of their observations, which should be devoid of psychological jargon or speculation. In other words, the instructor is advised not to speculate in writing about the disruptive student's putative mental condition.

Then, with as little editorializing as possible, the instructor should provide information that is concise, specific, concrete and chronological, emphasizing only the *behavior* of the disruptive student. Finally, if the instructor holds any particular preferences regarding the ultimate disposition of his complaints, he should state those preferences in the report. Upon completion, the documentation should be accurately dated and transmitted to the appropriate administrative officer for investigation and resolution. When a disruptive incident has already spiraled dangerously out of control, the instructor can be advised to report the matter both to an administrator and to the campus or city police.

NONINSTRUCTIONAL STAFF

In addition to instructors, the mental health consultant will receive requests from a great many other college employees for assistance with disruptive students. Counselors, support staff who work as secretaries, custodians, librarians, and managers of college book stores will, from time to time, seek help in resolving disruptive incidents. Therefore, it is essential that the consultant help these individuals determine whether the student is violating the code of student conduct in their specific workplace and then to advise them about their own prerogatives to initiate disciplinary proceedings.

Although they may not have the right to bar students from their work area on a unilateral basis, they certainly are entitled to report disruptive students to their supervisors and to expect that action will be taken to protect themselves from harassment and interference with their work assignments. As I have often stated to support staff, it is in no one's job description to suffer abuse. No one should put up with intimidation, bullying or violence. The mental health consultant can be very helpful in meeting with support staff and their supervisors in order to discuss these matters and to develop specific strategies for reporting and resolving incidents of student disruptiveness.

MENTAL HEALTH REFERRALS

It is quite common for those who report a disruptive student to question immediately whether the mental health consultant already knows the student as a client of the college's psychological services. Underlying the complainant's question is usually an assumption that, if the student is already known to the mental health service as a client, the mental health consultant will be in an advantageous position to understand and resolve the crisis.

Another, often unspoken, reason for this query is the complainant's wish to know if the disruptive student is a dangerous person. The complainant, therefore, hopes and expects that if a student is receiving psychological services at the college and is truly dangerous, the mental health staff will not only note that fact, but will duly report it to the proper administrative and law enforcement authorities in order to protect the college community from any known dangers posed by the student.

Unless a student is demonstrably a danger to himself or others, the information regarding students' use of psychological services ordinarily is confidential. How, then, should the consultant respond to queries about whether the allegedly disruptive student has already seen a college psychotherapist? My own tack has been respectfully to point out the fact that such information is confidential, but that I, in my role as a consultant, will nevertheless be able to help the complainant in a variety of effective ways—including a review of disciplinary procedures, the code of student conduct and the need for documentation—without having to disclose whether or not the student has ever utilized the college's psychological services.

It has been my experience that most complainants are quickly reassured by the offer of help and do not unreasonably persist in seeking confidential information. As May (1986) has cogently stated, in our consultation, as in our psychotherapeutic practice, our work is to help others explore and contain their anxieties rather than simply and inappropriately accede to their initial requests.

Quite frequently, when a complainant reports a disruptive student, the report is accompanied by a request that the student be seen for psychotherapy, perhaps involuntarily, by the consultant or another member of the mental health staff. Such requests are often motivated by the notion that disruptive students have obviously never before received psychotherapeutic help and should now, for the first time, avail themselves of the golden opportunity afforded them by a free and convenient psychological service on the campus. Often times, this assumption is made because the complainant—who thinks of psychotherapy as a treatment with a permanently civilizing effect—finds it impossible to believe that a student who has behaved in an outrageous manner could have ever been a recipient of a course of psychotherapy.

Yet, quite often, I have discovered that many of the students who have been reported by complainants for being disruptive had actually been clients of the college mental health program and, as well, were prior long-term patients of other psychiatric agencies in the community. Thus, it seems advisable to alert complainants, who are urging disruptive students to enter therapy, to the possibility that these students may already have their own therapist or, in some instances, have had a long skein of unsuccessful therapeutic experiences which may cause them to regard the prospect of additional therapy with a good degree of fear and skepticism.

Complainants frequently favor psychotherapy over the imposition of discipline for disruptive students because they consider it to be the kinder, more humane, intervention with which to deal with disruptive behavior. This viewpoint is, at best, arguable. As I have pointed out elsewhere (Amada, 1992), discipline is not inherently immoral or cruel. On the other hand, psychotherapy, as clients and therapists know full well, is not a painless or uncomplicated process. And, in some instances, to attain even moderate success, the therapy must continue for many weeks, months, or years.

I have known many students who would much prefer to receive a one-time form of just and proportionate punishment than to sit with a therapist week after week, undergoing the painful process of self-disclosure, however salutary the results might be in the end. In any case, the mental health consultant may find it advisable to point out to complainants that the choice between psychotherapy and discipline for disruptive students is not as clear-cut as it might appear at first glance, and that there often are decided advantages in disciplining rather than psychotherapeutically treating the disruptive student.

It is a common practice at many colleges and universities to require students who are disruptive to enter psychotherapy on an involuntary basis. Sometimes this practice is employed quite openly and explicitly, with little remorse or reservation regarding its potential dangers or drawbacks. At some colleges, where this practice is correctly recognized as coercive and authoritarian, it is conducted, to a degree, on a sub rosa basis, in hopes that it will not be generally discovered or legally challenged by students or their families.

Except in those cases that involve students who are a clear and imminent danger to themselves or others, there are cogent reasons for abolishing the use of mandatory psychotherapy as a form of, or a substitute for, discipline. Whenever a complainant, whether it is an administrator, instructor or a member of the college's support staff, requests that I, as the mental health consultant, countenance the use of mandatory psychotherapy in order to deal with a disruptive student, I strenuously object, while spelling out the following rationales for my qualms.

1. Requiring disruptive students to receive psychotherapy distorts and undermines the basis for corrective disciplinary action. The focus and impetus for disciplinary action is the disruptive behavior of the student, not the student's putative mental illness or disorder. When college administrators require the disruptive student to undertake psychotherapy, they are perforce making a psychiatric judgment using *psychiatric* criteria. Even if they were doing this with the benefit of having first consulted a mental health professional, the requirement is being carried out by means of the administrator's authority and, therefore, it is the administrator who is making the psychiatric determination that the student requires therapy.

College administrators generally do not possess the legal right or expertise to make psychiatric evaluations and determinations of this nature. On the other hand, they most certainly do have the legal right and prerogative to determine what is and is not acceptable student behavior on their respective campuses and to carry out nonpsychiatric discipline in cases of student misconduct.

2. The requirement of psychotherapy for the disruptive student is often motivated by fanciful and naive notions about psychotherapy itself. One such notion, for example, is the belief that once students receive psychotherapy, their disruptive behavior will abate or cease. Although this is sometimes true, it is also true that many persons who receive psychotherapy remain socially disruptive and at times actually become violent, despite their psychiatric treatment.

3. Requiring a disruptive student to receive psychotherapy is unequivocally a coercive measure that serves to instill in the student resentment toward the therapist and therapy itself. If such students comply

with this requirement, and on many campuses they do, they will agree to see a therapist, but frequently will make no personal investment in the treatment process itself. As a consequence, such students typically derive little from the therapy other than the impression that psychotherapy is a form of punishment that must be stoically endured.

4. For psychotherapy to work effectively, it must ordinarily be conducted on a confidential basis. Requiring a disruptive student to receive psychotherapy often removes this cornerstone of therapy because someone, either the student or the therapist, will eventually be expected to report to the college administration that the student is, indeed, receiving psychotherapeutic services.

Several safeguards can generally serve to protect confidentiality in such cases: (a) therapists may refuse to transmit substantive reports about students who have not given their voluntary, written consent to this procedure; (b) students who have been referred for psychotherapy may willingly, and in writing, authorize their therapists to transmit certain information about them to specified college officials; (c) students who are referred to therapists may be permitted explicitly to refuse, for whatever reason, the disclosure of therapists' reports about them to college officials without the threat of duress, penalty, or reprisal on the part of the college. In this regard, it is probably worth mentioning that there are significant differences of opinion among both mental health professionals and college administrators regarding what constitutes "substantive" disclosures that violate the confidentiality of students who receive psychotherapy.

In my own view, the simple fact that a student has entered psychotherapy is intrinsically substantive (and potentially inflammatory) information that should not be disclosed without the express voluntary and written consent of the student himself or herself. Although the disclosure of such limited information may seem quite innocuous, it can be used by the college, with or without intention, to embarrass, stigmatize, or manipulate students. I believe, therefore, that the student's decision to enter therapy should be given the same protections of confidentiality as are accorded the personal self-disclosures that later follow during the psychotherapy sessions themselves.

5. The administrative requirement of psychotherapy tends to transfer the responsibility and authority for administering discipline from where it rightfully belongs—the office of the designated administrator, to where it does not belong—the offices of counselors and therapists. Thus an institutional anomaly is created: Therapists and counselors (whose job it is to guide and heal) are asked or required, under administrative pressure, to assume quasi-disciplinary functions and responsibilities; and administrators (whose job, among others, is to administer discipline) are, instead, counseling disruptive students about

their need for mental health services. This anomaly is especially apparent when the evident purpose and expectation of the administrative referral are to have the therapist or counselor, by hook or crook, "stop" the student from being disruptive. Although there may be nothing wrong with an administrator's recommending psychotherapy to a student, it is ordinarily inappropriate and counterproductive to use such recommendations as a handy substitute for appropriate disciplinary action.

6. The requirement that disruptive students receive psychotherapy as a condition of continued enrollment is essentially predicated upon a policy that can exclude them because of their alleged mental or psychiatric disability. This is probably in violation of Section 504 of the Rehabilitation Act of 1973, which reads, in part: "No otherwise qualified handicapped individual shall, solely by reasons of his handicap, be excluded from participation in, be denied the benefits of, or be subjected to discrimination under any program or activity receiving Federal financial assistance." As Pavela (1985) has pointed out, Section 504 expressly prohibits discrimination against individuals suffering from a mental disorder and every relevant interpretation of Section 504 distinguishes between a simple diagnosis of a mental disorder and the behavior resulting from such a disorder. In other words, the antiquated practice of requiring disruptive students to receive psychological evaluations and/or psychotherapy on the basis of their putative mental illness is perhaps illegal and, in my view, definitely unethical.

When complainants seek to have the mental health consultant arrange for the involuntary psychotherapy of the disruptive student, it is essential that the consultant carefully and respectfully explain the many drawbacks to such an arrangement before denying such requests. In my experience, most complainants are completely satisfied with such explanations since they help them to recognize the greater efficacy of using a sound judicial/disciplinary procedure than of using the ethically questionable intervention of involuntary psychotherapy to deal with disruptive students.

AVERSIONS TO THE ADMINISTRATION OF DISCIPLINE

It is common to find that college instructors and administrators are averse to meting out discipline, even well-deserved discipline, to disruptive students. For this reason, many acts of serious disruption are trivialized and remain unreported, in some instances, even when they have reached truly dangerous proportions. Therefore, one of the most valuable services the mental health consultant can render to the college is to help those who must contend with disruptive students identify their own resistances to reporting disruptive crises.

Many faculty are reluctant to report a disruptive student because they one-sidedly believe that discipline has no positive value. They view disciplinary measures as necessarily punitive, harsh and harmful to students. When the consultant recognizes that it is this set of beliefs and viewpoints that has discouraged a prospective complainant from reporting a disruptive student, it may be helpful for him to point out that discipline, if applied in an even-handed and proportionate way, can have enormous positive value.

If necessary, examples can be provided to illustrate this point. For example, discipline can instill a sense of responsibility and accountability to others. It can serve as a reminder that no member of the college community possesses a license to abuse or interfere with the rights of others. In short, the prospective complainant is helped to understand that reporting a disruptive student is not an act of betrayal and usually does not have serious deleterious effects upon that student.

If, however, there is some likelihood that the disruptive student will be adversely affected by a certain disciplinary measure (e.g., expulsion), the consultant can help the prospective complainant understand that the rights of many individuals must be acknowledged and protected in dealing with disruptive incidents. If, as so often occurs, the disruptive student is not reported and continues to behave disruptively with impunity, it is likely that other students as well as the instructor will suffer adverse consequences. The instructor is then encouraged to consider the larger context of the problem, weighing the interests and rights of all those individuals who are in regular contact with and adversely affected by the disruptive student. Such considerations quite often are decisive in activating a prospective complainant to report disruptive behavior.

Some college staff are reluctant to report disruptive students because they anticipate that the resultant discipline will serve only to exacerbate and escalate an already inflamed conflict. Although this expectation should not be dismissed out of hand, it must be carefully scrutinized by the consultant for its potential flaws. For example, many disruptive crises have resulted from the fact that the instructor has passively and protractedly tolerated unacceptable behavior. Often, when instructors are questioned about the consequences of their inaction, they readily admit that their passivity has had, alas, a paradoxical effect.

Rather than being appreciated by the disruptive student as a gesture of goodwill and kindness, the disruptive student has viewed the instructor's passivity as emblematic of a weakness in the instructor's character and as an official passport to behave disruptively in the future. Therefore, when discussing with reluctant complainants the unwisdom of their passive posture, the consultant can point out that, apparently, it is their ongoing inaction that has inadvertently contributed to an escalation of the disruptiveness and that it is, therefore, high time to assert their institutionally conferred right to report student disruptiveness.

Of course, it is possible that a disruptive student who is reported to the college administration will react by behaving more uncontrollably and more offensively. Therefore, in recommending that the instructor report the disruptive student, the mental health consultant can point out that this intervention may, at least initially, cause an escalation of the student's disruptiveness. The consultant can then advise the complainant about how to proceed in the event that the initial use of discipline is ineffectual. For example, the instructor can then petition the college administration to remove and bar the student from the classroom immediately until a judicial hearing can be held in order to determine a proper course of action.

Another concern of prospective complainants is the potential litigiousness of the disruptive student. Stated plainly, the complainant fears that the disruptive student will sue him and/or the college if disciplinary action is taken against the student. Obviously, no college employee is immune from lawsuits at the hands of disruptive students, but there are times when such apprehensions are rather groundless. Many disruptive students are guilty of egregious misconduct and, being aware of their own culpability, would hardly consider suing the college for exercising its institutional right to enforce a reasonable code of student conduct.

Furthermore, even if a given disruptive student does threaten a lawsuit, the college should not be held hostage to such threats. If, in the view of the college—represented by the complainant, the designated administrator, the mental health consultant, the college attorney and the judicial advisor—the student has repeatedly or grossly violated the code of student conduct, it should by all means enforce its disciplinary prerogatives and let the legal chips fall where they may. The college that eschews this essential responsibility is guilty of moral cravenness and, as a kind of self-fulfillment of everyone's worst fears, invites legal retribution from disruptive students, who are often quick to detect a college's vulnerabilities, at the "drop of a hat." In any case, the prospective complainant who fears legal reprisals from the disruptive student can be advised by the mental health consultant to consult a private attorney or the college's attorney in order to determine the legal advisability of filing a complaint.

A quite prevalent concern of faculty who report disruptive incidents relates to the potential dangerousness of the disruptive student. Although this concern is sometimes disproportionate and groundless, it should never be dismissed out of hand. After all, many disruptive students are bigger, younger, and more vigorous than the instructor, and may, in extreme cases, have little compunction about using a weapon. When it appears there is a definite and imminent risk of physical harm to the complainant, the mental health consultant should recommend that the complainant report the student at once to the designated administrator and to the campus police. If the campus does not have a law enforcement unit, the assistance of the city police or sheriff's office may be enlisted. In such cases, an administrative investigation and assessment should be undertaken immediately to determine the advisability of allowing the student to remain in the instructor's class.

Another fear of prospective complainants that dampens their desire to report disruptive students is their worry that a disciplinary measure, no matter how mild and warranted, will be excessively harmful to the disruptive student, who is seen as too fragile psychologically to withstand any added pressure in his life. Therefore, it is usually very reassuring for complainants to learn from the mental health consultant that those disruptive students who are also apparently "mentally ill" quite often benefit and even flourish when rules and regulations are well defined and reasonably enforced. Conversely, those mentally ill persons with poor inner controls frequently languish and founder when they discover that their disruptive behavior is ignored or tolerated.

In short, it usually does disturbed students no favor to regard their disruptive behavior as simply pitiful, entirely uncontrollable acts committed by pitiable people. Defining and enforcing reasonable codes of conduct for all students, including the mentally ill, is one of the college's principal vehicles for expressing its dignified concern for the rights of all members of the college community. In my view, to hold mentally ill students to a less dignified standard of conduct conveys, not genuine compassion, but a form of contempt toward their personal capabilities. In any case, complainants who fear that they will irreparably harm the disruptive mentally ill student through the use of discipline can be told by the mental health consultant that in many cases it is precisely the use of external controls, via disciplinary interventions, that will aid the student to restore his sense of inner equilibrium and behavioral control.

Obviously, colleges should attempt to make reasonable accommodations to the mentally and physically disabled student. For this reason, the mental health consultant can recommend to the staff that they adhere to the following guidelines: When a student requests special accommodations on the basis of a disability, the college may, if it wishes, request that the student substantiate the disability by providing to the college psychiatric or medical records that attest to that disability. Then, if the college is satisfied that the request for special accommodations is both reasonable and practicable, it probably should be granted. If the disabled student, whose request for special accommodations has already been granted, is also a disruptive student, and his disruptive behavior continues after he has received special accommodations, the college has a clear right to initiate disciplinary proceedings against the student. If, for whatever reason, the college deems the disabled student's petition for special accommodations to be unacceptable at the outset, it must show *good cause* before denying such a request. If the request is ultimately denied with *good cause* and the disabled student subsequently behaves in a disruptive manner, the student is subject to the same disciplinary procedures and sanctions as are all other disruptive students.

Finally, the mental health consultant obviously should not presuppose that a complainant's allegations against a supposedly disruptive student are either accurate or valid. There are college employees who, for whatever reasons, develop an unwavering animus for particular students and use their complaints against them to carry out personal vendettas. Sadistic and mendacious college personnel may deliberately lie and distort the facts when submitting complaints against students.

Other college employees—racists, ageists, sexists, homophobes—may use their xenophobic prejudices to denounce and punish students who are different from themselves. Therefore, when dealing with complainants whose testimonies seem dubious, the consultant may wish to either temporize or, if necessary, recommend that no disciplinary action be taken. If this recommendation serves only to engender in the complainant more resentment and vindictiveness toward the student, the consultant might find it necessary to recommend that the complainant and the student part ways immediately and completely without, hopefully, causing the student to incur any penalty whatsoever as a result.

The Role of Mediator

Because complainants and administrators sometimes have widely different and conflicting viewpoints regarding the causes and the degree of the seriousness of disruptive crises, they may tend to favor and pursue disparate courses of action to resolve these crises. The mental health consultant can assist them by identifying areas of disagreement and, as a mediator for the contending principals, offer recommendations about how their differences and the disruptive crisis, itself, can best be resolved.

The role of mediator between sometimes contentious principals is often a problematic and delicate assignment. In my own experience, it is quite easy for one or the other principal, in the heat of trying to resolve an acute crisis, to attempt to enlist the consultant as a loyal ally. The consultant must take particular care to point out that he is doing his best to evaluate the situation on its own merits, has no vested interest in favoring one position or person over the other, and has formulated his recommendations according to the information he has received from all available sources.

Despite the best of intentions and the most eloquent attestations of neutrality and disinterestedness, the mental health consultant, who often will be placed in the rancorous crossfire between acrimonious adversaries, will probably find himself alternately accused of being "anti-administration" or "anti-faculty" from time to time. It has been the former charge that has sometimes been leveled at me. I've taken it with a large grain of salt because I know it is untrue. Frequently, one's personal integrity requires one to take bold and unpopular positions that may rankle those who do not understand or agree with those positions. That is, for better or worse, the ineluctable onus of the person who chooses to serve as a college mental health consultant.

The Mental Health Consultant and the Law

Obviously, the mental health consultant, unless he or she happens to be an attorney, should not dispense legal advice to college personnel who are coping with disruptive students. Nevertheless, it behooves each consultant to learn as much as possible about those federal, state and municipal laws and education codes that govern and shape college life. The consultant should become especially conversant with the rather specialized field of university and college law, not only to ensure that his advice and recommendations fall within the parameters of the law, but also to be able to inform his consultees about the various laws and education codes that may affect the outcome of judicial and disciplinary proceedings that are undertaken to deal with the disruptive students they have reported.

Finally, and most importantly, the mental health consultant should use his knowledge of the law to ensure that both he and his consultees fulfill the requirements of procedural due process—the legal principles requiring that the student be given oral or written notice of the charges against him and, if he denies them, an explanation of the evidence the school authorities have and an opportunity to present his side of the story.

References

Amada, G. "Coping with the Disruptive College Student: A Practical Model." *Journal of American College Health*, 1992, March; Vol. 40.

May, R. "Boundaries and Voices in College Psychotherapy." *Journal of College Student Psychotherapy*, 1986, Winter; Vol. 1, No. 2.

Monahan, J. *Predicting Violent Behavior.* Beverly Hills: Sage Publications Inc., 1981.

Pavela, G. *The Dismissal of Students with Mental Disorders.* Asheville, N.C.: College Administration Publications, Inc., 1985.

The Disruptive College Student: Some Thoughts and Considerations

I thought I would begin by telling something about how I first became interested in the problem of the so-called disruptive college student. I became a director of a college mental health program in the early 1970s, at a time of much political ferment on campuses across the nation. College students, in particular, were disillusioned and discontented with the "crackpot, duplicitous" actions of those in high government places. Not surprisingly, some of their distrust spread and began to include individuals who held authoritative positions at their own colleges. As the director of psychological services, I frequently heard from students, who were otherwise quite trusting and friendly, that they believed their college's mental health service would probably be used from time to time as a vehicle for imposing institutional control over their social and political activities.

Although I sympathized with the basis of the concerns they voiced, I covertly pooh-poohed such suspicions—largely regarding them as the standard agitprop of alert, bright, and radical students—and remained blithely confident that I would not allow my program to be used for such illicit purposes.

Over the next several years, I discovered that my facile confidence would be unexpectedly and severely tested and even shaken by certain prevailing institutional forces at my college, especially when it came to the college's handling of disruptive students. At first, a rather slight trickle, but later a fairly great wave, of instructors and staff sought my help with students whose disruptive behavior was frightening, baffling, and stymieing them during the course of their workday.

I soon noticed that these petitions for help developed into a disquieting pattern. They almost always bore the following characteristics:

159

1. The instructor had already appealed to the college administration for help in dealing with the disruptive student and had come away feeling disappointed and disgruntled by the results.

2. The instructor, more often than not, had not effectively adhered to the principles of due process in responding to the allegedly disruptive student. That is, the instructor did not: apprise the student specifically enough about what was objectionable or unacceptable in his or her behavior or how it was in violation of a code of student conduct; did not adequately warn the student about the possible consequences of his or her actions; and, moreover, had not adequately documented the course of disruptive events leading up to the instructor's request for administrative intervention.

3. Frequently, the instructor, not always groundlessly, was preoccupied with the disruptive student's potential for violence and mayhem.

4. Almost invariably, the instructor, understandably desperate for a resolution of the disruptive crisis, asked me to make arrangements and undertake procedures to whisk the student, whom the instructor deemed to be both disruptive and psychologically disturbed, into psychotherapy.

After consulting with these instructors, I would, with the instructors' permission, usually contact the administrator who had been designated to handle the case. These consultations far too often revealed very disquieting tidings that closely paralleled those that had emerged in my consultations with instructors. Administrators were frequently unfamiliar with the basic tenets of due process and did not sufficiently address essential issues in the instructor's report of the allegedly disruptive student's behavior. Sometimes, the administrator unwarrantedly and brutally blamed the instructor for the disruptive crisis or cavalierly dismissed the instructor's petition for help out of hand.

In quite a number of cases, flagrantly disruptive students were permitted to remain in classes where they predictably continued to carry on their unending campaign of disruptiveness. Finally the administrators, in search of a *deus ex machina* with which to deliver the college from a social plague, frequently turned to me with a request (sometimes couched in rather bullying and coercive terms) to get the disruptive student off everyone's hands and cured of his or her antisocial behavior by directing the student into psychotherapy in our clinic—if necessary, on a mandatory basis.

As I attempted to grasp the full mosaic of factors that impeded the resolution of these disruptive cases, I discerned another, quite important, determinant of outcome. Administrators, perhaps feeling uncertain and timorous about the possible illegality of their own actions in handling complicated cases of disruption, wisely turned to the college attorney, who in turn conferred legal advice relative to the disposition of these cases. I could never have a reasonable objection to this practice, but I found that the process was often highly flawed, cumbersome, protracted, and fraught with serious pitfalls. Although my legal training has been confined to being a plaintiff in the small claims court, I do not hesitate to say that much of the legal advice proffered to college administrators by their attorneys is, at best, questionable and, at worst, dangerous.

Having taken some nasty pokes at and offended just about everyone imaginable, I cannot, in good conscience, exempt my own profession—mental health and psychotherapy—from criticism. As I struggled to deal with the importunate and sometimes coercive pressures that arose in cases dealing with disruptive students, I turned to some of my mental health colleagues at other colleges for counsel, support, and direction. For the most part, I did not like what I saw and heard. What I learned was that many counselors and therapists were treating nondangerous but disruptive students on a mandatory basis, the mandate usually emanating from an administrator who was directly in charge of the counseling or mental health program.

I also learned that, although therapists generally resented and harbored ethical objections to the quasi-disciplinary role that had been thrust upon them, they unwillingly, uncomplainingly, and often guiltily acquiesced to administrative edicts for mandatory counseling or therapy. In short, what I observed on many campuses was, in my estimation, the rank bastardization of my profession. This angered me, and because imposing mandatory therapy upon nondangerous, disruptive students continues to be prevalent, I am no less angry today than I was more than 20 years ago.

I would like to share some of the observations and conclusions I have formed, stumblingly and incrementally, during my tenure as both an administrator of a college psychological service and as a consultant to the campus community on matters related to the disruptive student.

Ordinarily, the staff of an on-campus psychological service can serve the campus community most effectively, not by cooperating or colluding in a plan to direct nondangerous disruptive students toward psychotherapy, whether voluntarily or not, but by assisting colleagues to understand the basic principles of due process. We can show them the value of establishing and making use of a legally sound code of student conduct as well as the potential value of using discipline as a corrective and rehabilitative intervention.

The almost universal resistance to reporting disruptive incidents and to using disciplinary measures to cope with them usually has little to do with a lack of technical know-how. Instead, it has practically everything to do with powerful emotional factors. Among these emotional factors are fear of physical or legal reprisals from disruptive students; fear of inflicting psychic pain upon others, especially upon students who are deemed to be psychologically fragile; and fear of being blamed by administrators for instigating or causing reported cases of disruption. A final factor is the unfortunate belief that discipline, even mild and patently warranted discipline, is inherently cruel, and worse, evil. I would therefore suggest that one of the primary and most worthwhile tasks of the consultant in assisting complainants in coping with disruptive students is to help them address and overcome their fears about using disciplinary measures to resolve disruptive crises.

My observations have also led me to conclude that mental health professionals and their colleagues on campus have too often and too excessively overvalued psychotherapy and underestimated disciplinary measures as a means of coping with disruptive students.

Except for those students who can be accurately assessed as posing an imminent danger to themselves or others, it is almost always inadvisable and counterproductive to require disruptive students to undergo mandatory psychiatric evaluations or mandatory psychotherapy as a substitute for justifiable and proportionate discipline. Naturally, in some cases the degree of danger cannot be intelligently assessed until a mandatory evaluation has taken place. If it is already clear that the student is not dangerous but is merely disruptive, however, therapy should be offered on a strictly voluntary basis.

Mandatory psychotherapy is objectionable on both therapeutic and ethical grounds. It is objectionable because it is intrinsically coercive and ordinarily is conducted on a nonconfidential basis. That is, someone in the administration will expect to know whether the student is in therapy, keeps appointments, and is benefiting from the treatment. Mandatory therapy frequently misleads the student into believing an untruth—that his or her mental health is what is at stake when he or she is behaving disruptively. What the student does not recognize is the simple truth that his or her *misconduct* is what is really at stake and is all that must be corrected.

Finally, I believe that mandatory psychotherapy forces a student to do something that no one in our profession would stand for if it were done to him or her: It forces the student to identify himself or herself as an emotionally disturbed or impaired person rather than as simply a disruptive person. I do not think that mental health professionals should countenance such questionable practices, except in cases where students are clearly a danger to themselves or to others.

College psychotherapists who undertake mandatory psychotherapy with nondangerous, disruptive students usually do so reluctantly and with ethical qualms. They frequently do it under duress or pressure, either overt or covert, from administrative sources. The psychotherapists' dilemma is that those administrators who request this coercive measure are often in control of the budgets and the policies that govern and determine the ultimate destiny of the psychological services. In this regard, I am reminded of two things.

One, a recent survey indicated that the majority of college counseling directors who responded reported that their centers undertook mandatory drug and alcoholism counseling with students even though they believed that this form of therapy was largely inadvisable and ineffective. Two, when I discussed this matter with a psychotherapist at a large and quite prestigious university about a year ago, he indicated that his program cooperated with an administrative requirement that dangerous and nondangerous disruptive students alike undergo at least one mandatory evaluative session. This therapist asked what I thought of this practice, and my reply was that I thought it stank, or words to that effect. His response suggested that he agreed with me, and then he said, "You must have a very different political situation on your campus." He is no doubt right.

The political situation on our campuses is not a static or immutable set of sometimes unacceptable conditions that must be stoically tolerated or endured. Therapists and consultants can and should be agents of change on campuses. If we determine that our services are being misused, corrupted, or bastardized, we should object to those practices and, to the best of our abilities, boldly offer alternative and more effective means for dealing with disruptive students. For example, we could advocate the effective use of due process procedures rather than mandatory psychotherapy as a remedy for disciplinary problems.

Students who are chronically or grossly disruptive are ordinarily extremely averse to therapy and are generally very poor candidates for therapy, which requires a certain introspective and impulse-control capability they do not have. Admittedly, this generalization has exceptions, but not so many, I think, as to cause us to be sanguine about the potential success of treating the chronically disruptive student. A therapist at an East Coast university has pointed out that many of these students are "externalizers" who are bent on acting out and have little use for sitting down with a therapist to explore their inner workings.

The requirement that disruptive students enter therapy as a condition of enrollment or re-enrollment is archaic, groundless, uncalled for, and should be abolished. Why? First, it is the student's behavior that is the root of the problem, not his or her putative psychological condition, whatever that may be. Second, forcing students into psychotherapy as a condition of enrollment or re-enrollment breeds justifiable resentment toward the therapist and the therapy. Even if it can be argued that some students ultimately benefit from mandatory treatment, these ends should not justify the means, at least not in our field of work. Finally, schools that ask students to bring letters from psychotherapists in the community attesting to their readiness to reenroll are engaging in a sham or charade. These letters can be secured or "purchased" practically anywhere by students, have virtually no predictive value, and are deliberately written ambiguously. Deliberately vague communications protect the attester from a lawsuit and confuse the reader, usually an administrator who is seeking a definitive declaration about whether the student will return to the campus, possibly kill someone, and put the college in legal jeopardy.

The primary purpose of requiring suspended disruptive students who are seeking re-enrollment to enter therapy and procure letters from therapists attesting to their readiness to return to the campus is not generally altruistic. This requirement usually has little to do with a genuine interest in helping the student attain a desirable state of mental health. Rather, it is usually based upon the illusionary hope that a therapist will be capable of making a flawless, omniscient prediction about the student's level of dangerousness.

If the student actually returns to the campus and wreaks havoc that results in a lawsuit, the school will somehow be off the hook because a psychological expert predicted that the student would pose no danger. This is why no right-minded therapist would ever write a truly definitive statement about a potentially disruptive student. For that matter, I doubt that such a declarative statement would ever protect a college from a lawsuit because, ultimately, the college must take legal responsibility for heeding the expert's advice.

The decision to allow re-enrollment of suspended disruptive students should not be based on psychiatric criteria or on the fact that the student is or is not in psychotherapy. The length of suspension should, instead, be based entirely upon the gravity of the student's offenses and the length of time that has transpired since suspension was last imposed. Common sense would suggest that the graver the offense, the lengthier the suspension.

When the student applies for re-admission, a committee or an administrator can review the student's violations of the code of conduct and determine whether the length of suspension is proportionate to the offenses. If the student is readmitted, an administrator should inform him or her at once that a repetition of those offenses or any other form of misconduct will be dealt with immediately and affirmatively. Because of the cumulative history of disruptive behavior, the student should also be told that further violations will probably result in an even longer period of suspension than that previously imposed.

Requiring therapy in this case is often based upon two fallacious notions. First is the belief that the student in therapy is demonstrating good faith by agreeing to be treated. This may be true. It may, on the other hand, be completely untrue. The student understands the requirements of the game and is willing to play it, at least until he or she appeases the college authorities and gets back into school. In this regard, I am reminded of a recent incident at my own college. An administrator who was fairly new to his job dealt with a disruptive student by imposing nine or ten conditions upon him, all of which seemed to me to be eminently humane and sensible. All but one, that is.

The final requirement was mandatory therapy in our clinic. I called the administrator, with whom I had had a friendly relationship, and explained to him that, from the inception of our program, we have not accepted mandatory referrals, except for students who were deemed to be a danger to themselves or to others. Because this student clearly did not fall into that category, we could not accept such a referral.

When the administrator asked why, I explained that we did not consider such referrals to be either ethical or effective. He asked my advice. I told him to call or write the student immediately and tell him that all the other conditions must still be met but that he was not required to receive therapy, although he had the option to do so if he wished. In other words, he could refuse therapy with complete impunity. Later in the day, I noticed that the student had already scheduled an appointment with me. The next day, after receiving the dean's letter with my recommended addendum about eliminating mandatory therapy from the disciplinary menu, the student called and canceled his appointment.

The second fallacious notion is that all disruptive students who enter therapy will eventually learn something about what drives them to behave disruptively and will thereby cease to be disruptive. Perhaps this is true for some students, but surely many (if not most) of the seriously disruptive students who enter therapy will have great difficulty learning anything there. This is especially true when we consider their resentment that the therapy is mandatory. Many such students may very well continue to be disruptive, with or without therapy. The one murder that took place on my own campus, about 12 years ago, was committed by a man who was in psychotherapy at the time that he carried out his crime. As we all know, therapy is no surefire antidote for antisocial or disruptive behavior.

Mental health consultants can gain an important and sometimes decisive advantage by not providing treatment to disruptive students but by making recommendations to complainants based upon their observations. Admittedly, the consultants' ultimate recommendations will be based on a filtering process that begins with another person's subjective and perhaps even highly distorted perceptions of a disruptive crisis. If consultants are competent at using those interviewing techniques that normally allow them to arrive at the truth or near truth, they will be entirely free to state their opinions about the student to the complainant and to anyone else who is relevantly concerned, including an administrator. Why? Because the consultant's information is not based on a confidential psychotherapeutic contact with the student. Therefore, he or she is free, obviously within the usual bounds of professional discretion and with the utmost regard for the rights and safety of the complainant, to discuss the student with others without regard for the ordinary strictures of confidentiality that apply to psychotherapy.

If, by coincidence, the consultant is already familiar with the allegedly disruptive student through therapeutic encounters (as has happened to me on occasion), that fact should not be disclosed to the complainant. The information acquired in therapy sessions should not be a basis for the consultant's recommendations to the complainant, to the extent that this is realistically possible. An obviously sticky situation arises if the allegedly disruptive student is currently in treatment with the consultant. The consultant should then tell the student that he is consulting with the complainant and inform the student of the recommendations being made. Ideally, the consultant and the student's therapist should not be the same person. However, in some clinics and at certain times, such an arrangement may not be achievable.

In the matter of college attorneys, I think it behooves us to recognize that some college attorneys give very bad and even dangerous legal advice to colleges—as, for example, when they recommend against imposing strong disciplinary sanctions on demonstrably dangerous students. Why? Clearly, some college attorneys are simply bad attorneys, and a few are even bad people (as is the case in all professions, as Shaw suggested when one of his characters opined that all professions were conspiracies against the laity). Such attorneys obviously should not be in this line of work. In addition, many college attorneys have not been adequately trained in college and university law, a field of legal specialization that requires considerable training and experience.

To complicate matters further, many college attorneys spend little time on the college campus and therefore do not acquire an intimate, working knowledge of those institutional dynamics that can contribute to the evolution and possible resolution of some disruptive crises. An additional complication arises when college attorneys engage in the practice of what I have come to call jurisprudential roulette. Although I may be jaundiced and too cynical, I have often had the impression that the attorney's final opinion on complicated cases of disruption was formulated largely on the basis of a cold calculation regarding the potential litigiousness of the student. When disruptive students were, indeed, regarded as highly litigious, the legal recommendation disproportionately favored some form of leniency toward them. This is the grim game of jurisprudential roulette, with the attorney, more often than not, betting on the student, rather than the complainant, as the more likely principal to sue the college.

If I am correct in my observation and this practice continues, I foresee a time when college employees will begin to hire their own attorneys to litigate cases against their own colleges on the grounds that the colleges have not sufficiently protected their rights and safety. What can we, as mental health consultants, do about this situation? I think it is incumbent on us to learn as much as possible about college and university law and how it impinges on cases of student disruption. This is obviously not to arrogate to ourselves the role of college legal counsel. It is, rather, to keep an intelligent eye on the actions and recommendations of our legal brethren and to assist those complainants with whom we consult about disruptive students to meet the essential requirements of due process.

I would like to end on an optimistic note. In my own experience, I have seen great changes and improvements in the ways my own college has handled cases of student disruptiveness. Clearly, we and most other colleges have a long way to go. I have been told on pretty good authority that I have had much to do with some of the positive changes that have taken place at City College of San Francisco in dealing with disruptive students, and I suppose I can take justifiable pride in that fact. It has not been easy. There have been many serious disjunctions and misunderstandings between administrators and members of our mental health staff. Over time, our staff and I have been able fully to uphold our ethical and professional standards, and, I truly believe, we have come to be greatly respected for our pride, our accomplishments, and our moral courage. Speaking of moral courage, I wish to go on record as saying that I know of no personal quality that is more essential than this if one is to serve as a consultant on matters related to the problem of the disruptive college student.

PUBLISHER'S NOTE

A vignette illustrating many of the principles and opinions Dr. Amada has written about appears in his book *Coping With the Disruptive College Student: A Practical Model*; College Administration Publications, Asheville, North Carolina, 1994. (www.collegepubs.com)

You Can't Please All of the People All of the Time: Normative Institutional Resistances to College Psychological Services

The prevalence of on-campus psychological services throughout the country attests to the sympathetic support they receive from key constituencies—faculties, administrators, students, and boards of governors—at their respective institutions. However, on all college campuses there are also normative institutional resistances to the delivery of psychological services with which such programs must continually contend. This article describes those institutional resistances in discrete form using examples from the experiences of the author and some of his colleagues in various parts of the country.

The prevalence of mental health programs on college campuses throughout the nation perforce testifies to the fact that they enjoy at their respective institutions sympathetic constituencies—faculties, administrators, students, and boards of governors—that support their establishment and continuity. The reasons for this support are fairly self-evident.

Students support psychological services because the programs provide timely and vital assistance, usually at an affordable cost, that enables them to resolve their personal crises and get on with the task of successfully fulfilling their academic objectives. Faculties welcome on-campus psychological services because they are dedicated to educating and enriching the lives of students and recognize the significant role that psychological services can play in fostering and safeguarding the educational welfare of their academic charges. Additionally, it is often a decided relief to many college instructors to know that they can readily refer emotionally troubled students for help to trained professionals on their own campus rather than be required to undertake this often time-consuming and daunting task themselves.

Administrators support psychological services for many of the same reasons. As a professional group dedicated to administering institutional programs and implementing educational policies that advance the welfare and interests of students, they discern and respect the value of on-campus psychological services in meeting the personal and educational needs of students. As well, they too recognize that the pressures and exigencies of their own professional assignments, especially when they are required to deal with emotionally disturbed or disruptive students, can be alleviated and buffered through the intervention of the on-campus psychological service.

Boards of governors, when they are not overly beset by fiscal apprehensions that tend to eclipse all considerations save the need to trim institutional costs through campuswide retrenchment, will support the institution of an on-campus psychological service because they recognize that such programs have a stabilizing and reassuring effect upon the entire academic community.

Yet, despite the widespread support for on-campus psychological services, it would be patently self-serving and Pollyannaish for those who administer or serve in those programs to assume that there is universal enthusiasm for or advocacy of the psychological service on their respective campuses. A certain degree of wariness, skepticism, and even outright hostility toward college mental health services is expectable, commonplace, and multiformed on most campuses.

Among certain students, distrust of the campus psychological service may take the form of their eschewing assistance from the program, even when they are in the midst of an acute personal crisis. Among certain faculty, an attitude of leeriness or contrariness may be evidenced in their stolid unwillingness to refer students to the program and, in some instances, in their tendency to "bad-mouth" the service to the campus community, including students. Among certain administrators, a hostile or oppositional attitude toward the mental health program might surface in the form of a subjective reluctance to allocate adequate funds and personnel to the service or in an attempt to impose an administrative policy that is inimical to the interests of the program. Likewise, a board of governors may exhibit its opposition to the psychological service by severely defunding or, in extreme cases, entirely jettisoning the program. This urge to defund the college mental health service may be especially high-spirited and prevalent at academic institutions where the emotional or psychological life of students tends to be devalued and "even the scant resources devoted to psychological services are thought to be wasted" (Henry, 1986, p. 46).

In this article I will delineate and describe certain expectable, spontaneous, protean and, in my view, quite normative institutional resistances to college mental health services that generally manifest themselves on the college campus. In my own experience, these resistances are usually most acute and intractable in the earliest phases of the mental health service's historical development, during which time both its staff and the nature of the program's services may be perceived, especially within the context of the general educational milieu, as unorthodox, inscrutable, alien, intrusive and even dangerously threatening by some administrators, instructors, and students. Because these resistances, much like the psychological resistances of clients in psychotherapy, are largely dynamic and animated by complex intrapsychic and institutional forces, they are subject to change as trust and familiarity with the mental health program develop.

Of course, there will always be some individuals on the college campus who will harbor, seemingly on principle, quite intransigent and permanent resistances to the mental health service, no matter how familiar they become with the program or how long they have dealings with it. Let us now review some of these normative institutional resistances.

DISAGREEMENT WITH PSYCHOLOGICAL SERVICES' PHILOSOPHY, PRACTICES, POLICIES AND ETHICAL STANDARDS

Two quite polarized perceptions of mental health services may develop on the college campus, sometimes serenely cohabiting the mind of a single individual. At one end of the perceptual spectrum, the psychological service is regarded as the font of instantaneous solutions and remedies for whatever ails the campus. At the other end of the same spectrum the mental health service is viewed as an insidious, capriciously clandestine, and even rather renegade organizational entity. Viewed from this latter perspective, mental health services are sometimes regarded as the champion of sexual libertinism, irreligiosity, sinister clandestinity, and indiscriminate nonconformity. In particular, the policy of confidentiality which the service maintains is considered to be irrefutable evidence of renegade and nefarious goings-on within the program.

Those who maintain and protect the policy of confidentiality (a policy seen through the jaundiced eye as a hollow, shady and unnecessary form of secrecy) may, consequently, be viewed as amoral, anarchistic, mutinous and, perhaps worst of all, elitist. Additionally, if the policy of confidentiality is new and rather unique within the college setting it can be especially difficult to explain and justify to outsiders who cannot or wish not to accept its rationales. Machiavelli seems to have understood and appreciated this predicament well when he wrote, "It must be considered that there is nothing more difficult to carry out, nor more doubtful of success, nor more dangerous to handle, than to initiate a new order of things" (Machiavelli, 1952, p. 49).

An example from my own experience will illustrate this point. In one of my earliest meetings with a member of the college Counseling Department (an administratively separate department from the Mental Health Program), a counselor queried . . . "why is it that you don't want to talk with us, or won't tell us anything about what you do in the Mental Health Program?" In response to my question about why he believed our staff did not want to talk with counselors (a belief that was entirely belied by the initiative and time I took to arrange and attend this meeting), the counselor stated that the policy of confidentiality indicated that our staff were self-servingly worried that their professional colleagues would discover "something about how you really work with students." He added that he saw no particular reason for a policy of confidentiality other than to provide a "cover" for professional improprieties. The counselor did not spell out what he meant by the word "improprieties." However, I believe he was implying that the staff of the Mental Health Program were clandestinely fostering antisocial and aberrant behavior in students or, were simply attempting to hide their own professional incompetency from their colleagues.

Another imbroglio over confidentiality occurred at a large Southwestern university with, unfortunately, more disastrous consequences. Soon after a new director of the psychological service was hired he received a directive from an administrator requesting information about a student he believed to be a client of the service. The director informed the administrator that the clinic's policy of confidentiality precluded the disclosure of students' utilization of the program. The director was then informed by the administrator that his predecessor had had no such compunctions about disclosing this kind of information. The administrator explicitly and directly demanded the establishment of a policy of having this question answered about any student at any time—or, more accurately, he demanded the continuance of such a policy, if he was to be believed when he asserted that the previous director of the Counseling Center had cooperated in this matter.

The director, sensing that safety issues might be raised by the administrator, took the initiative to point out that, in considering the welfare of others, "no news was good news," i.e., the administrator could rest assured that if a duty to protect (or a duty-to-warn) situation arose, the director would legally breach confidentiality and apprise appropriate individuals (which might, depending on the circumstances, include the administrator). Indeed, the administrator offered no real rationale whatsoever for why he wanted the "disclosure-on-request" policy instituted.

To the contrary, he placed the burden of proof on the counseling director by demanding that he defend his refusal. For example, he asked "what possible harm" could be caused by agreeing to this policy, implying that the refusal was a slap in his face (i.e., the director did not personally trust him with this information). In the end, the director simply pointed out that he could not comply with the administrator's request for such disclosures.

The administrator, offended and infuriated by what he considered to be an act of crass insubordination, began a remorseless campaign of pressure and intimidation, all with the evident purpose of coercing the director into abandoning the policy of confidentiality and thereby relinquishing control of the program to himself. The harassment from the administrator became so severe that the director decided to hire, at his own expense, an attorney who was a specialist in mental health legal issues in order legally to defend his professional rights. The attorney sent a letter to the director, who forwarded a copy to the administrator, in which the legal requirement of confidentiality was explained and further pointed out that his client's non-compliance with this requirement could cost him his license and his career. The letter also wisely pointed out the liability risks to the institution if it coerced the director into doing something illegal or unethical.

Despite the distinct efficacy of the legal points contained in the attorney's letter, these arguments didn't faze the administrator in the least and, dismissing them out of hand, he went on insisting that the director submit to his demands for disclosures.

When it became obvious that the administrator had begun to regard the director's ethical stance with such repugnance that he would next proceed with attempts to have the director fired, the director found it necessary to convey the fact that he would deal with a dismissal by filing a wrongful termination suit against the college. Although the specter of a lawsuit brought threats of termination to an abrupt halt, the administrator's usurpatory onslaughts did not abate and eventually the work environment became so hostile and untenable that the director was forced to resign. In retrospect, he views this administrator's actions primarily as an attempt to test the "new kid on the block" by trying, immitigably, to wrest control of the counseling program away from him. The former director is fully convinced that had he acquiesced to the administrator's initial demands, other, equally unreasonable demands, would have followed in their wake.

Another scuffle over the policy of confidentiality, also with unfortunate consequences, took place several decades ago at Brandeis University (Hanfmann, 1978). An "anxious" administrator wanted to know if some very disturbed students were being seen by the psychological service, evidently for the purpose of keeping a close eye on them in the dormitories The psychological consultant caved in to the dean's importunate requests for confidential information about these students. That very day, over a few drinks, the dean's assistant divulged the dean's "victory" over the consultant in the presence of some students. Although news of this disclosure spread quickly, only the self-restraint and goodwill of the program's allies saved it from early extinction. It should be noted, however, that, subsequent to this incident, the psychological service suffered a decline in student utilization for the first and only time in its ten-year existence.

One final example will suffice. A therapist at a large Southern university was called by an administrator who wished to know if Jane Doe had used the program. The therapist felt that she had been placed "in a bind" and although she did not wish to reveal confidential information, she also did not wish to alienate the administrator by responding in a non-committal manner. She finally decided to disclose the fact that the student had had a few sessions in the psychological service, justifying the decision to herself on the basis of the dean's recognized "good judgment and good intentions." Based on my own experience with such incidents, I would have definitely and respectfully demurred to the dean's request-keeping in mind that the proverbial road to hell is often paved with such good intentions—and offered to assist the dean in some other, more ethically sound, manner.

In the final analysis, the mere fact that someone has utilized a psychological service connotes or implies nothing, absolutely nothing, about that person's character, trustworthiness, potential for dangerousness, or anything else. If the dean thought otherwise, he was clearly laboring under an unfortunate illusion and perhaps the therapist could have best served him by somehow disabusing him of that illusion.

Perhaps a caveat regarding this matter is appropriate at this point. College psychotherapists who are approached by colleagues who wish to know if particular students have utilized the psychological service, and wish to ascertain only that fact, should, I believe, consider the strong possibility that the inquirer is mentally attempting to mold that fact into some Procrustean bed of prejudices and stereotypes about students who use mental health services. Common stereotypes regarding student/clients of psychological services are the beliefs that they are more unstable, more prone to acts of violence and, in general, more untrustworthy than their academic counterparts. Since there is no evidence to substantiate these beliefs, it is generally incumbent upon college psychotherapists respectfully to deny requests for such disclosures rather than unwittingly countenance a will-o'-the-wispish pursuit of confidential information that only serves to reinforce pernicious social prejudices about psychotherapy clients.

A far better procedural alternative, I think, is to discuss with inquirers of confidential information why they are seeking such data in order to determine whether disclosure is truly warranted or whether the inquirer's fears and uncertainties regarding the student under question need to be carefully teased out and addressed. In my view, college psychotherapists who reluctantly accede to requests for confidential information from administrators do so mostly out of fear of these superordinate individuals, commonly rationalizing their own acts of ethical compromise by characterizing the administrators' intrusive behavior as innocuous and well-intentioned.

Most often, the psychotherapist who discloses confidential information to an administrator is committing an act of disservice both to the student (who, unknowingly, is being betrayed) and the administrator (who does not have his or her underlying concerns and fears about the student adequately addressed and resolved).

THE ROLE OF PSYCHOLOGICAL DEPRIVATION AND RIVALRY

The provision of mental health services to students sometimes meets with the intense ambivalence of college personnel. The staff of a college, although principally dedicated to fostering the welfare of students, at times harbors rivalrous feelings toward them, both consciously and unconsciously. When the mental health service extends help to students, these rivalrous emotions may become intensified. As a result, the program is then perceived as the "bad" parent who "plays favorites," i.e., one-sidedly nurtures "undeserving siblings" (the student clients) and at the same time deprives the "deserving sibling" (the staff member). One writer on the subject referred to this phenomenon as "hysterical identification with the fortunate rival," that is, with a person whom another individual envies and whose place he wishes to occupy (Fenichel, 1945).

Since the academic institution obviously cannot meet all the emotional and social needs of its employees, college staff occasionally turn to the mental health service for emotional sustenance. At times, the program can successfully meet the emotional needs of the distressed colleague. However, because the service is primarily designed for students, college staff sometimes feel emotionally deprived and excluded by the program, since their own psychological needs must be deferred and met elsewhere. This sense of emotional deprivation may become, in time, a basis for resentment and even virulent opposition toward the mental health service.

Several examples will illustrate this point. I have been introduced to many classes, usually by instructors who were enthusiastic supporters of the mental health service, in the following manner: "Dr. Amada works for a fine program. Don't forget, the program is right here on campus and very available to meet your psychological needs. You know, when I had to receive my own private psychotherapy, I had to pay a lot of money. You students are lucky, you don't pay anything (except a modest health fee). And, unlike my own situation, it's right here, at your convenience." In my experience, instructors who openly acknowledge and express such envy generally are able to maintain a positive attitude toward the mental health service. However, when such feelings are repressed or denied, they may fester and eventually find ill-disguised expression in oppositional attitudes toward the program.

For example, in a meeting with the Counseling Department, a counselor whom I hardly knew unexpectedly challenged the validity of an on-campus mental health service. There was, at that moment, little opportunity for a constructive dialogue between us, so I arranged to meet privately with him afterward. Later, in the privacy of his office, he enunciated his reasons for opposing the mental health service. He remarked caustically, "Your program coddles students. You give them more help than they want or need. This is a college, not a grade school. These students are adults and must stand on their own two feet. *I didn't get such help when I went to college, and I got by. Why should they get more than I got?"*

This counselor's sense of personal deprivation, rage, and envy was glaringly triggered by the psychological "coddling" of students by the program. His opposition to the service, when viewed in this light, was therefore understandable and inevitable.

Another example of the role psychological deprivation plays as a resistance to psychological services took place in a meeting of the entire student health staff, including several nurses. One of the psychotherapists had described a highly successful meeting which she had held with a group of student peer counselors. Her comments included specific examples of how she had effectively assisted the peer counselors during their meeting. At the conclusion of her remarks, one of the nurses responded by saying, "You know, I wish you were able to do for us what you just did for the peer counselors. We need that kind of help here too. I feel jealous." And sorely deprived, too, no doubt.

THE NEED FOR PERFECTION: THE "EMPEROR'S CLOTHES" SYNDROME

The mere existence of an on-campus mental health service is emblematic of the intrinsic and unavoidable imperfections and deficiencies of the academic institution. At times certain college administrators, especially those of an authoritarian bent, are wont to minimize or conceal the imperfections and dysfunctional aspects of their institutions from their Boards of Governors, students and the public-at-large. Although they may not necessarily depict their schools in Utopian terms, authoritarian administrators may only grudgingly acknowledge that their schools are beset by many profound, complex, and even insoluble problems. A major reason for this concealment and dissimulation is a dread that they will be held personally responsible for unsatisfactory results, even when the prospective untoward outcomes which cause their concern are actually outside their sphere of influence.

A mental health service can be perceived, especially by those preoccupied with the public image of the institution, as a clarion pronouncement that "all is not well" on the college campus. The program bespeaks the fact that there are dissatisfied, troubled and even severely disturbed students attending the college. A logical inference may be drawn from the mere existence of a mental health service that students are not having all of their psychological or emotional needs met elsewhere on the campus, such as in classrooms, academic counseling sessions, or through athletic activities.

This inference may affront the college administrator who strives to maintain an image of institutional near-perfection. As a result, he or she may then suffer irrational fears of being singled out for criticism over neglecting the academic and emotional needs of students.

If the mental health program demonstrates its pith and value by identifying and assisting dissatisfied and unhappy students, and the college administration demonstrates its pith and value by documenting and publicizing how well satisfied and contented are its students, a perceptual and even interpersonal conflict may ensue. The college administration may then attempt to disprove the contention that appreciable numbers of students are in need of psychological help. One means of achieving this end is to oppose the establishment or growth of a mental health service.

If, as a result, the psychological service is eliminated or reduced in size and effectiveness, the administration can then argue, deductively, that since students seem to be surviving the program's curtailment quite well, there is evidently little need for extensive psychological services on campus. The administrative emperor can then continue to wear the clothes of indefectibility, while keeping his or her regal fingers crossed that no incident occurs that will betray the institution's grandiose illusions and cover-up.

At my own college, over twenty years ago, two authors published an article based on a health survey of the student population. The findings of the survey suggested that the students generally suffered from a considerable number of physical, social and psychological difficulties, many of which were serious. The article was quoted in a local newspaper. Soon after, one of the authors received a telephone call from the Chancellor-Superintendent of the college, who proceeded to charge him with needlessly sullying the image of the college. He was also told that his research was unscientific and his findings unfounded and inaccurate. The verbal onslaught ended with the accusation that the entire matter "made me look bad." Although this Chancellor-Superintendent might be regarded as hypersensitive, his image-conscious behavior, I believe, is not far from the norm for many of those who occupy high administrative positions in academia.

THE FEAR OF PERSONAL EXPOSURE

The college psychological service is often perceived, with some degree of validity, as a pipeline to otherwise secret information about the inner workings of the institution. Because the divulgence of private and sometimes highly controversial matters is often psychotherapeutic, and is protected by a policy of confidentiality, the psychological service becomes a willing receptacle for many of the inner secrets of the college.

In all colleges there are varying degrees of indiscreet or unprofessional behavior, as well as outright delinquent conduct, among the staff. Sometimes sexual peccadilloes, for example, conflict with the role of the professional academician. The psychological service learns (or is believed to learn) of many of these matters through its intensive interviews with students. Of course, in some instances, students construct fanciful imaginings about the misconduct of college personnel which are obviously without foundation in reality. In other instances, students present indisputable proof of the errant behavior of the staff.

Occasionally, one can recognize the gnawing distrust which the psychological service induces in the college community by its willingness to learn the "secrets" of students. For example, I have many times been asked by instructors such questions as, "I guess you hear a lot of stories about how students don't like us or feel messed up by us, huh? " I normally answer such questions by truthfully saying that students generally speak to us in positive terms about their instructors. Nevertheless, to the extent that certain college personnel consider themselves guilty of unprofessional conduct, they may suspect that the psychological service is the recipient of information which is potentially damaging to their careers. Such suspicions may create irrational fears of exposure by the psychological service which, in turn, may become a basis for resistance to the psychological service itself.

For many years, until his retirement, one of the most venomous and trouble-making opponents of the psychological service was a colleague who had sexually exploited several coeds by convincing them that he could single-handedly bar them, if he wished, from a professional program in which they desired enrollment. A few of his victims became clients of the psychological service in an attempt to recover from their trauma. Although they were encouraged by their therapists to report the culprit, they refused to do so out of fear of public exposure and reprisal. In at least one case, the victim had told this man that she was seeing a college therapist in order to deal with the pain and harm he had caused her. Although this predatory man may have had many other reasons for opposing the psychological service, I had little doubt that he feared our service primarily because he understood that sooner or later we might become the long-tongued conduit through which he would be exposed. Unfortunately, despite our repeated attempts to solicit affidavits from these victimized women, their refusal to report this predator allowed him eventually to retire from the college with impunity.

TERRITORIALITY

It is common for those who work in modern organizations to regard their professional facilities and prerogatives as the amenities of their own personal fiefdom (Downs, 1967). As a result, there is always a degree of concern about territorial encroachment. Some of this concern is over the possible misappropriation of physical territory. This may be accompanied by a fear that others within the organization, especially those with superior ambitions and abilities, will provide services that will invalidate or replace their own professional services.

Clearly, mental health services have no legitimate monopoly in carrying out the mission of meeting the emotional or psychological needs of students. Students' emotional needs are constantly and effectively dealt with by a wide and diverse range of college personnel throughout the campus. Many instructors and administrators valuably spend considerable amounts of time with students who wish to discuss their personal concerns. Obviously, not all students who feel emotionally upset are suitable candidates for formal psychotherapeutic services. Many, quite sensibly, prefer to share their most intimate concerns with instructors or administrators whom they already know and trust, rather than turn to a psychotherapist who is a complete stranger to them.

Nevertheless, on many college campuses there are instructors and administrators who tend to fear that the psychological service will erode or usurp their prerogatives to engage students in discussions of a personal nature. Conversely, college staff may also fear that, by engaging students in intimately personal conversations, they are encroaching upon and violating the prerogatives of college psychotherapists.

For example, it was not long ago that I was called by a counselor in another department who asked if it was permissible for her to conduct a personal counseling group for students who suffered from social shyness. I asked why she needed my permission to undertake such a worthwhile project. She indicated that the Chairman of her department thought it advisable to "clear" it with me since the program was akin to those conducted by the psychological service and therefore might be regarded as competitive and interloping. I, of course, told her that there was always room for more human services on campus and that she need not, in the future, clear such programs through me. And I sincerely wished her good luck with the new endeavor.

The concerns which some segments of the college community harbor that the psychological service will devour their professional prerogatives to intervene psychologically with students are not always without basis. For example, an instructor was consulted by one of his students who was in serious conflict with one of her parents. His first inclination was to talk extensively and painstakingly with the student about her concerns. In a short time, the student's problems grew worse, despite (or because of) the instructor's assiduous but floundering assistance. At that juncture, the instructor turned to me for help.

I told the instructor that I would be willing to help the student directly. When asked my opinion as to what role he should maintain with the student, I suggested that he support her involvement in psychotherapy and attempt to focus his discussions with her upon academic matters. This appeared to be satisfactory to him. The instructor referred the student to me and after I had seen her twice, she had a serious clash with her parents. She fled from home, traveled to the city in which the instructor lived and called him in a state of desperation. She had no money or shelter for the evening.

What the instructor did in response to this student's crisis is, I believe, highly relevant to the point under discussion. Rather than call me to consult about how we might best proceed (I am, as he knew, easily reached through my answering service), he discarded our agreement by offering the student personal advice. He recommended that she seek shelter in a nearby hostel. The student followed his advice, went to the hostel, and attached herself there to a man who had exhibited an immediate interest in her.

The student submissively left the hostel with this man later in the evening, ostensibly to see a movie. After a long, meandering walk, he led her to a darkened side street where he raped her. In a subsequent talk with the instructor he admitted, without prompting from me, that he should have consulted me before advising the student that traumatic evening. This example illustrates the resistance which some college personnel have to relinquishing to the psychological service certain prerogatives to attend to the emotional needs of students, even when such relinquishment may be necessary.

There are instances when the psychological service may be called upon to usurp the prerogatives of other college personnel, despite the inadvisability of such action. For example, I participated, with several instructors, a dean, and a counselor, in a conference which was called to determine whether a dental hygiene student should be retained in that program. Although I did not know the student, based upon the reports of the other participants, I recommended strongly that she be dropped from the program and be given an opportunity to graduate by taking courses in other programs. This student had a positive, long-standing relationship with the counselor, who recommended that she be retained in the program. My recommendation, however, was enthusiastically endorsed by the instructors, who viewed her work as irretrievably substandard, and eventually they adopted it.

The discussion next turned to the subject of how tactfully to inform the student of the adverse decision and the need for someone to commiserate with her expected disappointment. One of the instructors urged that I undertake that unsavory responsibility. I immediately noticed that the counselor grimaced at this suggestion. I replied that the counselor had far better credentials than I for such an assignment since he knew the student well and she trusted him. With some relief, I thought, the counselor eagerly volunteered to talk with the student. He and I left the conference on positive terms with each other, despite our contrary recommendations.

This example illustrates how a psychological service may be viewed as a threat to the professional prerogatives of a colleague. Although fears based upon territorial issues may sometimes be exaggerated and unfounded, the staff of the psychological service may give their colleagues justifiable cause for territorial worries if they truly disregard, disrespect or trespass upon the professional prerogatives of others.

ECONOMIC CONSIDERATIONS

Obviously, all colleges set budgets for their various programs with finite financial resources. The funding of a psychological service, in particular, can present highly idiosyncratic challenges to a college administration. First, unlike many academic programs, it is usually impossible to offer ironclad proof of the cost-effectiveness of a mental health service. The inability to measure precisely the cost-effectiveness of a psychological service may then lead to the belief that the service is nothing more than a costly luxury or frill.

Second, even when vigorous attempts seem successful in establishing economic justifications for a psychological service, such as its ability to increase student retention, it is not difficult for opponents of the service to adduce seemingly cogent arguments that can debunk and erase these justifications in a trice. For example, in the 1980s a Midwestern college eliminated the post of a clinical psychologist held for over twenty years. Since this was the only clinical assignment on the campus at the time, the elimination of this post brought about the demise of all psychological services at the college.

In a personal communication with this author, the psychologist informed me that the Superintendent of the college was recruited to the campus expressly for the purpose of cutting and eliminating the costs of instructional and student services programs. Since, in the opinion of the psychologist, the Superintendent had a non-humanistic background and philosophy, it took him little time to target the psychological service for total elimination. Despite glowing testimonials from students who publicly extolled the many achievements of this gifted psychologist at a board meeting, the Board of Governors (some of whom, ironically, had children who themselves had received invaluable psychotherapy services from this psychologist) summarily ratified the Superintendent's recommendation to eliminate the psychological service.

Although the psychologist was protected by tenure and therefore was able to remain at the college in an instructional assignment, the gaping cavity of unavailable psychological services that was left behind by this reassignment was viewed by many as nothing less than tragic. It was apparently small vindication to those who suffered from this injustice that the Superintendent quickly fell into extreme disrepute with his colleagues, was actually jeered at by them in public gatherings, and soon thereafter left the campus, having served the shortest tenure of any Superintendent in the history of the college. His role, as mandated by the Board of Governors, was unquestionably one of hatchet man and in the wake of his detrimental handiwork the psychological service was permanently amputated from the array of programs provided by the college.

THE ROLE OF DISAPPOINTMENT
WITH ONE'S OWN PSYCHOTHERAPY

Certain members of the staff of a college may regard the mental health service with distrust and trepidation due to their own unfortunate prior experience with psychotherapy. Because psychotherapy is an intricate intense process of interaction between two or more complex personalities, even the best method of treatment does not necessarily produce satisfactory results, at least not immediately. Mental health practitioners are continually confronted with the doleful accounts of many clients who regularly report their dissatisfactions and disappointments with their therapy and their therapist. To a degree, these accounts may be distorted and exaggerated, or they may be quite natural manifestations of a painful psychological process which is intrinsically fraught with periodic disillusionment.

On the other hand, as most candid therapists will readily admit, psychotherapeutic failures may also result from therapists' blunders that stem from narcissistic, erotic and sadomasochistic countertransferences [Robertiello and Schoenewolf (1987)]. Flaws in the psychotherapist's training or personality can interfere with or perhaps even destroy a patient's considerable potential for psychological growth and improvement. A myopic or uncharitable psychotherapist may self-servingly attribute all cases of psychotherapeutic failure to his patients' "resistances" to personal change and growth.

During my tenure as an administrator of a college psychological service I have detected that some college personnel assumed an almost immediate belligerence or aversion toward the very concept of an on-campus psychological service. In my later dealings with them or some of their intimates on the campus, I discovered that some of these individuals had previously suffered serious personal crises in the past and, in their view, had been treated shabbily by the mental health professionals they had consulted at the time. In most instances, I could not clearly perceive whether their bitter and antagonistic attitudes were the result of the gross mishandling of their personal difficulties by therapists or were more the consequence of their own regrettable inability to derive benefit from the services which were extended to them.

Whatever the causes for their abortive attempts to acquire beneficial psychological services to deal with their own psychological crises, some college personnel will immediately and inevitably identify the college psychological service with those other "unfit" therapists who, in their view, so badly disserved them. This identification can become a potent factor in engendering strong resistances to the psychological service itself.

TRANSFERENTIAL EXPECTATIONS

A psychological service, especially one that is regarded as a reliable authoritative resource on the campus, may induce perceptible transference reactions among certain college personnel. As a result, the program may activate in these individuals strong infantile wishes which were originally harbored in relation to the significant figures of one's childhood. For example, it is not unusual to detect indications in some co-workers of a genuine conviction that the mental health staff have omniscient and omnipotent powers. A corollary of this conviction is the magical belief that those who practice psychotherapy can actually "see through" others. Naturally, such beliefs can cause one to feel psychologically transparent and highly vulnerable in his relations with a college psychotherapist. As one authority on the subject has pointed out, the tendency to view a therapist as an omnipotent parent is one of the most powerful resistances that confronts the work of a therapist (Strean, 1990).

The "parental" aura which often surrounds a college mental health program may incite highly charged emotions towards its staff. Infantile longings and fears may cause segments of the college community to perceive the program as a paragon of perfection and beneficence. As well, there may also be an underlying contempt which accompanies such a distorted viewpoint, and this contempt sometimes surfaces when the psychological service reveals its disappointing shortcomings and imperfections.

The transference attitudes which are animated by a psychological service can have many and sometimes subtle implications for the interpersonal relationships which develop between its staff and the rest of the college community. For example, college psychotherapists may be approached on an interpersonal basis as if they were larger-than-life, all-knowing and bounteous personages. In this case, they may be treated with a strong degree of adulation and obsequiousness. This places immeasurable interpersonal hardships upon college psychotherapists who may feel it incumbent upon themselves to repeatedly and even ostentatiously give evidence of their own self-doubts and weaknesses in order to demonstrate their mere humanness.

PREJUDICES AND AVERSIONS REGARDING "MENTAL ILLNESS" AND PSYCHOLOGICAL DEFECTIBILITY

The mere presence of a psychological service on campus may provide incitive reminders of the fact that the college educates some students who are less than whole psychologically. For those who fear for their own mental health or have extreme prejudices regarding the nature of mental illness, the specter of students who have serious emotional problems and may even be "mentally ill" attending classes and freely mingling with other students and staff can be a frighteningly anathematic one. In the minds of such persons these students may be irrationally identified as potentially dangerous or in some other respect peculiarly unfit to avail themselves of the educational offerings of the college. In the extreme, this attitude may lead one to viewing the emotionally disturbed student as a pariah or social malignancy that needs to be barred or excised from the college, by hook or crook.

When the psychological service officially and proudly welcomes the emotionally disturbed student to utilize its services, it is, in the estimation of the prejudiced observer, encouraging and even directly generating the influx of "undesirables" to the campus. At some campuses I have visited there seems to be a fairly widespread alarm among faculty and administrators alike that the campus eventually will be inundated with strange and implacably disruptive students, all because their "bleeding heart" therapists in the community and at the college have conspired to arrange that they receive hospitable care on the campus. When the on-campus psychological staff are viewed as being responsible for opening the campus floodgates to students who, through their unusual behavior, complicate the professional lives of their colleagues, there is likely to be resentment for the role and mission of that staff. If such is the case, a vigorous educational campaign regarding the rights and needs for accommodation of the psychologically disabled student will probably be essential for the welfare of all concerned. Two vignettes will illustrate the above-described dilemma.

A psychological service at an Eastern university established and sponsored a supportive educational program for psychologically disabled students. During the initial phase of this program stereotypes regarding the psychologically disabled student led to concerns about whether such persons were "appropriate" for the campus. However, since the President of the college supported the program, no organized resistance emerged.

When the President took a position at another college, an interim President was hired. The interim President was a horse of a different philosophical color. She viewed the program for the disabled students as lacking in credibility and, believing that such students put the college "at risk," requested that the program be discontinued. The director of psychological services rejoined by informing the interim President that the program was wholeheartedly supported by a large coalition of community agencies which would be extremely unhappy with its termination. When the President realized that she had a highly delicate political situation on her hands, she sought a path of negotiation and compromise which ultimately led to the restoration of the program. Nevertheless, the stigma and stereotypes regarding the psychologically disabled student that originally inspired the opposition to the program continue to be expressed, albeit somewhat more circumspectly than before.

At a college in the Southwest a counseling center was in the process of appealing for a new position during a major fund drive. The outcome of these negotiations was the allocation of a substantial amount of money for refurbishing athletic facilities and nothing for the counseling position. The director of the counseling center assessed the situation as follows. She believed that the institutional priorities favoring athletics over human services represented institutional uneasiness with programs that stand for illness or damage. "Our very existence," she says, "punctures the illusion that all the students are healthy and doing well. We then come to stand for such unpleasant realities as anxiety, defect, or craziness, and then we are marginalized in the institution as a way of trying to fend off those issues."

To summarize, those who administer or practice psychotherapy in college mental health or counseling centers will inevitably encounter institutional resistances—mild, moderate and sometimes virulent—to their philosophy, policies, practices and even to their very presence throughout the course of their tenure on campus. Although institutional resistances were described in this article in their discrete form for the purpose of clarity and elucidation, they rarely, in my view, occur in complete isolation from one another. Rather, like the defense mechanisms of the human personality, they usually combine, overlap and appear in rapid concatenation with one another, making them all the more confounding and formidable to deal with (Amada, 1995). It is for this reason that I have long believed that the most essential personal quality for fulfilling the professional responsibilities and ideals of the college psychotherapist is moral courage (Amada, 1995).

References

Amada, G. (1995). *A guide to psychotherapy*. New York: Ballantine Books.

Amada, G. (1995). The disruptive college student: some thoughts and considerations. *Journal of American College Health*, 43 (5): 232-236.

Downs, A. (1967). *Inside bureaucracy*. Boston: Little. Brown and Company.

Fenichel, 0. (1945). *The psychoanalytic theory of neurosis*. New York: W.W. Norton & Company, Inc.

Hanfmann, E. (1978). *Effective therapy for college students*. San Francisco: Jossey-Bass Publishers.

Henry, P, (1986). Psychological services challenges the academy. *Journal of College Student Psychotherapy*, 1(1), 1986.

Machiavelli. N. (1952). *The prince*. New York: The New American Library of World Literature. Inc.

Robertiello, R. and Schoenewolf, G. (1987). *101 common therapeutic blunders*. Northvale, N.J.: Jason Aronson. Inc.

Strean, H. (1990). *Resolving resistances in psychotherapy*. New York: Brunner/Mazel, Publishers.

The Disruptive College Student: Recent Trends and Practical Advice

In recent years there has been a disquieting rise in the numbers and gravity of disruptive incidents involving college students. This trend reflects and closely parallels in character the upsurge of violence and disruption that we regularly witness throughout contemporary society. This article first identifies some of the more common forms of student disruptiveness and then provides practical advice to college personnel for dealing with the formidable challenge of student misconduct.

———

In recent years the phenomenon known as the "disruptive college student" has reached almost calamitous proportions on many college campuses. The hallowed and seemingly impermeable university walls of yesteryear now evidence, even at our most prestigious colleges and universities, visible porosity in the face of many of the disruptive and violent forces that prevail in the extramural world. Tragically, within the past few years brilliant and highly promising students have committed murders—of students and/or faculty—on the campuses of Harvard (Thernstrom, 1996), Simon Rock, and Iowa (Matthews, 1993), to name just a few.

Although, for obvious reasons, student-committed homicides are usually the most dramatic and disquieting forms of disruptive behavior that can afflict a college campus, it would be patently misleading and parochial to define disruptive behavior only in terms of conduct that is violent or lethal. In my consultations with instructors, administrators and psychotherapists at colleges and universities throughout the United States and Canada, I have been informed of a wide range of behaviors that have surfaced, especially in recent years, that perplex, stymie, and even terrify college personnel. I will first describe some of these behaviors and then conclude this article with some suggestions for remediation.

187

CLASSROOM MISCONDUCT

There are certain student behaviors that occur in the classroom that, at first glance, appear innocuous or frivolous, but when one considers their cumulative and adverse effect upon the educational process, are really highly disruptive. For example, it is quite common for cliques of students to engage in chattering during lectures, ignore admonitions to desist, and even openly challenge the instructor's authority to insist upon respectful attentiveness during lectures. Other students use the classroom as a convenient refuge to escape from their harrying or fatiguing personal pressures, whatever they might be, by snoozing in their seats, oblivious to the possibility that such behavior might legitimately be construed as disrespectful to the instructor as well as to their fellow classmates.

One form of seriously disruptive behavior that has become almost ubiquitous on college campuses is the problem of lateness. Almost always, when I mention this issue to audiences of instructors, it resonates immediately and gratefully with them. Many students are chronic and blatant in their unpunctuality. They may enter class by unapologetically passing right in front of the instructor during the early phase of the lecture and, taking their seats with some additional fanfare, wave to their classmates while carelessly and noisily scraping their chairs so as temporarily to drown out the lecturer's words. It has interested me to discover, largely through their own testimonials, the great number of instructors who are sorely outraged by students who are excessively late to class, yet undertake no decisive measures to deter or remedy this problem.

According to the anecdotal reports I have garnered from instructors and administrators at various schools, student disrespect for institutional authority is waxing at a worrisome rate and can take many forms within the classroom environment: inappropriate eating, drinking, smoking, and loud gum chewing; personal conversations during class presentations; unannounced and extended bathroom breaks; carrying on one's person beepers, pagers, and cellular phones whose unexpected cacophony can bring a lecture to an abrupt halt; the use of profane, hostile, and abusive language; the indiscriminate expression of racist, agist, sexist, and homophobic sentiments; note-passing, signaling, gesturing, or whistling across the room; unauthorized doctor, dentist, counseling, or registration appointments during class time.

PHYSICAL INTIMIDATION

Instructors on many campuses are increasingly beset by disruptive forms of behavior that can be physically intimidating. There are students who are not loathe to threaten an instructor with bodily harm or even death in retaliation for such perceived slights as a bad grade or evaluation. On my own campus an instructor warned and admonished a student for sexually harassing a classmate. The student responded by asking the instructor if he knew the meaning of the word "vendetta."

Bullying behavior can take many forms, not all of which are physically threatening but some of which, nevertheless, cause instructors considerable consternation. For example, a Hispanic instructor who teaches at a southwestern university reports that her Hispanic students repeatedly hector her over her grading system, suggesting to her that since she and they share a common cultural heritage it behooves her to grant them, preferentially, more favorable grades. Fortunately, she did not succumb to this stratagem, but she did have her twinges of doubt and guilt whenever she conferred deservedly substandard grades upon some of these students.

Many instructors report a growing number of incidents that involve students who brazenly interrupt lectures with long harangues of their own and belligerently resist the instructors' efforts to curb their verbal onslaughts. As well, on practically every campus I have visited (about 70 altogether), there are multiple reports of students who stalk instructors and other students. These stalkers don't necessarily confine their stealthy handiwork to the campus itself, they often pursue their quarry to the off-campus streets and even to their homes. Many faculty throughout this country receive late-night, anonymous phone calls from students (often clearly identifiable as student-placed calls through the types of academically oriented messages that are left), who leave cryptic messages about the impending dangers confronting the instructor.

Of course, certain types of disruptive behavior on the part of students are almost exclusively directed at other students. One such example is that of date rape, which has reached within the last decade or so almost epidemic proportions. A 1985 national survey by Koss, Gidycz, and Wisniewski (1987) of 7,000 students on 35 campuses revealed the following findings:

1. One in eight women have been raped;

2. Eighty-five percent of these incidents occurred among students who knew one another and 5% of the attacks involved more than one assailant;

3. Seventy-five percent of the victims of acquaintance rape did not identify their experience as rape and none of the males involved believed they had committed a crime;

4. Forty-five percent of the males who committed acquaintance rape said they would repeat the experience; and

5. More than one-third of the women raped did not discuss the experience with anyone and more than 90 percent of them did not report the incident to the police.

COMPUTER MISCHIEF

In this age of cyberspace, there is a considerable amount of mischief that is perpetrated through the misuse of college computers. Some malefactors use computers to send hate mail to others, usually anonymously. By stealing passwords in the computer labs, some students purloin accounts, modify or erase the files of other students or overwhelm the resources of a particular program so that it becomes totally useless to its hapless owner. Some send unsolicited and unauthorized E-mail through the stolen files of other students.

The college computer has also become a modern-day appliance with which some students are able to carry out a newfangled form of sexual harassment: retrieving pornography from the Internet, introducing it into a woman's program and displaying it on her screen. On my own campus, a student in a computer lab deliberately sabotaged the computer system of a large library, shutting it down for an entire day.

DRUG AND ALCOHOL ABUSE

The ubiquity of student alcohol and other substance abuse constitutes a formidable challenge to colleges which must deal with their standard concomitant: aggressive and antisocial behavior. It is estimated that one in ten college students has or will have a problem with psycho-active substance abuse during college (Eigen, 1991). This represents an obvious health hazard to the self-abusing students themselves and a social and institutional threat to those who must control or contend with the aggressiveness that at times is catalyzed by substance abuse. Two researchers have concluded that it is reasonable to conclude that as many as 20-30% of the students who use college psychological services have problematic involvement with alcohol or other drugs (Meilman and Gaylor, 1989).

CAMPUS CRIME

Although crime on the college campus is not by any means a new phenomenon, it seems to be on the rise. In recent years, the Federal Bureau of Investigation has annually reported from 2,000 to 2,500 crimes of personal violence (homicide, aggravated assault, forcible rape, and forcible robbery) and in excess of 100,000 serious property crimes (burglary, larceny, and arson) on college campuses (Smith, 1989). Although these figures in themselves provide cause for concern, they are generally understood to represent only a small percentage of the actual criminal offenses committed on campuses each year, since the totals were based upon voluntary self-reporting of a relatively small number of colleges. Also, lest we try to gain small comfort from the notion that on-campus crime is committed by preying perpetrators from the local communities outside the college campuses, it should be noted that perhaps 80% of campus crimes appear to be student-on-student (Matthews, 1993).

PRACTICAL SUGGESTIONS

Before presenting suggestions for the remediation of student disruptiveness, I should first point out that this list of suggestions is not, of course, intended to be exhaustive or binding and therefore should be augmented by the recommendations of my colleagues on other campuses, according to the particular characteristics and exigencies of their own college environment. Also, as I have stated elsewhere (Amada, 1993), many of the principles inherent in the following suggestions are utilized in my daily work as a consultant to faculty and administrators on my own campus. I sincerely hope they will be relevant and applicable to other college mental health administrators and psychotherapists.

1. The centerpiece for dealing with student disruptiveness is the college code of student conduct. This is the "law" of the college and therefore legally determines what is acceptable or unacceptable student conduct. Therefore, all colleges should strive to have in place codes of student conduct that are clear, coherent, fair, comprehensive, mutually compatible, legally enforceable, and generally applicable.

2. The code of student conduct should be regularly reviewed by all college staff with the purpose of determining their relevance and efficacy for resolving disruptive incidents throughout the college campus.

3. The code of student conduct should prohibit not just those forms of disruptive behavior that are most visible and overt, such as defacing property, verbal abuse of staff, or the possession of dangerous weapons, but should also allow for prohibitions of the more subtle, covert forms of disruptive behavior, such as sleeping or persistently whispering in class. The more covert forms of disruptive behavior do not necessarily require separate codes but could be subsumed under the rubric of a broad code that proscribes behaviors that "interfere with the educational process," for example.

4. Each school should develop a clear system or set of procedures for the reporting of disruptive incidents. All college employees should be regularly apprised of the procedures by which they can report disruptive behavior as well as the range of options and prerogatives that are ordinarily available to them to resolve a disruptive crisis.

5. It is ordinarily essential for colleges to have in place a hierarchy of specified sanctions for particular acts of disruption. The hierarchy normally begins with the mildest form of sanction, such as a verbal warning to the student and then ratchets up to more severe sanctions for graver acts of misconduct, such as written warnings, suspensions,

and expulsions. The college should strive to make the sanctions commensurate with the seriousness of the misconduct. For example, a one-time act of rudely interrupting a lecture might warrant a verbal warning. Unprovokedly assaulting an instructor, however, would probably warrant expulsion. Naturally, attempts should be made to allow for extenuating or mitigating circumstances, such as a student who "inexplicably" erupts with an offensive temper tantrum on the day he has learned that a parent has been diagnosed with a serious illness.

6. To deal with the prospect of disruptive behavior in the classroom, instructors should state in their syllabi those behaviors that are discouraged or prohibited. For example, smoking, eating, and excessive lateness might be included among the list of prohibited and sanctionable behaviors. Naturally, different instructors have different sensibilities regarding certain forms of social behavior. For example, an instructor at a college I visited in Texas disliked and resented a student for wearing a baseball cap in class. Rather than inform the student at the outset of the semester about his objection to this particular dresswear, he seethed over it for many weeks. Then one day he launched an angry broadside at the student, shouting at him to remove his cap. The student complied but was no doubt frightened and humiliated. After hearing about this unpleasant tale, I was left with the impression that the student, like most students who attend college, would have willingly complied with a reasonable request from the instructor had it been stated clearly at the beginning of the semester in the syllabus.

7. Since plagiarism is a widespread, odious, and seriously punishable form of misconduct on many campuses, it needs to be addressed emphatically and early on with students. To avoid casting unnecessary aspersions or arousing hostile defiance, it is perhaps best for instructors to approach this problem by informing students at the beginning of each semester that, since they are in an academic environment that is apt to engender intense competition for good grades, they may fall prey to the temptation to cheat. This temptation may ebe spawned, they might be told, less by a flaw in their character than by a long-held and powerful ambition to succeed academically in order to fulfill the hopes of their loved ones. However, the ethical compromise and the risk that accompany plagiarism are incalculably grave and therefore they should never resort to plagiarism.

good example

8. In defining and evaluating incidents of disruption, college personnel may take two essential criteria into account: (1) Is the misconduct repetitive, and (2) is the misconduct extreme or gross? In weighing the first criterion, we might consider the example of chattering in class. If a clique of students chatters only very infrequently, it is perhaps best simply to ignore this behavior. However, chattering, when it takes

place on a regular basis, can be extremely distracting and nullifying to a lecturer and therefore can be defined as genuinely disruptive conduct that warrants disciplinary intervention. In considering the second criterion, let us use the unsavory example of a student's unprovoked physical assault upon an instructor. Physical assaults are generally gross or extreme forms of misconduct and when a student attacks an employee of the college, this gross misconduct need not be repeated before some form of discipline is imposed.

9. It is essential that all college employees understand that they have the prerogative—one might legitimately call it a responsibility—to establish behavioral standards for their workplace, whether that workplace is the classroom, the library, the bookstore, the instructor's or administrator's office, or the student health center. Naturally, in establishing behavioral standards, college employees must heed legal and administrative requirements that ensure adherence to due process procedures. This adherence can be achieved through close collaboration between the administrative staff and all other employees of the college.

10. The administrative staff must provide a safe and hospitable climate throughout the college for the reporting of disruptive incidents. This does not mean, of course, that all requests for the imposition of discipline should be administratively granted. It should mean, however, that all requests for the administrative evaluation of alleged incidents of disruptiveness are dealt with promptly, thoroughly, and with due respect for the complainant's fears, concerns, and sense of urgency over the reported behavior. Generally, the administration can best assure the safety of staff and students alike by immediately and vigorously investigating all threats, veiled or explicit, verbal or written, direct or conveyed through third parties. Perpetrators of serious threats should either be severely disciplined or reported to a law enforcement agency for investigation and, if necessary, prosecution.

11. The important role of documentation in dealing with disruptive behavior should be stressed and demonstrated throughout the college, as often as necessary. Careful documentation should be advocated for the following reasons: (1) Human memory is fallible and if complainants are later called upon to testify, at either a college hearing or in a civil or criminal courtroom, it is advisable that their testimonies be well fortified with contemporaneous documentation of the events under investigation and (2) documentation regarding certain disruptive students, particularly those who commit multiple acts of disruptiveness, greatly assists the designated administrative staff in resolving disruptive crises. Without the availability of adequate documentation, students who repeatedly engage in disruptive behavior do so with relative impunity and, even if they are eventually disci-

plined, it is often for an isolated incident of disruptiveness rather than for their cumulative history of misconduct.

12. Because most schools extensively depend upon attorneys for sound legal advice in resolving cases that involve disruptive students, it is imperative that they retain attorneys who are conversant with college and university law as a specialty (Amada, 1994). Also, college attorneys should be encouraged to spend time on the campus, informally as well as formally, in order to familiarize themselves firsthand with the various aspects of campus life that perforce will impinge upon the legal advice they confer in cases of disruption.

13. Generally speaking, referrals for mental health services of students who are deemed disruptive should not be carried out as a substitute for discipline. Disruptive students who are referred to the college's psychological service should be referred strictly on a voluntary basis (apart, perhaps, from those who are demonstrably a danger to themselves or others). Ordinarily, they should neither be rewarded for utilizing the psychological services with a mitigation of the discipline their misconduct warrants nor should they be additionally penalized for their refusal to avail themselves of psychological help.

14. Disruptive behavior that is also apparently unlawful, that is, violates municipal, state, or federal law, should be reported to the proper authorities for investigation and resolution. All college employees should be helped to understand their legal rights and responsibilities with regard to reporting incidents involving acts of criminality. Also, all college personnel should be apprised of their legal obligation to report "reportable" cases that come to their attention, such as child abuse or threats of bodily injury to another person.

When it is unclear as to whether or not a particular form of misconduct constitutes an actual crime, the matter should normally be referred to the college attorney for clarification and disposition. It should be borne in mind, however, that an on-campus crime committed by a student is, from both a legal and moral standpoint, no less a crime than an equivalent one committed by an ordinary citizen in the off-campus community. In other words, students should not receive immunity from prosecution for crimes they have committed simply because of their supposed privileged status as students. Of course, a college may opt to deal with ambiguous offenses by enlisting the college disciplinary system rather than the resources of the police or courts if, for example, the more lenient standards of evidence that are generally applicable in a college investigation of misconduct are likely to bring about an earlier and more just outcome than a badly backlogged and overworked court could achieve.

15. Colleges that do not presently have an on-campus psychological service and are attempting to cope with ongoing incidents of stu-

dent disruptiveness are at a decided disadvantage. Of course, the college psychological service will never be a panacea for the burgeoning tide of disruptive incidents with which many schools are now beleaguered. However, an on-campus mental health service can play a significant role in stanching some of the destructive force of this tide in the following respects: (1) Many students who are potentially disruptive due either to disturbances inherent in their personalities, and/or in their interpersonal relationships, seek psychological help and become less antisocial and less disruptive as a result; (2) The role of the on-campus psychological consultant can be pivotal in assisting college staff to understand and resolve disruptive crises (Amada, 1993). For these reasons, colleges that do not yet have the benefit of an on-campus psychological service may need to earmark some of their future funding in order to establish such an essential program, not only to deal with the unrest caused by disruptive students but also, of course, to assist all students to cope optimally with the stressful vicissitudes of college life.

Two particular arguments that favor the reliance upon off-campus psychological services for college students are frequently adduced; one is largely fiscal, the other philosophical. The fiscal argument contends that an on-campus psychological service is excessively expensive, cost-ineffective and an unnecessary drain on the institution's financial resources. Those of us who serve in a college mental health service can readily recognize some of the serious flaws in this argument. Many students who utilize on-campus psychological services will not turn for help to similar resources in the community, usually because of the costs, inconvenience, or red-tapeism they expect to encounter there. What price should be placed on the value of the help they receive from their college psychological service if it enables them to overcome, for example, a serious depression or even suicidal intentions? And at what point does this help become "cost-ineffective," even when it continues to alleviate terrible human misery?

The philosophical argument often contends that it is not the proper role or mission of a college or university to provide mental health services to students. Rather, the college provides the requisite educational programs and whatever psychological help students require should be the responsibility of the local community and/or their families. This viewpoint disregards, of course, a serious moral obligation on the part of the college; namely, to assure that all students have ready access in times of crisis to a psychological resource that will enable them to recover, learn, grow and become better students. In short, since mental health is the bedrock upon which the edifice of academic success is founded, colleges must do their utmost to establish and safeguard those programs that foster the psychological well-being of students.

16. Finally, colleges must boldly and relentlessly honor an institutional credo—publicly stated and disseminated and buttressed by the entire panoply of legal, administrative, instructional and clinical resources of the campus—to protect all staff and students from bullying, intimidation or violence.

References

Amada, G. (1993). The role of the mental health consultant in dealing with disruptive students. Chapter in *Campus Violence: kinds, causes, and cures*, L.C. Whitaker and J.W. Pollard (Eds). New York: The Haworth Press, Inc., pp. 121-137. Published simultaneously in *Journal of College Student Psychotherapy*, 8(1/2)(3).

Amada, G. (1994). *Coping with the disruptive college student: A practical model*. Asheville, N.C.: College Administration Publications, Inc.

Eigen, L., (1991). *Alcohol practices, policies, and potentials of American colleges and universities*, An Office of Substance Abuse Prevention White Paper, U.S. Dept. of Health and Human Services, Office for Substance Prevention, Rockville, MD.

Koss, M., Gidycz, C. and Wisniewski, N. (1987). The scope of rape: Incidence and prevalence of sexual aggression and victimization in a national sample of higher education students. *Journal of Consulting and Clinical Psychology*, 2, (2), 162-170.

Matthews, A. (March 7, 1993). The campus crime wave. *The New York Times*, Section VI, National edition, 38-47.

Meilman, P.W., and Gaylor, M.S. (1987). *Dartmouth College 1987 alcohol and drug use survey*. Unpublished data, Dartmouth College.

Smith, M.C. (1989). *Crime and campus police: A handbook for police officers and administrators*. Asheville, NC: College Administration Publications, Inc.

Thernstrom, M. (June 3, 1996). Diary of a murder. *The New Yorker*, 72, (14), 62-71.

The Formulation
of a Therapeutic Paradigm:
A Professional Odyssey

*Following is a description of the development of a therapeutic paradigm
through the course of the author's career as a college psychotherapist. The
paradigm that is described incorporates a variety of (sometimes disparate)
theories, but is essentially psychoanalytic. The paradigm is viewed by the
author as a dynamic process that is subject to change and elaboration as
the therapist's understanding of social and psychological factors grows and
undergoes refinement.*

When the editor of this journal suggested that I write an article
explicating my own psychotherapeutic paradigm, I was both flattered
and a bit unnerved. After all, trying to explain how one has arrived
at a particular therapeutic model is, I think, as difficult to explain as
it is to describe how one's own personality has evolved and crystal-
lized into the complex psychological entity that now presents itself
to the external world. I deliberately use this particular analogy because
I strongly believe that each therapist's choice of a therapeutic paradigm, regardless of its well-formulated and empirically tested theoretical underpinnings, is powerfully motivated and shaped by the very
same forces that have served as the psychological building blocks of
his or her personality—i.e., deep-seated hopes, prejudices, disappointments, terrors and fears, illusions, confusions, resentments, triumphs,
hostilities, etc.

Atwood and Stolorow (1993) have trenchantly explained how various psychological theories can be interpreted as psychological pro-
ducts embedded in the life history of their partisans. With this thought
in mind, I will now attempt to provide a somewhat psychoautobio-
graphical explanation of how I have conceived of and practiced psychotherapy during the course of a career that now spans almost forty
years.

197

My initial interest in psychology and psychotherapy was born out of frustration and discontent. Duteously following a misguided parental suggestion that I pursue a career in accounting (because I could swiftly add long columns of numbers), I enrolled in the business college of a university. At the end of two years, I had discovered what the comedian Bob Newhart had learned after his own brief stint as an accountant; namely, that I couldn't care less whether the ledgers balanced.

Thus, I visited a college psychologist, who administered an aptitude test that grandly confirmed my unsuitability for business studies, but blessedly revealed some evidence of a nascent interest in and aptitude for "working with people." Armed with the authority of these findings, I was able to convince both my parents and the university that a transfer to the liberal arts college, where I could major in psychology, was the most humane way to salvage my college career.

I found two psychology courses especially interesting: Abnormal Psychology and Introduction to Psychotherapy. Although the psychotherapy course was not taught by a clinician, and the instructor was a painfully insipid lecturer, the assigned readings caught my fancy immediately. Especially intoxicating, from an intellectual standpoint, was Robert Lindner's *The Fifty Minute Hour* (1955). Lindner's book was inspiring not only because he told fascinating stories about his psychiatric patients, but also because he was, through the telling of these tales, able to beautifully depict how he could enter the deeper inner sanctums of his patients' psychic life in order to psychologically travel and empathize with them through their travails. Lindner, through this book, taught me, quite unforgettably, a wonderful truism about psychotherapy. I learned that, if therapists permit themselves the opportunity, providing help to suffering patients can be a unique, exciting adventure, and, moreover, should always be regarded as a singular privilege. This view of the unique role, responsibility, and vantage point of psychotherapists toward their patients has always served as a kind of bedrock, guiding principle of my own work ever since.

FREUD

I was first introduced to psychoanalytic theory as an undergraduate, but at first glance the readings, including Freud, were a bit too formidable. By no means was I shocked or repelled by the concepts of the Oedipal complex or infantile sexuality. As a matter of fact, I accepted these theories with equanimity as largely valid. Yet, I simply considered these ideas to be too abstract and overgeneralized, and therefore, for the time being, unembraceable. Seeking another iconic light to illuminate my search for the Truth, I briefly flirted with the theories of Carl Jung, but his concept of the collective unconscious struck me as being highly implausible and otherworldly (it still does), and when I later learned that Jung had once been insufficiently unsympathetic to Naziism, he lost all credibility with me and I forever threw away, for better or worse, most of his concepts along with the dirty historical bathwater. (For a number of years, Jung obligingly served as the president of a psychotherapy association and editor of a leading periodical that recognized the "scientific" principles espoused in *Mein Kampf* as the basis of their activity. Jung claimed that he could not in good conscience decline these assignments because to do so would be an act of disloyalty to his friends and medical colleagues in Germany! Moreover, in the pages of the journal of which he was editor he declared that National Socialism, if not too categorically dismissed as an ideology, might have something "better" to teach the world.)

I grudgingly returned to psychoanalytic theory in graduate school in a course called Human Growth and Behavior when one of the instructors assigned a book by Otto Fenichel. This book, *The Psychoanalytic Theory of Neurosis* (1945), was a dense thicket of quite abstruse psychoanalytic concepts, and the technical jargon, especially with curious terms like "narcissistically hypercathected" interspersing the entire text, was nearly indecipherable to my neophyte capacities. It was then that I decided to give Freudian theory one more try before turning to yet another set of theories to explain the psychological foibles of humankind. I decided, quite sensibly I now believe, to quench my thirst for psychological understanding by drinking from the original wellspring of psychoanalytic theory; the writings of Sigmund Freud himself.

Over the course of about a year I read many of Freud's writings, including his collected papers (1959). Although I did not always grasp the nuances and implications of his many theoretical formulations, I was definitely awed by the elegance, trenchancy, and ingenuity with which he stated his views. Keeping in mind that practically every subject Freud broached was of a pathbreaking nature, I wondered how one human being could make so many delicious discoveries.

My greatest disappointment with Freud, however, related to how he sometimes treated his patients, according to his own accounts in case histories. At times he seemed to browbeat patients with too many interpretations, rather simplistically expecting, I thought, to break down their self-armoring defenses and achieve an early cure through intellectual insights. I have since forgiven Freud for this proclivity, for, as one of my former interns wittily pointed out, "After all, Freud had no supervisor."

Reading Freud deeply and immutably changed my perspective about psychology, psychotherapy, and most importantly, about myself, in the following respects. First, although at the time I vaguely knew about and believed in the human unconscious, it was Freud's microscopic excavations into the unconscious that provided me with a greater awareness of the potential of this psychological netherworld to guide a person toward a life of either fulfillment or misery. Throughout my career I have never worked with a patient, regardless of the therapeutic milieu, without giving serious thought to how he or she is driven by unconscious forces and I attribute much of my interest in and understanding of the role of the unconscious to Freud's inspiring example.

Second, although I do not think Freud paid sufficient attention to the quality of family life as determined by the specific interplay of family members day after day, he did place due emphasis upon childhood as the forerunner of the adult personality. Perhaps he overstressed the pathological nature of the Oedipal complex, but his dogged plumbing and sleuthing through the labyrinthine pathways of his patients' memories of childhood, although not necessarily bull's eye-accurate, expanded my appreciation for the vast possibilities and complexities of childhood's contribution to the development of the human personality. Thus, I rarely work with patients, even on a short-term basis, without inquiring into their early childhood experiences, and usually I find some valuable means for incorporating this vital information into my therapeutic interventions. Here, too, Freud deserves considerable credit.

To my mind, Freud's discovery of transference is indisputably of monumental importance. At first, Freud considered transference, the tendency of patients to revivify and relive, through feelings, memories, and various sets of behavior, their early childhood experiences with their therapists—to be an impregnable barricade to a successful analysis. Ultimately, however, Freud recognized transference to be an invaluable diagnostic and therapeutic tool, if properly understood and utilized by the therapist.

I suppose one can never really "prove" the existence of transference, much as one can never "prove" most of Freud's theories, but, after working with thousands of patients over the years, I cannot recall a single session in which some important manifestation of transference did not become palpably evident. This, of course, is not meant to suggest that I regularly use transference interpretations with each and every patient; it is to suggest, however, that, without a single exception, I use my awareness of transference phenomena to assess and treat patients throughout the course of their therapy. Again, my indebtedness to Freud.

Finally, for those who favor the preciseness of the "hard" sciences, Freud's theoretical writings might be viewed as no more than discursive speculations. As a matter of fact, he has been pejoratively

negative

rambling

referred to by certain detractors as the century's Great Speculator. His detractors notwithstanding, I praise and admire Freud for his courage to speculate, boldly and innovatively. As a therapist, I myself can do no more than engage in a speculative process with my patients regarding the obscure origins of their psychological conflicts and the true nature of their current emotions and thoughts. I recognize that it is precisely this process of mutual speculation that fertilizes the imagination, and, when it is successful, ultimately generates self-awareness, understanding, and healing. Thus, I regard the courage to creatively and intelligently speculate—perhaps Freud's greatest legacy—to be an essential quality for therapists who, like myself, desire to explore deeply the murky depths of the human psyche.

Professional Supervision

In the mid-1960s I began to moonlight at a private psychotherapy clinic, a formative experience that provided me with my first opportunity to practice psychotherapy on an individual basis with adult patients. I was assigned a supervisor who was a psychoanalytically trained psychologist. He and I worked together for seven consecutive years, almost exclusively analyzing my work with the same patient. The wise and patient guidance and mentoring provided by this supervisor enabled me to see with greater clarity the significance and applicability of psychoanalytic theory, as well as its curative potential.

Perhaps of more importance, however, was the supervisor's confidence, his unswerving conviction, that the process of psychoanalytic therapy actually works, as conveyed through his soft-spoken yet penetrating recommendations regarding how I might unravel a therapeutic impasse or meaningfully connect with my patient on deeper and deeper levels. From this supervisor I was able to learn the importance of acquiring and exercising non-directive patience, persistent curiosity, non-possessive warmth, abiding respect for the complexity of the human personality, and the requisite moral courage to investigate the forbidden regions of the mind. By the time this supervisory experience had ended, I had become a fully devoted adherent and admirer of psychoanalytic therapy, a devotee for a lifetime.

Brief Psychodynamic Psychotherapy

In the early 1970s, I came to work as a director of a college mental health service. Although I, of course, had to carry out administrative duties, my primary responsibility was to treat students in crisis. Because the students were many and the staff relatively few, it was necessary to provide students with short-term treatment (usually a maximum of twelve sessions). This abbreviated therapy presented a personal and professional challenge. There were pressures from the student patients (and from their significant others, including instructors and administrators) to resolve their crises quickly and even to provide them with some form of therapeutic prophylaxes against relapse, if at all possible. In later years, as community agencies were retrenched and even entirely liquidated due to drastic defunding, the pressures for faster and better "cures" only intensified. With the advent of managed care in recent years, the ethos of providing a short-term treatment that affords both early symptomatic relief and far-reaching, transformative benefit has come to predominate.

While faced with this challenge, I heard loud and recurrent rumblings from many sources in the psychiatric community that the most promising wave of the future of psychotherapy, the one that was to carry clinicians to the most pristine beaches of their professional dreams, was some form of cognitive-behavioral treatment that provided rapid, practical, and realistic remedies for short-term crises.

Despite the highly touted blandishments of the cognitive-behavioral orientation (and after reading several books by well respected cognitive therapists, all of which I found to be painfully uninspiring), I had no difficulty maintaining my psychoanalytic convictions. (This is not to suggest that I never enlist some of the theories and techniques of cognitive-behavioral therapy in my work with patients. It is to suggest, however, that I regard cognitive therapy, as a delimited psychological orientation, to be theoretically straitjacketing and inordinately wanting in its lack of vision and depth, and I usually find behavioral modes of therapy to be much too authoritarian to suit my personality as well as my therapeutic style and objectives.) I decided, therefore, to modify and tailor my therapy with students to accommodate the limitations and exigencies of time-limited therapeutic encounters, without abandoning my original theoretical underpinnings.

I first had to ask myself a fundamental question: Could psychoanalytic theory be suitably yoked to or merged with a short-term therapeutic model? A brief review of the literature indicated that this had already been accomplished quite well (Lewin, 1970; Malan, 1972, 1982; Sifneos, 1979). Nevertheless, I wanted to try my own hand at formulating certain concepts and principles of short-term psychodynamic psychotherapy and eventually did so in a published article (Amada, 1977).

The following principles were highlighted in this article: (1) attending, with heightened therapeutic activity, to the limitations of time (in the form of, for example, highly pointed questioning and a willing opinionatedness on the part of the therapist), (2) establishing with the patient a reasonable chronology of those events that precipitated the presenting crisis, (3) utilizing, if necessary, ancillary resources (such as an off-campus legal service), (4) maintaining, if possible, a relatively consistent positive transference in order for the therapist to be looked upon and depended upon by the short-term patient as a credible source of help, (5) interpreting historical material forward in time (in contrast to what a therapist is apt to do in long-term therapy) in order to place reasonable constraints upon psychological regression and to clarify the contemporary context so that the patient may more effectively deal with the current source of his or her crisis, (6) using a flexible schedule, if necessary, in order to troubleshoot in a timely manner the many acute upheavals experienced by some patients who are in the throes of a serious crisis, (7) providing, when necessary, ready telephone accessibility to patients who cannot safely tolerate their anxiety without gaining some access to their therapist between sessions, (8) extending practical advice to some patients, who simply cannot extricate themselves from demonstrably dangerous situations, regarding a prospective course of liberating action, (9) actively attending to the patient's regressive feelings and behavior regarding the early (and perhaps premature) termination that is inherent in all abbreviated therapies, and, finally, (10) acknowledging with short-term patients that they, much like characters at the end of Checkhov's plays, will leave the therapy with some feelings of disappointment and incompleteness.

The Interlude Between
Short- and Long-Term Psychotherapy

Feeling fairly well equipped with this set of principles for doing short-term psychodynamic psychotherapy with college students, I gradually began to discern a clinical phenomenon that at first eluded my prized principles and the reach of my psychological understanding. I observed that most students, after receiving perhaps 4-8 sessions, predictably experienced a dissipation of and release from the crisis that initially prompted them to seek therapy.

At this juncture they began to evidence discomfort and anxiety, often manifested in their confusion about the future goals of treatment. A seeming impasse would develop in the therapy, characterized by the manifestation of heightened resistances and an intensification of the patients' emotional responses to the personality and techniques of the therapist. When the resistances were not adequately addressed and resolved as they presented themselves, it was quite common for the patients to bolt from the therapy, often without notice or explanation.

At first, I thought this clinical phenomenon was somehow peculiar to the particular therapy I was conducting with students. Perhaps, I mused, the acute restlessness, confusion, anger, and urges to flee the therapy soon after the resolution of their crisis were the students' adverse reactions to serious flaws in my particular personality, conduct, or techniques. I was given cause to reconsider this notion, however, when I discovered from large numbers of students who had previously received therapy elsewhere that they had experienced a quite similar reaction to their other therapists soon after the resolution of the crisis that had brought them into treatment.

The Formulation of a Therapeutic Paradigm: A Professional Odyssey　　203

On the basis of this finding, I began to view therapy as a kind of developmental process, marked by certain recognizable and quite predictable phases. In an article I published at the time (Amada, 1983), I referred to the phase following the resolution of the initial crisis as the "interlude between short- and long-term therapy." As I viewed the matter, many patients, as they entered this interlude phase, experienced a heightened state of confusion, anxiety, and anger in response to an evolving ambiguity with respect to therapeutic goals. In short, they quite often suffered from an unclear perspective regarding the purpose of continuing in therapy.

A second factor that contributed to the patients' deepening anxiety was the intensification of their emotions in direct relation to the therapist. The patients' feelings, both negative and positive, were intensified, first by having spent several intensive hours in the presence of a nurturing, empathic professional who was obviously dedicated to their well-being. Moreover, the help they derived from the therapist to overcome their crisis, although usually deeply appreciated, also tended to engender in patients an even deeper quest for signs of special caring and regard from the therapist, accompanied by disappointments, frustration, and anger when the patients felt, as they often did, that the therapist was not fulfilling their heightened emotional expectations.

The sources of these feelings, which at bottom were highly transferential in nature (i.e., they reflected earlier wishes, hopes, fears, and expectations that originated in childhood in relation to the child's primary caregivers), were usually quite unconscious and therefore the patients felt piloted by emotions they could neither understand nor control especially well. It is for this reason, I believe, that they often felt the impulse to flee the therapy before they felt compelled to reveal something about themselves that, in their view, they would come to regret.

I have incorporated this developmental view of therapy into my therapeutic work with students in several crucial respects. First, by anticipating the "interlude" phase, I can be more reposeful and prepared to deal with the turmoil of patients as they manifest heightened anxiety during this phase, thus providing them with a hospitable, healing presence. Second, by recognizing the fear that many patients feel in response to the ambiguity of therapeutic goals, I am prepared to review, reevaluate and, if necessary, modify the goals of therapy in collaboration with them in order to ensure that the goals of therapy remain realistic and achievable. Third, by understanding the nature of the "interlude" phase myself, I can assist patients to appreciate therapy as a developmental process that entails somewhat predictable phases that can, as one phase passes into another, generate emotional upheaval. I have found, repeatedly, that this demystification of the therapeutic process has enabled me to assist many of my patients to weather the turmoil that sometimes accompanies their journey through the "interlude" phase.

Object Relations and Self Psychology

Although steadfastly committed to a psychoanalytic model throughout my career as a therapist, I had never become, strictly speaking, a Freudian. In my view, Freud's overemphasis upon instinctual drives in ego development does not provide a sufficiently thorough understanding of the intrinsic nature of the human personality. I have, of course, never denied the reality or potency of drives to shape the lives of human beings, but I have repeatedly discovered that my interpretations of drives and their derivatives to patients, no matter how well timed, intonated, substantiated empirically, and rendered intelligible, seemed to be of little value and utility to them (or me).

As object relations theory gained currency and stature in the field of psychoanalytic therapy, I studied its central concepts and found them to be penetrating and therapeutically indispensable (Kernberg, 1984, 1985; Masterson, 1976; Ogden, 1982). The central concept that the human personality is an expression of an internal drama that continuously reenacts memories (and fantasies) of early interactions with the caretakers of one's childhood (Pine, 1985) is, in my view, an indisputable psychological fact about human beings and, moreover, can serve, if properly put to use by a therapist, as a powerful therapeutic tool. My understanding of this concept continually enables me to explain to patients how their early laid-down memories still affect their behavior, their idiosyncratic longings for gratification, and their subjective perceptions of the world and of me.

Finally, my theoretical foundations were forever shaken and restructured by the theories of self psychology, especially as they had been expounded by Heinz Kohut (1971, 1977, 1984). Although I, along with many of my colleagues, found Kohut's style of writing to be turgid practically to the point of sheer unintelligibility, his salient concepts, it seemed to me, profoundly explained the deepest yearnings of the human heart. I learned from Kohut about the origins and pathways of both normal and pathological narcissism. I gained insight from him into the sources and manifestations of my patients' vulnerabilities.

More importantly, I derived from Kohut a deeper appreciation for the formidable challenges presented by narcissistic patients, including the need for therapists to withstand the great interpersonal pressure generated by the grandiosity, devaluation, and massive rage of many of these patients. In addition, I found Kohut's strong faith in and advocacy of the therapeutic power of empathy to be truly inspirational and a guiding light with which I could better understand and serve narcissistically vulnerable patients.

Although I have attempted to integrate the psychoanalytic theories of object relations, ego psychology, drive theory, and self psychology, my therapeutic work decidedly tilts toward the utilization of the theories of self psychology. I believe I am most effective with patients when I am especially empathic and in close attunement to their needs and conflicts. From my studies and therapeutic use of the theories of self psychology, I have come to the conclusion that one of the most fundamental needs of human beings, apart, of course, from the gratification of certain instinctual drives, is the quest for celebration from others—i.e., being recognized as a unique individual with very special qualities and aspirations—in the form of their acknowledgment, acclamation, validation, respect, empathy, and understanding. When this quest is thwarted or shattered through experiences of gross adversity and disappointment, it only becomes more pronounced and unruly. In my view, therapists who closely and intelligently attend to their patients' quests for celebration in all its myriad, exquisite forms will not stray far from the task of providing a healing presence to their patients.

Feminist Theory

I owe a debt of gratitude to feminist theory for certain modifications I have made in my thinking, my theoretical outlook, and in my therapeutic style in recent years. I have been enormously impressed with feminist theory that recognizes and protests the historical injustices that have been perpetrated by men and male-dominated institutions in our society (Greer, 1971). Each day, in the college student health center, I work with women who have been treated inhumanely by men; their fathers, brothers, husbands, doctors, coworkers, and employers.

It is true of course that psychoanalytic psychotherapy and its founder, Sigmund Freud, have been heavily bashed by many proponents of feminist theory (Shainess, 1970). Freud's chauvinism toward his wife and his female patients has been widely documented and sometimes enlisted as an argument against a set of theories that are essentially the brainchildren of Freud, and in themselves—like the theory of penis envy—may serve only further to stigmatize and demean women.

As the heated controversies about feminism versus psychoanalytic therapy whirled about my profession, I sometimes felt defensive and self-conscious whenever I was asked to disclose my own theoretical orientation (and the orientation of the college clinic, which largely remains psychoanalytic). If I embraced psychoanalytic theories, did that not establish me as the "enemy" of women? How could I be sympathetic to Freud's theoretical viewpoints and yet maintain respect for women?

One day, while mulling over some of these issues, I attended a lecture by Jeffrey Masson, a well known Freud scholar and detractor. Toward the end of a lecture in which he repeatedly accused Freud of cowardice for retracting his earlier beliefs in the seduction and sexual abuse of his female patients, Masson let fly a strong, quite categorical statement: to wit, no woman should ever receive psychotherapy from a male therapist, especially one that subscribes to psychoanalytic theories. To my discomfort, this statement met with considerable applause from an audience mostly comprising graduate clinical psychology students.

Soon after the lecture I found myself in a rage. I soon realized why. It was clear to me that Masson was posturing as a champion of women by suggesting that only women therapists would possess the requisite compassion and understanding to help other women. But, as I and much of the audience failed to realize at the time, Masson's remarks bespoke a profound contempt for women. He was, I realized, cleverly disguising an insidious form of misogyny that needed to be challenged. After all, if one were to extend his thoughts to their logical conclusion, it was obvious that he was suggesting that the many thousands of women who were receiving therapy from male therapists in this country were really dupes, hapless victims of men who were corruptly trained to use a body of chauvinistic theories to dehumanize them.

Extending Masson's viewpoint even further, one would then have to assume he must believe that the many thousands of women who felt enriched and strengthened by the services they received from male therapists were really deluding themselves; were either not intelligent or psychologically sophisticated enough to know that, even if they experienced appreciable benefit from their work with male therapists, they were really being gulled and disserved. Evidently, Masson would recommend that these women, despite their positive feelings for their male therapists, should immediately decamp from their therapy and find a woman therapist who would necessarily provide them with a more hospitable therapeutic relationship. Clearly, when one closely scrutinizes Masson's opinions about women patients, one discovers that he demonstrates a profound disdain for their judgment, intelligence, and their inalienable right to choose their own therapist, regardless of gender.

Masson's viewpoints notwithstanding, I have often asked myself the question: Can a male therapist actually conduct a psychoanalytic therapy that demonstrates full respect for the rights and integrity of women? I believe I now can confidently answer that question in the affirmative. The most important psychoanalytic theories—transference, the role of the unconscious, the influence of childhood and childhood memories—do not in themselves demean or discriminate against women.

Many men discriminate against women, and, indisputably, some male therapists are inordinately disrespectful of their women patients. But it is the attitudes and behavior of the disrespectful male therapist, not his theories, whatever they may be, that usually cause the harm. There is no evidence, for example, that male therapists who are trained psychoanalytically are any more or less chauvinistic than therapists trained according to the theories of other theoretical persuasions.

I believe that my therapeutic philosophy and my clinical interventions have been vastly informed and transformed by feminist theory. I cannot presume to know whether the advocates of feminist theory would accept me, a male therapist, as a feminist ally, but I would like to think so, as evidenced by the quality of my work with women. As I each day work with college women who, tragically, are enmeshed in relationships with men that are degrading, abusive, and grindingly oppressive, I zealously explore with them the many factors, psychological, social, and economic, that shackle them to tyrannical men, while doing my utmost to provide them with the insights and courage to confront and emancipate themselves from malignant relationships. I should add, parenthetically, that I have been pleased to see, in recent years, thoughtful and well researched studies by feminists who vouch for the efficacy of a therapeutic paradigm that weds feminist theory to psychoanalytic theory (Prozan, 1992).

The Role of Therapist / Advocate

Before concluding this article, I would like to include one further point about my view of therapy. There are times, in my view, when it is absolutely essential for therapists, especially those of us who work in college mental health clinics, to step outside of our traditional roles, and assist patients by collaborating with other agencies. There are other times, however, when mere collaboration is inapt and insufficient to resolve highly complicated clinical situations. I have described in a prior article that appeared in this journal how I had served as a social advocate for two rape victims, each of whom was a student patient of mine (Amada, 1989). By maintaining continuous contact with the Rape Crisis Unit of the city police, the district attorney's office, and the administrative staff of my own college, I was able to help coordinate a joint investigative effort that ultimately led to the arrest, conviction, and incarceration of the perpetrator.

More recently, I served as an advocate for a student patient who was charged with the crime of defrauding the department of social services. This student had made it abundantly clear to me that if she were convicted of the charges and had to undergo even a short period of imprisonment, she would definitely commit suicide. I was entirely convinced that she meant exactly what she said. Because I believed her claim that she was innocent of the charges and because I simply could not let her take her own life, I advocated her innocence to the court and actively served as a character witness for her. After many months of therapy during which she dismally anticipated her conviction (followed by the compulsion to fulfill her vow to kill herself), she was exonerated of the crime. She is no longer in therapy, but, on the basis of a recent phone conversation we had, I can confidently vouch for the fact that her outlook on life is extremely positive. Each day she is making a positive and very rewarding contribution to the community by serving as a volunteer tutor for children and views the future with realistic optimism.

The traditional psychoanalytic model appears to discourage extramural activities on the part of therapists in behalf of their patients. Arguments that are commonly adduced against these activities suggest that they tend to contaminate the therapeutic relationship and interfere with the essential neutrality of the therapist. I am of the opinion that there is nothing inherent in this theoretical model that precludes the use of the role of advocate when such a role is essential to the well-being of the patient. In my own experience, when the therapist advocates appropriately for patients, the therapeutic alliance is normally strengthened and the essential neutrality of the therapist is not at all compromised. Therefore, although the average therapist may only rarely be called upon to serve as a social advocate for patients, this role, in my view, should be considered an entirely legitimate and at times essential part of the therapist's clinical armamentarium.

The Dynamic Nature of a Therapeutic Paradigm

It is perhaps best to end this article with my conception of a psychotherapeutic paradigm that I believe is fundamental to all theoretical frames of reference. I think of a therapeutic paradigm as a dynamic process, not a static, rigid, and sacrosanct set of concepts and procedures. Because the essential nature of a therapeutic paradigm is dynamic, it is continuously subject to modification and elaboration, as our understanding of social and psychological conditions expands and undergoes refinement. It is well to keep in mind, I believe, that a therapeutic paradigm is never more than an approximation of social and psychological reality. It therefore must undergo a continuous process of scrutiny, re-evaluation, and refinement if it is to remain relevant, realistically applicable, and truly therapeutic to our patients.

References

Amada, G. (1977). Crisis-oriented psychotherapy: Some theoretical and practical considerations. *Journal of Contemporary Psychotherapy*, Vol. 9, No. 1, 104-111.

Amada, G. (1983). The interlude between short and long-term psychotherapy. *American Journal of Psychotherapy*, Vol. 3, 357364.

Amada, G. (089). Date rape on the college campus: the college psychotherapist as activist. *Journal of College Student Psychotherapy*, Vol. 4, No. 2, 89-93.

Atwood, G. & Stolorow, R. (1993). *Faces in a cloud*. Northvale, New Jersey: Jason Aronson, Inc.

Fenichel, 0. (1945). *The psychoanalytic theory of neurosis*. New York: W.W. Norton & Company, Inc.

Freud, S. (1959). *Collected papers*. New York: Basic Books, Inc.

Greer, G. (1971). *The female eunuch*. New York: McGrawHill Book Company.

Kernberg, 0. (1984). *Object relations theory and clinical psychoanalysis*. Northvale, New Jersey: Jason Aronson, Inc.

Kernberg, 0. (1985). *Borderline conditions and pathological narcissism*. Northvale, New Jersey: Jason Aronson, Inc.

Kohut, H. (1971). *The analysis of the self*. New York: International Universities Press, Inc.

Kohut, H. (1977). *The restoration of the self*. New York: International Universities Press, Inc.

Kohut, H. (1984). *How does analysis cure?* Chicago: The University of Chicago Press.

Lewin, K. (1970). *Brief encounters*. St. Louis, Missouri: Warren H. Green, Inc.

Lindner, R. (1955). *The fifty-minute hour: a collection of true psychoanalytic tales*. New York: Rinehart.

Masterson, J. (1976). *Psychotherapy of the borderline adult*. New York: Brunner/Maze], Publishers.

Malan, D. (1982). *Individual psychotherapy and the science of psychodynamics*. Boston: Butterworths.

Ogden, T. (1982). *Projective identification and psychotherapeutic technique*. New York: Jason Aronson.

Pine, F. (1985). *Developmental theory and clinical process*. New Haven: Yale University Press.

Prozan, C. (1992). *Feminist psychoanalytic psychotherapy*. Northvale, New Jersey: Jason Aronson.

Shainess, N. (1970). A psychiatrist's view: images of woman-past and present, overt and obscured. In R. Morgan (Ed.), *Sisterhood is powerful*, pp. 257-274. New York: Vintage Books.

Stiffens, P. (1978). *Short-term psychotherapy and emotional crisis*. Cambridge: Massachusetts: Harvard University Press.

Sifneos, P. (1979). *Short-term dynamic psychotherapy*. New York: Plenum Publishing Corporation.

Disqualifying Specified Students from the Campus Psychological Service: Some Considerations and Guidelines

Inasmuch as college mental health programs are ordinarily mandated and designed to provide a wide range of services, modalities of treatment, and a competent professional staff determined to assist students in various states of crisis, there is usually little thought or attention given to denying services to particular students. Nevertheless, most college mental health programs are, from time to time, beset by students who attempt to utilize their services in a manner that is highly inappropriate, sometimes quite disruptive, and, in extreme cases, even dangerous. This article will provide certain guidelines and criteria that may be used, when and if necessary, for disqualifying such students from utilizing the campus psychological service.

It is only natural that most articles and books that are written about college mental health programs extol the virtues of establishing, broadening, and enhancing the range of services provided by these programs. After all, the *sine qua non* of a college mental health program is, unquestionably, to help as many students as possible cope with and resolve their current crises in order to get on with the primary purpose of their matriculation: the attainment of their educational goals.

Yet, there are times when it becomes necessary for a psychological service to deny, disqualify, and exclude some students from receiving assistance due to the following reasons: (a) the service itself lacks sufficient wherewithal to assist the student adequately (for example, a given student requires or requests long-term treatment and the service provides only crisis-intervention or brief therapy), (b) a student's behavior in the therapy situation is so blatantly disruptive or aggressive that any benefit he or she might potentially derive from it is being entirely nullified or, worse, the emotional or physical welfare of the therapist is being endangered, (c) the student's behavior while in the clinic facility is so antisocial as to constitute a serious disruption to the professional work of the clinical or clerical staff, (d) the student's application for therapeutic services is based upon causes and rationales that are incompatible with the policies of the clinic (for example, the student is being required to use the psychological service by an instructor or administrator and the clinic maintains a policy of seeing students strictly on a voluntary basis), and (e) the student's purpose in seeking psychological services is deemed unacceptable or illegitimate (for example, the student seeks therapy simply to avoid disciplinary penalties for acts of misconduct or academic penalties for substandard work or absenteeism).

At this juncture, I will introduce some case examples to illustrate how and why some of the above-mentioned considerations were used when certain students were denied psychological services in the City College of San Francisco Mental Health Program.

DENIAL OF SERVICES ON THE BASIS OF A MISMATCH BETWEEN THE STUDENT'S NEEDS AND THE PROGRAM'S WHEREWITHAL

Ms. Smith was for many years a perennial student at the community college. At several different campuses she took one of two courses. She had no particular academic or career goal in mind but, nevertheless, found the overall college environment to be a hospitable and nurturing one. In the early '70s Ms. Smith received a few sessions in the college mental health program. She was diagnosed as having a schizophrenic disorder and received a referral to a community practitioner for further treatment. During the ensuing years she saw many different therapists, most for a relatively short time. Despite the multiplicity of her therapists and the brevity of her therapies, she was for the most part able to sustain herself fairly well (with the help of a disability subsidy).

A few years ago Ms. Smith returned to our clinic requesting services because she had reenrolled at our campus and was experiencing "some nasty crises." I was away on sabbatical at the time and when I returned I had learned from the staff that Ms. Smith had come into the clinic many times maintaining that she was in crisis and making importunate demands for an immediate session with one of the staff. Each time, she was obligingly assigned to whichever therapist was most readily available. Invariably, at the end of each session the therapist, cognizant of the chronicity of her condition, would recommend to Ms. Smith that she seek long-term therapy in the community. Ms. Smith each time gratefully thanked the therapist for the referral and then returned to the clinic in yet another putative crisis.

The staff and the clinic receptionist were in a quandary about what to do with these repeated appeals for help. The receptionist found it difficult to conveniently fit Ms. Smith into the staff's busy schedule and the staff felt after each session with her that little was accomplished other than fostering her mistaken belief that our clinic was an appropriate resource for her. The hope that by seeing her in crisis each time it would be possible to effect a referral for long-term treatment was clearly an illusory one.

It was at this point that I was asked to intervene when Ms. Smith next returned to the clinic. We did not have to wait very long. When she returned, she was assigned to see me. She began her session by announcing that she was in crisis. I acknowledged that she seemed to be having a great many crises lately and wondered why she was returning each time to the clinic against the advice of the staff. She replied that I was not entirely correct.

The first therapist she had seen had informed her that, although she needed long-term treatment, she could return to our clinic in the event of an on-campus crisis. Aha! I now realized what had happened. Ms. Smith had been given a double, contradictory message. She should go elsewhere for treatment but return to our clinic (for treatment) in the event of a crisis. It was understandable, then, that this student, who had over the years formed a powerful institutional transference to both the college and our clinic, was opportunistically using the catchword "crisis" as the only legitimate passport into the clinic.

I then apologized to Ms. Smith for any confusion our advice may have caused her. I told her that henceforth, however, she could no longer use the services of our clinic even when in crisis. It was, I added, imperative, given her evident susceptibilities to crises, that she seek a therapist in the community and whenever she experienced a crisis she should initiate contact with that therapist instead of our clinic. It was quickly apparent that Ms. Smith would not readily accept defeat of her own blueprint for acquiring psychological services.

She pointed out that she had so many crises in her personal life that it simply might not be possible for her to wait until she could see a community therapist to resolve them. Unpersuaded by her (in my view) disingenuous argument, I informed her that if she had as many genuine crises at the college as she had claimed, then it seemed to me that it would be in her best interest to take a leave of absence from the college at this time, returning whenever she felt strong enough to withstand academic stresses. Obviously annoyed but undaunted by the logic of my statement, Ms. Smith then tried another tack.

She said that she still might need to return to our clinic in order to talk with our staff about available community resources for herself. I then lightly told her that in all likelihood, considering her extensive prior therapeutic experiences in the community and in our clinic, she probably knew more about community resources that anyone on our staff. Therefore, it really wouldn't be necessary for her to consult with us any further. With a knowing smile, she acknowledged the validity of my observation and agreed to seek services elsewhere.

I do not know whether Ms. Smith actually sought psychological services in the community. After my meeting with her, I had seen her in the clinic many times, amiably chatting with friends and, if I'm not mistaken, keeping a watchful eye on the doings of our staff. In any event, our staff is no longer besieged with requests for crisis intervention from her.

DENIAL OF SERVICES ON THE BASIS OF A STUDENT'S BEHAVIOR IN THERAPY

A student, Mr. Stone, had received a round of psychotherapy several years ago with a (at the time) relatively inexperienced psychotherapist on our staff. I had learned about what had transpired in this therapy only a few years later. The student, a very large, hulking man with a gruff and highly aggressive manner, entered therapy with a woman therapist who had recently completed her training in our clinic and was serving in her first stint as a staff psychotherapist. Mr. Stone, who, according to later descriptions of his behavior and personality, was probably a paranoid character, quickly turned the therapy into a ferocious battleground of wills.

From the very inception of the therapy, he insisted and demanded that the therapist discuss her personal life with him. The therapist, in response, evidently set appropriate limits by refusing to disclose personal facts about herself. By means of interpretations, confrontations and, probably, exhortations, she attempted to induce the client to trust her enough to share his own personal concerns with her. He adamantly refused, however, declaring each time that he could share with this therapist, a total stranger, nothing personal about himself until she would first shed her professional persona by discussing her personal life with him. Needless to say, each session ended in a tense stalemate.

At the end of the therapy, Mr. Stone evidently derived little benefit from the experience other than, perhaps, a kind of quixotic gratification that some patients feel when they take sadistic pride in maintaining an aura of secrecy with their therapists. The therapist, unquestionably, felt a great sense of relief when the therapy ended, evidently feeling not only frustrated and enervated by the bullying and abuse that the client exhibited but also because she had come to fear this man who was intent upon frightening and humiliating her week after week.

A few years later, an instructor came to see me about a harrowing experience she was having with one of her students. This man was constantly interrupting her lectures, ridiculing her remarks, and generally denigrating her personality and her right to teach. When she issued warnings to him to desist, he blithely ignored them. It was then that she sought my advice. At the time of our meeting this instructor was so distraught that she was seriously considering quitting her job. I advised her to request an administrative investigation immediately since the student's misconduct clearly warranted strong disciplinary sanctions.

The instructor, based upon my recommendation, planned to impose a two-day "removal" from class upon the student. (A "removal" in California is a kind of short-term suspension that can be used by instructors, without administrative authorization, to remove highly problematic students from classes. It is legally sanctioned by an education code and is usually a prelude to an administrative investigation.) The instructor asked me what should she do if the student flouted the "removal." After all, he had displayed a disdain for all her other attempts to contain him. I told her to contact the campus police in order to have them at the site in the event that he might attempt to enter the class. The instructor followed my advice and, fulfilling her worst apprehensions, the student, in direct contravention of the "removal" notice, did indeed attempt to attend the class. When he arrived, to prevent his ingress, the room had already been cordoned off by the campus police, he was taken into custody, and an additional charge of misconduct was added to those previously reported by the instructor.

About one or two days after this incident, a student came to the clinic for therapy and was randomly assigned to see me. His chart in which his earlier therapy was recorded was retrieved and when I read it I immediately recognized this student to be the one who had been making demands for personal disclosures upon his previous college therapist. At the outset of our session Mr. Stone stated that he hadn't been sleeping well lately. When I asked why, he said he had recently had a run-in with an instructor that was upsetting him. From his few remarks it became abundantly clear that this was the very student who had been harassing the instructor with whom I had been consulting that week!

Before I had even a chance to let the student know of my role in recommending that he be reported as a disciplinary problem, he targeted me with a fusillade of questions about my personal life. How old was I, did I like my job, how much did I get paid, what did I think of my academic colleagues, etc. Entirely expecting this diversionary maneuver, I calmly informed the student that he should understand that no matter how many personal questions he asked me, I would answer none of them; that my personal life was just that, personal, and if he wished to tell me something personal about himself, that was his option. The student rejoined by asking how I could expect him to reveal personal matters about himself if I would not do likewise. I told him that I did not expect him to tell me anything personal. He could tell me whatever he wished about himself but if our conducting therapy together was conditionally based on my sharing personal information with him, we clearly had no work to do together. None.

Moreover, I informed him, I knew, from our written records, how he had misused his previous therapy sessions at the college and no therapist in our clinic, including myself, would repeat that untoward experience with him now. (Here, I was assuming the prerogative to speak for my colleagues who, I was quite confident, would be highly averse to providing therapy to such an implacably unamenable and frighteningly aggressive individual.) I then apprised the student of the fact that I had recently consulted with his instructor about him and had recommended to her that he receive disciplinary sanctions for behavior I regarded to be extremely offensive and disruptive.

The student and I, given the inextricably adversarial nature of our relationship, agreed to terminate our work together at the end of this session. Not surprisingly, he has never returned to the clinic. Should he, he would probably be denied services unless, by some extraordinary means, he could conduct himself less incorrigibly in his sessions. Following the above-mentioned episode, the student added a rather quixotic footnote to this tale. As expected, he was administratively suspended from his class. In an act of reprisal, he filed a suit in small claims court for damages related to the suspension. The court refused to grant his claim due to the patently preposterous nature of the suit.

Although the following case, extensively described elsewhere (Amada, 1998), does not, strictly speaking, fall into the category of "denying a student services based upon the student's behavior in therapy," it does illustrate how a college therapist might use his or her prerogative to discontinue therapy with a student based upon the discovery of intimidating information in the student's personal history during the course of therapy.

Mr. Wood, a rather large, muscular man, entered therapy with fairly mild grief reactions to the breakup of his relationship with his girlfriend. Mr. Wood, quite conventional in dress and behavior, was at the time planning to attend graduate school in order to prepare for a career in one of the health professions and gave every indication of being an upstanding person. Thus, it was a great shock to discover in our third session, as the student began to reminisce about his past, that he had an erstwhile career as a hitman. His description of his brutal handiwork on the street as a hitman was quite remarkable in two respects. First, he graphically described how he had brutalized unsuspecting victims, some to the point of their requiring a prolonged period of hospitalization. But even more remarkable was the rather phlegmatic and unremorseful manner in which he described his savagery.

By the end of this tale of inhumane and callous victimization, I had come to despise and fear Mr. Wood. I said nothing to him about my feelings, but, given my fears and my repugnance for him, I did not think I could work productively with him any longer. Whether my fears were largely countertransferential in nature (that is, exaggerated and largely based upon my own personal memories and mental associations connected to images of violence) or not, it simply was not possible for me to maintain the requisite level of empathy and objectivity toward this student that would enable me to be of further assistance to him. Thus, I informed the student that it was my impression that he had overcome his initial crisis and that we need not continue to meet. Because my assessment of his emotional status at that time was probably quite accurate, the student readily agreed with the suggestion to terminate our sessions without, I believe, fully grasping the true reason for the suggestion. (One could, of course, reasonably argue that the student did intuitively sense my disquietude over his horrific tale and agreed with my recommendation to terminate for that very reason.)

Certainly an ethical question might be raised in a case like this one regarding the ultimate welfare of a student who is terminated for the sake of the therapist and not the student. What should a therapist in my situation do if, for example, the student, in disagreement with my recommendation to terminate therapy, requests that the therapy be prolonged? In considering such a scenario, it might seem best, taking into account the reality of my own emotional limitations to help the student, to tell him in vague terms that my crowded clinic schedule precludes my offering him additional sessions—a blatant fib, of course, but one that can avoid unnecessary controversy and distress, to both the student and myself.

If the student then requests that he be allowed to continue therapy instead with another therapist in the college clinic, it would be best, I think, to temporize by telling the student that I will consult with other staff to see if they have openings in their schedules. I would take this tack rather than simply referring the student to a colleague because it is quite possible that his or her reactions to the prospect of working with an unrepentant ex-hitman would be quite similar to my own and therefore such a referral might conceivably meet with an adamant demurral from other staff as well. If no other therapist on our staff is willing to treat the student, I would then suggest to the student that he seek services elsewhere and give him information regarding community resources. In any event, I think it is the prerogative of college therapists to refuse to work with students whose past histories are so abhorrent and horrific as to constitute a realistic emotional or physical threat to the welfare of the therapist.

DENIAL OF SERVICES BASED UPON
THE STUDENT'S BEHAVIOR IN THE CLINIC FACILITY

A student, Ms. Jones, entered therapy with me during the time her therapist in the community was on vacation. I agreed to see her two times, that is, until her therapist returned from vacation. The two sessions were for the most part unremarkable and seemed to serve well as a handy bridge back to her regular therapist.

Soon after these two sessions I discovered, however, that they had engendered in this borderline student a significance and an attachment I had not anticipated. The staff of the clinic was celebrating a holiday with a buffet lunch when Ms. Jones suddenly appeared in the lunchroom with a large shopping bag. She began foraging for food, stuffing it into her bag in great quantities. When one of the staff asked her why and where she was taking this food, she replied that she had been sent and given permission by Mr. Y of the English Department to bring some of our food over to his staff.

Knowing Mr. Y as well as I did, it hardly seemed plausible that he would enlist a student in the capacity of a food courier without first telling someone on our staff. Therefore, I called him in order to ascertain the truth. He informed me that the student was guilty of a bald lie; he had known nothing about our holiday party. Although the student's behavior caused some annoyance among the staff, no one considered it necessary to pursue the matter any further.

Several days later one of the receptionists discovered Ms. Jones atop a stepladder in the clinic from which she was attempting to change a light bulb. The receptionist ordered Ms. Jones down from the ladder, pointing out that there were college custodians who were responsible for carrying out such tasks and, furthermore, the clinic did not want to incur legal risks by having a student, such as herself, injured in the act of improperly performing custodial work in the clinic. Reluctantly and rather huffily, the student climbed down off the ladder.

Soon after this incident the same receptionist placed a basket filled with candy on the ledge near her window. Over the basket she placed a sign which read, "Please take one." Soon after, Ms. Jones came to the window and was seen scooping up a large handful of candy that she carried out of the clinic. When she next came into the clinic, ostensibly to talk with a nurse about a headache, she again attempted to liberate a handful of candy and desisted only when the receptionist advised against it. On at least two other occasions she was seen repeating this behavior.

A more serious incident involving Ms. Jones ensued shortly thereafter. The receptionists had locked the doors of the clinic at closing time. As they were preparing to go home, Ms. Jones arrived. Irate at finding the doors locked, she began pounding on the doors and yelling obscenities at the receptionists. She was not admitted and the incident was reported to me the following day. It was definitely time to take measures to halt Ms. Jones's misconduct in the clinic.

I reported the skein of disruptive incidents to the designated administrator along with a request in behalf of the entire clinic staff that he take immediate action to curb Ms. Jones's misconduct in the facility. The administrator cooperated by warning Ms. Jones not to enter the clinic except in instances of absolute medical necessity. Ms. Jones countered this directive by stating that she needed to use the clinic restrooms because she was allergic to the tobacco smoke of the other campus restrooms.

When she was asked to substantiate this allergy with medical documentation, she failed to do so. She then alleged that she had some form of a psychiatric disability that required that she be allowed to use the more private restrooms of the clinic. When asked by the administrator to produce some evidence of this disability, perhaps through the Disabled Student's office, she failed to comply. Then, in direct contravention of the administrator's directive, she returned to the clinic for the purpose of using its restrooms.

On her last visit I intercepted her and asked that she meet with me in my office. In the privacy of my office I informed her that, given her pattern of highly disruptive behavior in the clinic, her current visits for the purpose of using the restrooms were not only unwelcome but in clear violation of an administrative directive. Ms. Jones angrily retorted that she had documentation that supported her need to use the clinic restrooms. I asked if she had this documentation with her. With that, she withdrew a piece of paper from her purse. It was a shriveled letter from a social agency in the community, correspondence about setting up an appointment, barely legible and completely devoid of any content that related to a disability. I told Ms. Jones that her "documentation" carried no weight in this matter and that if she returned to the clinic one more time for any reason other than a medical necessity I would personally request that the dean suspend her from the college.

She then said something about the fact that my actions were certainly peculiar since I had been her therapist for a short time and we had once had a very positive relationship. (In all likelihood, of course, my supportive and empathic work with this borderline student had inadvertently spawned a highly eroticized and proprietary attachment to the clinic and to me.) I openly acknowledged that her assessment of our prior relationship was quite correct but because her behavior in the clinic had somehow become so offensive and disruptive to our staff, she was no longer eligible for our psychological services. She left in a huff and returned to the clinic only infrequently, usually in order to speak with a nurse about a minor ailment. She never again behaved disruptively toward the staff.

DENIAL OF SERVICES BASED ON A CLINIC POLICY

Soon after the inception of the psychological service in the early '70s, an incident occurred in the men's gym that prompted a call to me from a dean. An altercation had taken place between an Hispanic student and an instructor. Evidently, in the course of chewing out the student for some form of perceived misconduct, the instructor had used a few ethnic slurs. This naturally inflamed the student who in turn behaved threateningly toward the instructor.

The dean asked me if someone on our staff could see the student as soon as possible, preferably a Spanish speaking or Hispanic therapist. Although at the time there was such a person on staff, it was not clear why this student should be seen in therapy at all. When I asked the dean why he thought the student needed a therapist, he simply said that the student was extremely upset. I then pointed out that if, as I had been told, the student had been slurred by the instructor, he then had good reason to be upset, but there was no cause thus far to assume that the student either wanted or needed a therapist.

The dean, who, I later came to discover, was often inclined to be heavy-handed in such matters, stated with annoyance that I was not doing my job when I refused to see the irate student. With some annoyance of my own, I pointed out that I was not absolutely refusing to see the student; rather I wanted first to know if the student actually expressed an interest in receiving therapy in our clinic in order to ensure that his therapy would be voluntary—one of the essential conditions of our program. The dean acknowledged that the student had not evinced an interest in therapy, but then asked if he could be sent over to the clinic anyway.

I told the dean that "sending" someone over to the clinic in that manner was tantamount to mandatory therapy and the clinic had an official policy against mandatory therapy (except, of course, in cases where students are an imminent danger to self or others). The dean, now evidently in a rancorous mood, informed me that, by refusing to comply with his request, I was not doing my job. After all, he said, the clinic staff had been hired as mental health experts to handle complicated situations just like this one. I then pointed out to the dean that if, as he had just acknowledged, the staff and I were indeed mental health experts, he should accord us the respect and the right to establish ethically sound policies for our clinic and to maintain a policy of declining mandatory referrals.

I further pointed out that in a case such as this one, the instructor who had used ethnic slurs in his argument with the student should be referred himself to, for example, a cultural sensitivity workshop. The student, on the other hand, could be told that the campus psychological service on campus would be quite willing to see him if he wished, but he should understand that he had the right to refuse our services. The dean, in obvious disagreement with my advice to give the student a choice about therapy, said he would take the matter up with the student. He either did not do so or the student declined the offer, since the student never came to the clinic.

In another case involving a disciplinary matter, a student who had been suspended from the college was being readmitted by one of the deans on a highly conditional basis. The dean outlined a long list of conditions, all of which appropriately referred to behavioral standards. All but one, that is. The final item on the disciplinary menu was a condition that the student enter psychotherapy in the college clinic. The dean, who at the time was a relative newcomer to the college, was understandably not yet aware of the clinic policy against mandatory therapy. I first learned about his condition of mandatory therapy when the dean mailed me a copy of the readmission "contract" with the student. The student, who evidently was determined to fulfill all the terms of his agreement with the dean, had already been scheduled, by coincidence, to see me within a few days.

I called the dean and informed him that our policy against mandatory psychotherapy had been violated by his written agreement with the student. He apologized, admitted that he had been unaware of the policy, and asked how he could make amends for his mistake. I advised him to rewrite the "contract," retaining all its conditions save the requirement of psychotherapy. I also advised him to let the student know that he could cancel his appointment with me without penalty if he wished. The dean amiably consented to follow my suggestions and the student, not surprisingly, cancelled his appointment the next day.

One final, rather brief, example will suffice. A student was ordered to see a therapist in our program by one of his instructors. The coercive, mandatory nature of the referral came to light early in my session with the student. When I asked the student why he had come to the clinic he blandly and somewhat resentfully stated that his instructor had "forced" him to come. He said that the instructor had told him that if he wanted to pass the course he would have to receive therapy from our clinic. She evidently believed that some emotional impediment in this student was interfering with his academic work. Although she was perhaps correct, her way of going about helping this student was definitely heavy-handed and damaging to the student.

I asked the student what he would do if he had the freedom to choose between seeking or declining therapy. He made it very clear that he would decline. I then told him that he had that very freedom and that his instructor was mistaken when she ordered him to come to our clinic. She could, I informed him, lower his grades for substandard academic work but could not legitimately impose academic penalties for failure to enter therapy. I promised the student that I would, with his permission, discuss the matter with the instructor very soon. Gratefully, he gave his consent and left the session straightaway. I called the instructor, whom I knew rather well and she confirmed that she had indeed required the student to seek therapy in our clinic. I informed her that her tack with this student, although well intentioned (actually, I really wasn't so sure), was not only in violation of a clinic policy but was designed to sour the attitude of such a student toward our service due to its coercive nature.

The instructor, although she apologized for running afoul of our policy, gave me the decided impression that she did not consider my position a particularly principled or collegial one. I, for my part, was confident that I had acted properly in making it clear to this instructor that she could not use the campus psychological service as a quasi-disciplinary agency with which to coercively goad students toward certain academic objectives and that our clinic would decline all such referrals in the future.

DENIAL OF SERVICES ON THE BASIS OF
ILLEGITIMATE RATIONALES FOR ENTERING TREATMENT

Mr. Kent, a student in his early forties, came to the clinic on the very first day of school. A homeless man, he carried all of life's possessions on his back. Although obviously intelligent and articulate, he spoke discursively throughout our session about a variety of mundane subjects that, oddly enough, did not seem at all bothersome to him. As hard as I tried, I simply could not in the least pinpoint the reason for Mr. Kent's visit. Somehow there seemed to be a hidden agenda somewhere but none that I could definably intuit.

I saw no more of Mr. Kent until almost the end of the semester. When he returned it was to inform me that he had not attended any of his classes. He seemed strangely blasé about this and then, as before, began to ramble about a variety of fairly irrelevant subjects. If my feelings were not betraying me, they suggested that his rapid and idle chatter was being used as an artifice to lull or gull me into conspiring with him in a scam of some kind, but as yet I was not ready to identify the nature of the scam.

Finally, taking the liberty to interrupt him, I asked Mr. Kent if he had returned to the clinic in order to ask a favor of me, perhaps a favor connected with his unexcused absences from class. His startled reaction suggested that my first fling of the arrow had hit near the bull's eye. At first, he sputteringly denied that he needed my intervention in that matter, but a moment later gave himself away by asking me point-blank whether I would provide him with a letter that could, on authoritative psychiatric grounds, justify his absences from class.

I told Mr. Kent that, given the fact that I had seen him only once before and that he had seen no reason to work with me in order to overcome his difficulties in attending class, I could not in good conscience provide him with such a letter. I then asked him why he was intent upon receiving a letter to excuse his absences since attending and passing his courses, if I might say so, seemed rather unimportant to him. Mr. Kent then admitted that he had never intended to attend his classes. Puzzled, I asked why, then, had he enrolled in the first place. Rather sheepishly, he mumbled something about financial aid.

Now I understood the scam! Poor Mr. Kent had no regular or reliable source of income. By enrolling as a full-time student he qualified for financial aid. If he could now have his unexcused absences expunged from his record by means of a psychiatric report attesting to some form of disability he could, he hoped, return to the college in a subsequent semester and once again qualify for financial aid. By means of this clever scheme he could go on indefinitely supporting himself; that is, until the scheme was detected and thwarted. For the remainder of our session Mr. Kent rambled on about a great many trivial subjects.

Then, at the end of the session, in one last die-hard attempt to salvage his plan, he asked if he could return to see me one more time in order to justify receiving a letter from me that would excuse his absences. I told Mr. Kent that I, regrettably, would not see him again on such a basis. To the best of my knowledge, he has never returned to the clinic for any purpose.

In a similar situation, a student, Mr. Forest, came to the clinic for his first session close to the end of the semester. He spent most of the session discussing his contentious relationship with his girlfriend but I was puzzled by the fact that there seemed to be no discernible crisis taking place within the relationship nor did the student seem to be in any particular turmoil about his situation. On the contrary, he was fairly jolly and optimistic about the prospects of his relationship with his girlfriend. In short, there was a highly incongruent and inauthentic quality to the student's presentation of his concerns. At the end of the session, because the semester was almost over, we scheduled no other appointments.

The next day, as I was passing through the waiting room, Mr. Forest buttonholed me by asking if he could be seen immediately for a brief session. When I asked why, he stated that he had neglected to mention the day before that he had failed some courses and now wanted me, based on the single session of therapy he had just received, to give him a letter attesting to the fact that his failing grades were caused by psychological stress and therefore should be expunged from his academic record. I told the student that I would definitely not do such a thing on the basis of just a single session with him, therefore, I would not meet with him. He angrily stated that he had a right to receive such an accommodation from me; after all, that's what mental health programs are for, he averred. I told him I disagreed and that if he wanted such a letter he would do better to go to another psychological service or a private practitioner instead. He left in high dudgeon and, as far as I know, never returned to our clinic.

Another case involving a questionable rationale for therapy occurred in our clinic about ten years ago. A student in her first session, Ms. Rose, amiably and lightheartedly discussed a wide variety of everyday subjects with me without any sense of worry or urgency. Each time I attempted to focus upon an area of her life that might represent a source of concern to her she demurred by moving on to another safe subject. Quite perplexed by all of this strange lightheartedness and apparent dissimulation, I finally admitted to the student, very near the end of the session, that I had no idea why she had come for therapy. Ms. Rose then stated, with some abashment, that perhaps she should have mentioned it earlier but her reason for seeking therapy was to receive extra credit in one of her courses, a health education course. With that, she withdrew a form from a folder and asked me to sign it.

When I inquired about the purpose of my signing this form, the student pointed out that my signature would be verification that she had received therapy from me. I told Ms. Rose that we had no agreement or understanding with her instructor, nor did we even receive prior notification from her, that such a form existed or that our staff would be asked to provide therapy on such a basis. I then told the student that I would not sign the form since therapy in our clinic was provided only for its own sake, had its own intrinsic value, and, therefore, I could not, in good conscience, honor a practice that extended extra academic credit for our services. Visibly disappointed, Ms. Rose attempted to have me sign the form anyway. I repeated that, for ethical reasons, I could not do so. I also informed her that I would be contacting her instructor to let her know that henceforth she should not extend extra academic credit to students whom she referred to our service. Finally, I asked the student if she would like to schedule another appointment with me despite the fact that she would not derive academic credit for doing so. Pleasantly, but without hesitation, she declined my offer.

The next day, I contacted the instructor, with whom I had a very friendly relationship for many years. I told her that her strategy of using academic blandishments to induce students to enter therapy, although creative and obviously well-intentioned, was not, unfortunately, compatible with the principles and rationales our staff used in undertaking therapy with students. In response, she explained that her motive for using those blandishments was to increase the numbers of ,students who would use our service and she believed that the ends (increased student utilization) justified the means (the carrot of extra academic credit). Although I don't believe my discouragement of this practice disabused her of this belief, she amicably agreed to rescind her use of the credit-for-therapy offer to students and continued to make many referrals to our program afterward.

By the way, over the years I have heard a large number of anecdotes from colleagues with private psychotherapy practices about patients who enter therapy primarily for the purpose of uncovering some flaw in the therapist's techniques or personality with which to construct the edifice of an expensive civil suit against the therapist. These litigious patients are essentially present-day bounty hunters and their therapists are their hapless quarry. I do not know firsthand of any case of a student who has preyed upon a college psychotherapist in this manner, but if a student were detected to enter therapy for the primary purpose of damaging the reputation and economic well-being of the therapist for financial or any other kind of gain, that student, doubtlessly, should be terminated and excluded from the service as soon as possible.

DISCUSSION

Although it is not a widely discussed subject, college mental health programs can and do exclude certain types of students from receiving treatment in their clinics. The fact that this subject does not receive much attention or publicity in professional conferences or journals is perhaps reflective of the fact that most therapists pridefully view themselves as bountiful and practically unconditional "givers" of service, certainly not excluders and deniers of assistance to the psychologically needy. Thus, it may cause some college therapists a good degree of discomfort, embarrassment, and incertitude before they can admit that there are some students whom they will not treat.

I believe it is important for college therapists not only to acknowledge that they, from time to time, are required to exclude some students from utilizing their programs, but also to endeavor to establish clear and definable criteria and standards for denying their services to certain students. As well, these criteria and standards must, by all means, be ethically and legally defensible. It is not entirely paradoxical that a college psychological service that, for *good cause*, denies its services to certain highly problematic students, will ultimately provide better services to the students it does serve. After all, if the staff of the psychological service becomes deeply mired in the frustrating, time-consuming, and largely fruitless endeavor of assisting students who are inordinately abusive, manipulative, mendacious, intimidating, fraudulent, delinquent, or generally amoral in their conduct toward them, they are bound to suffer a degree of demoralization that will spread to and undermine their work with other, more deserving, students.

Reference

Amada, G. (1998). *The mystified fortune-teller and other tales from psychotherapy.* Lanham, MD: Madison Books.

Liberal Censorship on Campus: A New Form of McCarthyism?

When, earlier in the year, the public print was flooded with the xenophobic effusions of John Rocker, ace relief pitcher of the Atlanta Braves, there was, in response, a torrent of protest and vituperation from civil libertarians decrying this man's ignorance and bigotry. Ordinarily, such a prodigious outpouring of ecumenical indignation would be heartening to anyone who condemns acts of racial and ethnic hatefulness were it not for the fact that John Rocker, we must acknowledge, is not some kind of mutative social anomaly that has somehow brooded itself in our midst. He is, instead, a rank-and-file member of that vast and nebulous group of American citizens that might best be described as narrow-minded and self-interested nativists who have little tolerance for or truck with those who are dark-skinned, speak with foreign accents, or depend, even temporarily, upon governmental assistance in order to survive.

What, I believe, is more newsworthy than John Rocker's frenzies of simple-mindedness is the nature of the avenging backlash with which they were met, as reported in the newspapers. It was not enough, it seems, to condemn, excoriate, and vilify the ignoramus. No, there must be further sanctions, penalties, and remedies in order to complete his rehabilitation. What were the principal sanctions and remedies that were recommended? First, to ban him from baseball —that is, to take away his job and destroy his career. Second, that he be required to undergo either some form of sensitivity-training or psychotherapy in order to uncover and resolve the particular pathology in his character that germinates his bigotry. This from civil libertarians!

It requires historical amnesia of serious proportions, I believe, to forget the fact that about fifty years ago in this country thousands of our citizens became innocent victims of colleges, businesses, and governmental agencies that fired them simply because of their heterodox

227

social and political opinions and associations. Are we now about to revive and rejuvenate McCarthyism in the name and spirit of cultural pluralism and diversity? Is it not possible to champion the value of inclusion, cultural pluralism and diversity without stripping people— even bigots—of their occupations and livelihoods, not to speak of their precious constitutional rights? Let's face it, if we as a society set out to disemploy all the bigots amongst us, vast numbers of schools, agencies and corporations throughout the country will suffer serious retrenchment and the unemployment roles will grow exponentially. As well, the courts would be bloated with cases litigated because of the mass infringement of constitutional rights.

As for the efficacy of psychotherapy in metamorphosing bigots into latitudinarians—forget it. First, the bigot who is involuntarily corralled into psychotherapy is likely to learn nothing from the experience other than the fact that therapy is an unpleasant form of discipline that must be endured until the disciplinary monkey is finally removed from his or her back. Like the proverbial light bulbs of a now-popular joke, bigots are not about to change unless they want to and no form of mandatory treatment is going to alter that fact.

Furthermore, since when did bigotry enter any diagnostic manual, including the venerable DSM-IV, as a form of psychological disorder requiring psychiatric treatment. It may be hard to swallow, but there really are well-adjusted bigots who do not require treatment and, for all we know, John Rocker may be one of them. In any case, it is ironic and sad that some civil libertarians, including many psychotherapists themselves, believe that therapy should be foisted on Rocker, conveniently forgetting that it was just such inquisitorial horrors that were visited upon citizens of the erstwhile Soviet Union when they manifested political viewpoints that were deemed inimical to their government.

What does this preamble about the Rocker affair have to do with life in academia? A great deal, I am afraid. As a consultant to hundreds of faculty during my thirty-year tenure as a psychotherapist at City College of San Francisco, I was often questioned about the rights of instructors to abridge or restrain the speech of students. At times, this issue arose when instructors evaluated written essays. A student would, for example, write an essay in an English or social science course in which he or she engaged in a long, hateful (and usually discursive and irrational) diatribe against various groups such as African- Americans, Asians, Hispanics, or gays. The instructor, in high dudgeon, would consider failing the paper based solely on its invective slurs and overall noxiousness, forgetting to attend to the matter of whether the paper met reasonable standards of scholarship.

Nevertheless, the instructor almost always felt queasy about taking this tack because it would likely lead to an nasty casuistic showdown between the racist student and the teacher as to the matter of whose opinions about race were really the more substantive and credible —something that can be extremely difficult to prove. When, however, the instructor was advised to evaluate the paper strictly on an academic basis—that is, based on its demonstrable level of scholarship— the problem was immediately resolved. Without a single exception, these papers were written atrociously, argued illogically, and totally lacked any semblance of scholarship. Thus, a failing grade was incontestably fair and warranted, entirely irrespective of the viewpoints espoused in the paper. These experiences suggest that instructors who adhere to a viewpoint-neutral position in evaluating written assignments by grading papers solely on the basis of the quality of scholarship exhibited by the student will fare quite well, while at the same time respecting students' constitutionally protected speech.

Of course, if one wishes to imagine the worst, a given professor might some day encounter, for example, a Nazi student who can logically and articulately argue, based on "sound research," that Hitler and the Holocaust never existed. Yet, even in such an extreme case as this one, adherence to a viewpoint-neutral standard of scholarship is the soundest approach from both a practical and legal standpoint. After all, proving the nonexistence of Hitler and the Holocaust would be a Sisyphean challenge for even the most brilliant student.

During a recent lecture to instructors at a Midwestern university I was proudly informed by a professor that he had his own special way of handling bigots in his class: he simply shouted at them to keep their disgusting opinions to themselves. I briefly and politely demurred and will explain my reasons in this article. First, to dogmatically censor a student's social or political opinions, however repugnant they may be to the ears of a civil libertarian, is to treat that student as irredeemably uneducable. Would it not be better to assume, instead, that the student is in a formative phase of his or her academic career and might be open to discussing, debating and even reevaluating the merits of his or her social opinions? After all, that's one of the primary reasons students attend college—to learn, change, and grow. To denounce and censor the bigot in a classroom is an act of despair, arrests the potential for the student's intellectual growth, and results in a hollow victory.

Second, when an instructor suppresses and censors the opinions of a bigot, that teacher is, perforce, failing to fulfill an important academic mission. Instructors are supposed to be exemplary scholars who foster and facilitate discussion, inquiry, controversy, argumentation, and the courageous exploration of topics that are generally considered anathematical in the extramural world. Therefore, by shunning and banning certain opinions because they offend one's sensibilities is to defeat one's own fundamental purpose for being an instructor. Therefore, this may be the time, I believe, to consider the censorious intolerance for intolerance to be just another form of bigotry.

Finally, there are far too many cases of censorship on campuses throughout the country that violate the constitutional rights of faculty and students alike (see *The Shadow University*). Therefore, college instructors and administrators must be especially respectful of constitutionally protected rights of speech in order to avoid running afoul of the law and incurring either disciplinary sanctions or career-damaging litigation.

Do these caveats mean that there can be no abridgement of classroom speech under any circumstances? Of course not. If a bigoted student targets another student with racist (or any other) epithets in the classroom there are probably several codes of student conduct that can be enlisted to harness that behavior; for example, those that prohibit verbal abuse, interference with the educational process, and an unwillingness to respond to the duly delegated authority of the instructor.

Those students whose speech tends to monopolize classroom discussions can and should be actively discouraged from doing so. Students whose speech is glaringly irrelevant (for example, the student who is discussing personal and intimate autobiographical details during a discussion of a psychological concept) should be firmly curbed. Students whose speech has reached an intolerable decibel level will need to be stopped and warned. Students who incessantly interrupt lectures with attention-getting questions or who distractingly chatter in class should also be stopped and warned. Students who verbally level dangerous or lethal threats at instructors should be reported and possibly charged with a crime.

Most of these examples, one may note, involve cases that are viewpoint-neutral. However, before disciplining students solely for their opinions, racist or otherwise, instructors should tread carefully and consult with knowledgeable authorities on their respective campuses.